Voices of Their Own

Voices of Their Own

Contemporary Spanish Narrative by Women

Elizabeth J. Ordóñez

Lewisburg
Bucknell University Press
London and Toronto: Associated University Presses

863.09
O65v

Associated University Presses
440 Forsgate Drive
Cranbury, NJ 08512

Associated University Presses
25 Sicilian Avenue
London WC1A 2QH, England

Associated University Presses
P.O. Box 39, Clarkson Pstl. Stn.
Mississauga, Ontario,
L5J 3X9 Canada

The paper used in this publication meets the requirements
A⌣of the American National Standard for Permanence of Paper
for Printed Library Materials Z39.48-1984.

Library of Congress Cataloging-in-Publication Data

Ordóñez, Elizabeth Jane, 1945–
    Voices of their own : contemporary Spanish narrative by women / Elizabeth Jane Ordóñez.
        p.   cm.
    Includes bibliographical references (p.   ) and index.
    ISBN 0-8387-5203-9 (alk. paper)
    1. Spanish fiction—Women authors—History and criticism.
2. Spanish fiction—20th century—History and criticism.   I. Title.
PQ6055.O7   1991
863'.6099287—dc20   90-55690
                                                                                      CIP

PRINTED IN THE UNITED STATES OF AMERICA

To my mother and my daughter,
the unbroken matrilineal chain.

Contents

Acknowledgments

I have come to think of this book as a kind of Darwinian project. It represents what I hope may be considered the survival of some of my fittest work, and the evolutionary process of theory and practice that culminates herein I would wish to contribute, however modestly, to the further survival and evolution of not only my own work, but that of numerous others without whom this particular project would not have been possible: writers, colleagues, students, and friends. It is from them that I have received inspiration, and for that I would like this book to be an expression of appreciation.

Through the years that my research interests have centered on the cultural production of contemporary Spanish women, I have had the good fortune of sharing many a pleasant hour of "café" and conversation with a number of the writers represented in this book—among them Carmen Laforet, Elena Soriano, Elena Quiroga, Ana María Matute, Carmen Martín Gaite, Concha Alós, Carmen Kurtz, Esther Tusquets, Lourdes Ortiz, Montserrat Roig, and Marta Portal. For their hospitality and generosity I am grateful; with the insights their sharing has conferred, I am forever enriched.

I would also like to thank the many colleagues and students who, over the years, have offered valuable comments and welcome encouragement as the ideas in these essays first emerged tentatively, and then evolved and transformed into their present shape. Special gratitude goes to Carol Maier, who read the present manuscript with great care and helped smooth its stubborn rough edges, and to Julian Palley, my mentor and friend for more years than either of us might care to remember.

Acknowledgment is also due the Ministerio de Asuntos Exteriores of Spain, which—together with the American Association of Teachers of Spanish and Portuguese—made my first extended stay in post-Franco Spain possible. To the Dean of the Graduate School, the Dean of Liberal Arts, and the Chair of the Department of Foreign Languages at the University of Texas at

Arlington, and to the American Council of Learned Societies, I express gratitude for support contributing to travel and research.

Most of all, this book is for Guido and Veva, who spent more of their hours in the kitchen so I could spend more of mine in the study, and for my father, Leon Fischer, who never made apologies for having a daughter.

The following publishers have generously given permission to include revisions of earlier versions of my work in this book:

- Parts of the Introduction and Conclusion appeared in "Inscribing Difference," *ALEC* 12 (1987): 45–58.
- A portion of chapter 1 contains revised material from a previously published article, "*Nada:* Initiation into Bourgeois Patriarchy," in *The Analysis of Hispanic Texts: Current Trends in Methodology*, II, edited by Lisa E. Davis and Isabel C. Tarán (New York [Tempe, Arizona]: Bilingual Press/Editorial Bilingue, 1977).
- Chapter 3 contains material that previously appeared as "Reading, Telling and The Text of Carmen Martín Gaite's *El cuarto de atrás*," in *From Fiction to Metafiction: Essays in Honor of Carmen Martín Gaite*, edited by Mirella Servodidio and Marcia L. Welles (Lincoln, Nebr.: Society of Spanish and Spanish American Studies, 1983).
- Chapter 4 contains material that previously appeared as "The Female Quest Pattern in Concha Alós' *Os habla Electra*," *REH* 14 (1980): 51–64, and "A Quest for Matrilineal Roots and Mythopoesis: Esther Tusquets' *El mismo mar de todos los veranos*," *Crítica Hispánica* 6 (1984): 37–46.
- Chapter 5 is a revised version of "Rewriting Myth and History: Three Recent Novels by Women," in *Feminine Concerns in Contemporary Spanish Fiction by Women*, edited by Roberto Manteiga, Carolyn Galerstein, and Kathleen McNerney (Potomac, Md.: Scripta Humanistica, 1988).
- Chapter 6 contains material from "*Los perros de Hécate* as a Paradigm of Narrative Defiance," *ALEC* 13 (1988): 71–81.
- Chapter 7 contains material from "Writing Ambiguity and Desire: The Works of Adelaida García Morales," in *Women Writers of Contemporary Spain*, edited by Joan L. Brown (Newark: University of Delaware Press, forthcoming).

Voices of Their Own

Introduction
Pricking Up Our Ears—Toward a Perception of Multivocality

> These women are necessary to Arimneste, for they know
> something that she has yet to learn—her silence can be bro-
> ken—and thus can instruct her in the prior tragedy that con-
> sists not of acting and mirroring but of doing and saying
> nothing, or of looking in the mirror and finding no face there.
> She pauses and waits for examples. Eventually the murmur of
> women's voices—whispers at first, and then a many-languaged
> chorus—swells and inhabits the room. Her page begins to fill.
> —Lawrence Lipking, "Aristotle's Sister"

Until quite recently to combine the roles of North American
Hispanist, student of feminist theory, and woman writing about
Spanish women writers, it was necessary to occupy a position not
unlike that of Aristotle's putative sister, Arimneste. Like Arimneste, this multiplicitous scholar looked at reflections of herself
and saw either nothing or images that neither approximated the
men she was supposed to resemble nor the woman she was supposed to transcend. To be a feminist scholar of Spanish women's
writing was to inhabit, like Arimneste, a cultural space in which
those writing women were "assumed to be a subspecies of men"
and most "poetics" or literary theory was not necessarily "con-
temptuous but oblivious of women."[1] The woman, as feminist
scholar of Spanish women writers, was thus nowhere yet
seemingly everywhere at once. In her role as dutiful daughter, she
followed all the -isms as they arrived in the critical arena. Yet
somehow she found only fragments of herself in them. It was
enough to either drive her crazy or intimidate her into silence, but
she waited, gathering evidence like Arimneste, until the times and
the texts were ripe for her, or until the voices of the women she
read welled up so richly that they could no longer be ignored.

The preceding allegory, inspired by Lawrence Lipking's poignant revelations on the exclusion of women from literary theory,

is at once a plaint about Spanish literary theory and its inattention to the writing of women and a commentary on how this book came to be. It is also an apt portrayal of my own experiences as a North American woman reading the contemporary Spanish novel by women, and I suspect that I am far from being alone in my feelings of uneasiness and dislocation in this position. As Constance Sullivan, another North American reader of Spanish women writers lamented in 1983: "Hispanists have not yet begun to question on a wide scale the male assumptions of Hispanic culture."[2] Certainly, there has been no lack of women novelists in contemporary Spain; by the early sixties, a routine review in *La estafeta literaria* proclaimed that "el panorama de las mujeres novelistas es vastísimo" (the panorama of women novelists is quite vast).[3] That being so, why did Janet Pérez still conclude in 1984, more than twenty years and a generation of writers later, that "little attention" had "been accorded" twentieth-century Spanish fiction by women, "whether in Spain, the United States or elsewhere"?[4] I suggest that this lack is due, at least in part, to a paucity of relevant theories that would have made paying attention to this body of texts more compelling, and that would have opened them to a reception process more disposed to reading sense into what may have appeared as non-sense to earlier theories or nontheories of the narrative text.

Postwar Spanish literary criticism has been, in a word, problematical. Women are far from being the only plaintiffs of its oversights. Beset with the limitations of a highly controlled political system, the period following the Spanish Civil War until the death of Franco left little room in Spain for dialogical critical positions. Writing shortly before 1975, Fernando Alvarez Palacios characterized the state of Spanish literary criticism as unidimensional and deeply rooted in conservative values of the past:

refiriéndonos a España, en los treinta largos años que nos separan de la finalización de la guerra, la crítica literaria ha optado principalmente por seguir el sagrado fuego de determinados clásicos, propiciando con ello la revigorización de los presupuestos clásicos de la cultura burguesa

(referring to Spain during the thirty long years that separate us from the end of the war, literary criticism has opted principally to follow the sacred flame of certain classical writers, favoring through that the revitalization of the classical assumptions of bourgeois culture).[5]

When culture critics like Alvarez Palacios express their indignation at the monopoly of traditional literary criticism, they do so from an opposing, though not necessarily inclusive, position. Representing the boom of social-realist criticism and writing, they occupy the other side of a sociocritical polarity from those consecrated pundits that they assail. Though these social critics contributed significantly to the destabilization of bourgeois Falangist hegemony by problematizing class and ideology in literature, woman was still largely invisible within the terms of their arguments. The battle lines were drawn rather between what John Butt has called "modernism" and "social realism," two -isms whose concern with gender was only marginal.[6] Though Alvarez Palacios speaks in the generic masculine, his revised description of the literary critic is telling: "el crítico no es un ente amorfo o un ser mítico, sino un hombre con las mismas implicaciones sociales que el oficinista o el director de empresa, el pintor o el obrero" (the critic is not an amorphous or mythical being, but rather a man with the same social implications as an office worker or an executive, a painter or a worker).[7] Without putting too fine a point upon it, Alvarez Palacios's critic is a man; the verb of being places equal signs between gender and professional function, rendering even the progressive critic implicitly unmindful of woman's presence as writer.[8]

As a result, when women's narrative is included in studies of the novel, it often appears curiously unmanageable. A number of well-known and respected studies of contemporary Spanish fiction during the last two decades seemed uneasy about where or how to include works by women. Their categorizations revealed a certain theoretical instability and provisionality vis-à-vis the works of women. For example, in a fine contribution to social-realist criticism, Gonzalo Sobejano classified Carmen Laforet, Elena Quiroga, and Dolores Medio as authors of existential novels and Ana María Matute and Carmen Martín Gaite as creators of social novels. In many ways, the categories for locating each writer could just as easily have been reversed with a mere sleight of the critical hand. In fact, this is precisely what happened when M. García Viñó approached Laforet in terms of her personal development and Matute as a deviant from the realist mode. Matute did a complete flip, then, in this theoretical context from the category she occupied in Sobejano's schema. José Corrales Egea included Martín Gaite as an author of the "new novel" (the Spanish, not French, variety), yet needed to qualify that she occupied a "lateral" position with respect to that category. Matute, in light of Corrales

Egea's categories, became a marginal, compromise figure, strad-dling his categorical fence through a personal synthesis that re-sisted placement on one side or the other. And *Nada* made Corrales Egea most uncomfortable because it purportedly failed to be what his consigned category required: committed and trans-formative. As another "subspecies" of the social-realist novel, it failed to meet that category's criteria. (Chapter 1 of the present study should reveal, on the other hand, just how relative to under-lying theoretical and ideological assumptions the concept of trans-formative in *Nada* may turn out to be.)[9]

Another problem in postwar Spanish criticism has been the age-old one of judging quality. The predilection for classical values left many living writers at best ignored, at worst despised. As Juan Goytisolo has commented with bitter humor: "respecto a los es-critores de hoy, razones de clima y temperamento favorecen el imperio de esa mentalidad Far-West que denunciaba justamente Castellet en uno de sus primeros ensayos: para los amigos, elogios que harían enrojecer a Cervantes; para los enemigos, el insulto, la mofa, la hiel, el veneno" (with respect to today's writers, reasons of climate and temperament favor the rule of that Far-West mentality that Castellet justly denounced in one of his first essays: for friends, praises that would make Cervantes blush; for enemies, insults, ridicule, gall, and venom).[10] Elena Soriano utters a sim-ilarly negative assertion: "no creo que exista en España una crítica responsable, orientadora y clarificadora" (I don't think that a responsible, orienting and clarifying criticism exists in Spain).[11] It would probably not be overstating the issue to say that the per-sonal subjective nature of traditional postwar Spanish criticism has affected, in one way or another, all living writers of the period.

Still, the problem of literary criticism and assessment proves especially vexing when women are considered a subset of the male species. The implied masculine yardstick has led to such curi-osities of judgment as Olga Prjevalinsky Ferrer's critique of Laforet's *La isla de los demonios*, in which the novel's shortcomings are described as "deficiencies of the feminine style."[12] This un-questioned equation of inferior with feminine led the same critic to assess the flaws of other women writers with much the same bias, a bias that emerged most clearly by the conclusion of the same article: "la novela femenina revela por una parte los carac-teres dominantes de la novela contemporánea española, sin que lleguen a constituir muchas veces tendencias que hayan alcanzado grado de perfección en manera alguna" (the feminine novel exhibits, in part, the dominant characteristics of the contemporary Spanish novel, without, by any means, frequently achieving a high level of perfection in those tendencies).[13] Whether or not these novels are good or bad should not be the central issue here. What should concern the reader most is that they are categorized as a subspecies of *the* contemporary novel (presumably as authored and authorized by the "universal" [male] writer and reader). Within that frame of reference their differences are almost inevitably consigned to appear as deficiencies. By any other measuring device those same deficiencies might even be redefined as strengths, which is indeed the case of Carmen Martín Gaite's excruciatingly appropriate use of banal language in *Entre visillos*, a masterstroke that the same critic judges negatively as feminine and intranscendent.[14]

Certainly, it is not my objective to heap criticism on poor Olga. She just happens to offer a clear and unassailable example of the pitfalls of value judgment when the theoretical or ideological underpinnings of the critic or reader remain unenunciated or undefined. And I am also aware that I may be reproved for beating an historically dead horse; recent publications are, undoubtedly, supplementing the oversights of the past.[15] But today's Arimneste finds herself empowered thanks largely to a recent confluence of both Spanish and non-Hispanic theoretical influences in her field of inquiry. So at this juncture, it seems only fair to acknowledge those influences—traces of a critical intertext as it were—that are now spurring this Arimneste to reconsider the previously indecipherable and, upon redefining the terms of her own critical pages, fill the pages of this book.

When I and others in my generation of Arimnestes began "thinking about Spanish women" (to borrow and adapt a phrase from Mary Ellman), the focus of our attention was largely on the effects of the traditional, politically repressive, patriarchal Spanish society on women's lives and literature. Conversely, or as an inevitable corollary, this social criticism also interested itself in the possible effects that literature might have on social change. In many ways early feminist criticism of the contemporary Spanish novel by women attempted to adjust the social realist paradigm so that it would consciously and conscientiously include women, women as an oppressed class in itself, and women as members of different social classes. The temptation inherent in this position was that the critic tended to cast herself as the vanguard of women and issued prescriptive recommendations for "transformative praxis" to writers whose inspiration was often less pragmatic. It was my experience during interviews with Spanish women novelists in 1977 and 1980 that theories of feminist "praxis" were frequently given a polite hearing at best, a wry smile of skepticism at worst. Youthful ardor and my own position as a North American feminist left me at that time less than prepared to read what was actually written or to give a fair hearing to voices that might not have fit into my zealous scheme.[16] And yet my position was not unlike that of other social critics who, as David Herzberger has assessed, have viewed novels "more as literary sociology than as artistic objects with their own structures and energies."[17]

So feminist criticism, in order to better hear the undistorted voices of contemporary Spanish women, had to become more conscious—as Herzberger has also proposed for social criticism—of "textual norms as esthetic mediators of social vision."[18] It was not, then, a question of "giving up" entirely on social criticism, but of acknowledging that all texts—even those non-Utopian ones that spoke of undesirable social realities—were inextricably linked to a complex series of signifying practices. Feminist criticism, along with other forms of social criticism, came to realize in this way that narrative does not simply reflect society or history; it textualizes it, or as Fredric Jameson concludes, it makes of it "a symbolic meditation on the destiny of community."[19] But how or through what means does this mediation and meditation occur?

It is now difficult to conceive of any symbolic meditation or mediation without echoes of Lacan and his theory of the Symbolic Order of language and culture. In fact, as Juliet Flower MacCannell has observed, the Symbolic Order "stands in the role of the mediator" of the patriarchal ideological order, governing and regulating desire.[20] It seems, then, that the narrative text in its function as symbolic mediator of the culture will somehow be linked to the Symbolic Order from which it is unavoidably generated. If one agrees that this Lacanian proposition is suggestive as an opening to the mediating functions of the narrative text, then it seems that one must buy into the rest of the controversial package wherein it comes included; that is, Lacan's assertion that the phallus is "the privileged signifier."[21] Whether or not one agrees with this disturbing Lacanian proposition, the claim stands before us in all its challenging insolence. We may be vexed by it, yet we are caught up by it for it glides still further into Lacan's other concept of the Law (the Father's Law as the Other that governs desire). As each theoretical notion overlaps with the other, it substantiates an interdependent network of external and internal signifiers that

Lacan has traced to "the dawn of history."[22] While the Symbolic Order is buoyed up by the "name of the father," it conversely privileges its supporter in a symbiotic relationship that ties together patriarchal ideological or cultural order with its internal support structure, the Symbolic Order. Through this play of interests, the demands of culture (the Other or the Father's Law)—by means of its institutions and symbolic structures—delimit (and even repress) the boundaries of desire.]

In this study, echoes of these Lacanian mediating networks surface and resurface in voices that tell of (or grow silent because of) the restrictions and demands that the symbolic ordering of culture places on woman. These echoes are an important source of my readings in chapters 2 and 7. Chapter 2, "Feminine Plots and Their Undertow," juxtaposes three mature women at mid-century who mourn the effects of frustrated relations and impossibility.[23] As they regard the various threatening images of aging, [they become deeply enthralled by the discourse of the Other, by reflected images and alien voices that have undermined the confidence and integrity of their own. From their ambivalent positioning between the acceptance of definitions of desire as spelled out by the Symbolic Order and their own desire to somehow express themselves outside these boundaries, they grow increasingly silent.]Yet that very silence is suggestive: it intimates something beyond reflections of the Other's desire, something less immured in the silence of self-deprecation (*La playa de los locos*), immobility (*La enferma*), and exile (*La trampa*). In chapter 7, "Beyond the Father," the three young female protagonists of Adelaida García Morales's *El Sur, Bene,* and *El silencio de las sirenas* respond ambivalently and often uncontrollably to the powerful presence of Lacanian signifiers: *El Sur*'s protagonist is initially bedazzled by the Father's Law, *Bene*'s ghostly apparitions suggest evasions from its legislation of cultural meaning, and *Silencio*'s meditation on an impossible love and the perils of love story writing becomes inextricably enmeshed within the merciless demands of the Symbolic Order.

Yet in spite of the Symbolic Order's omnipresence, it appears that Lacan has left something out of his seemingly omnipotent scheme: the desire to voice, through, in spite of and even beyond the Symbolic Order, does assert itself.[24] Derrida has contributed
✓ much toward clearing out a space for this voicing (or according to the terms of his discourse, this "writing") by destabilizing the secure moorings of Western culture's binary oppositions, the props of its logocentrism or belief in the transcendental signifier

or absolute (read: masculine) truth.[25] So sure is Derrida of this attack, that he coined what might be seen as a self-deprecating neologism to stand for the blindness of the culture under fire: "phallogocentric." As Terry Eagleton humorously interprets, this new word "might roughly translate as 'cocksure.' It is this cocksureness by which those who wield sexual and social power maintain their grip."[26] These words push us beyond Lacan's definitions to displace or dislodge fixed or phallocentric notions of truth. In this way, Derrida further unlocks the text and opens it to the play of other "truths" that may have been previously silenced or repressed. Derrida's decentering of the consecrated Book, his dislodging of the text from the Book, and ultimately of "radical illegibility" from the text, serves as a model gesture for those engaged in reading texts by women (texts so often classified as illegible).[27] From among the uncanonized and illegible, the silent "supplemental" voices of women emerge from absence into a decentered presence. Derridean notions of "differance" and "displacement" thus refuse encirclement into ordained notions of truth and knowledge; instead, they dislocate sites of established power and release a chorus of textual voices iterating "difference" through their challenges to phallogocentrism.[28]

Derridean echoes are also present throughout this study, particularly in its unrelenting attention to the ways in which postwar Spanish women novelists have confronted and responded to phallogocentrism in their writing. Chapter 3, "Talking Herself Out," explores how Carmen Martín Gaite in many ways answers for her more silent precursors by working out in her own way the Derridean anxiety with binary oppositions. In that chapter, I proceed from the assumption that Martín Gaite's major novels, *Retahílas* and *El cuarto de atrás,* in many ways respond to earlier, more agonized attempts to skirt the restrictions of the symbolic contract or phallogocentric discourse. Both novels express what might be called a Derridean desire to dislodge and displace the prison houses of textual and cultural order with a self-defined play of "differance" (or, in the metaphorical terms of Martín Gaite's own text, a "room at the back"). Chapter 4, "In Search of Her Mother's House," also engages in a process of Derridean difference or supplementarity, this time in order to decenter patriarchal or paternal sources of myth and archetype. In Chapter 6, "Parody and Defiance," Gómez Ojea's *Los perros de Hécate* defies the consecrated Book, shocking and amusing its readers with playful gestures of insolent difference.

With a move in social criticism away from homology, or structural parallelisms between society and text, to more dynamic and complex notions of the text as process, the narrative text by woman reveals itself still further as a diverse web of cultural discourses enhanced by the range of its voices.[29] Foucault has made readers particularly attentive to the idea of "discursive fields and practices" that shape the cultural networks within which all texts are necessarily inserted. Now text and context appear intertwined into a more heterogeneous network of discursive practices, and the use of the word "discourse" is expanded by complex interrelationships among sites of authority or power that weave themselves in and out of the culture and its texts. We find ourselves obliged to ask: who is really speaking? Who is deemed qualified or authorized to do so?[30] The loci of meaning thus shift and collide and undergo constant repositioning. For now, after Foucault, a book "constructs itself, only on the basis of a complex field of discourse," and that field includes the "not-said" along with the "already-said."[31] Our ears thus become attuned not only to what can and is said, but also to the ways in which texts may respond implicitly to silence and incorporate the unsaid among their gaps and folds./

Echoes of Foucault's theories resonate in my approach to *Nada* in chapter 1. "The Double Voices of Youth" discloses a variety of discourses, thus picking up voices still inaudible during feminist criticism's more homologous stage. /A more socially overdetermined reading/exposes the lure of the good father as the savior of damsels in distress, and places the mother and daughter figures securely within the boundaries of his power and discourse. But a second reading, /or perhaps "strategic misreading" (to borrow from Gayatri Spivak),[32] discovers a less audible alternative to the authority of dominant paternal or patriarchal discourse. When we perceive the differing positions of these varied discourses, when we hear who really is speaking, the very meanings of the text shift and reposition themselves/Other chapters of this study also bear the influences of these theories: Chapter 2 reveals that silence is the "not-said" repressed or left out of the omnipresence of phallo(go)centric discourse, and chapters 3 and 4 proceed to explore how such discursive omnipresence in the culture—in the forms of gender polarities, textual conventions, myths, and archetypes—can be decentered and countered.

With these theories, Arimneste has begun to hear ever more clearly than she did without them, but a certain unshakeable uneasiness remains. Does this distilled summary of French poststructuralist influences on her reading simply prove that our contemporary Arimneste has traded one set of unsatisfying fathers for another more to her liking, for one that has proffered a more seductive line or lure? Will she continue to regard herself as other in the mirror that they hold out before her? No. I believe she need not fear such bedazzlement, for the very concept of "difference" would foreclose such a move. It would instead spur the inevitable countermove that has been executed by French feminist theorists, women ready to dispute with alacrity. One, Luce Irigaray, has entered the fray with an ostensible reading of Plato, but I suggest that through the Greek philosopher, she is defending her (woman's) terrain against her paternal colleagues. Though they may have problematized their status as privileged subjects, though their irreverence may have cast them as "fellow-travelers," Irigaray is aware of the dangerous lure concealed within the mirror that they hold before her/us. Though they have shaken the foundations of phallogocentrism, they, as subjects, are still the "re-source of specularizations; . . . the 'subject' of discourse is the father . . . the father is, always has been, pure speculation."[33] Irigaray's play on the word for mirroring, her pun on speculum and speculation, bares the dangers of accepting mirrors from these new fathers just because they have said what we may have wanted to hear. There is much in the poststructuralist project that *is* pure speculation, an investment in the paternal academic enterprise, and this is where woman enters to crack or subvert the speculum of the speculators and where Arimneste begins to find a familiar face in the mirror.

French feminist theory and its concept of "l'écriture féminine" has been in recent years one of the most influential countervoices of poststructuralism. Responding first to Freud's reading of female sexuality as a lack, a problematic and even inferior version of masculine sexuality, and then to Lacan's controversial positing of the phallus as the ultimate signifier of desire, French feminist theorists have attempted to circumvent the Symbolic Order of language and culture seemingly mandated by Lacan's Law of the Father. They have sought to devise a mode of expressivity beyond such dominant or paternal discourse, working to structure a language closer to the female body and identified with the mother rather than the father. Their "écriture féminine" thus endeavors to write "difference" as an insistent transgression of paternal Law and as an empowerment of mother and daughter, repositioned now as claimants of redefined subject status through the production of their own discourse.

While the details of each French feminist proposal obviously vary, for the purpose of the readings in this study, their most suggestive resonance is their desire to displace with the primacy of a redefined and self-defined feminine that reigning hierarchy which their male colleagues unveiled and even denounced. Julia Kristeva may stress the subversion of "male orders of logic, mastery, and verisimilitude" through a nonsymbolic "jouissance maternelle"; Hélène Cixous may call for an escape from "male desires for mastery and domination" through a rewriting of woman's place in history; and Luce Irigaray may urge women to affirm their difference through a new mythology of the "(re)productive earth-mother-nature."[34] The precise wording and strategies may differ among them, but all together the goals of these and other French feminist theorists counsel a suggestive triadic process of subversion, escape, and affirmation, one that works to establish what Ann Rosalind Jones has named a "site of 'différence,' a point of view from which phallogocentric concepts and controls can be seen through and taken apart."[35] And these theoretical strategies point to similar gestures in contemporary Spanish narrative by women, especially that of the present decade.

References to Kristeva's nonsymbolic Mother surface in chapter 2 in order to elucidate the painful contradictions of La trampa's protagonist. In chapter 5, the protagonist's decision in Una primavera para Domenico Guarini is made more comprehensible, indeed legible, through Kristeva's insights into the maternal, and in chapter 7, Kristeva's theories help the reader discern the predicament that makes love story living and writing such a chilling challenge. Cixous's call for a rewriting of history provides a framework for chapter 5, "Writing 'Her/story,'" in which the protagonists of three novels find themselves at what Cixous has called "the beginning of a new history" and within a process in which rewritten personal history intersects and blends with that of national and world history, indeed of all women's history, in order to change the shape of women's textualization of her collective story.[36]

Essential for the writing of this proposed new history is the recuperation of close ties between mother and daughter, or more broadly, with woman's matrilineal heritage. On this issue Irigaray queries rhetorically: "How can the relationship between these two women [mother and daughter] be articulated?" In response she proposes: "Here is one place where the need for another 'syntax,' another 'grammar' of culture is crucial."[37] The core of this study is poised to provide multiple answers to Irigaray's query and quest for a language of "woman's desire": from *Nada*'s less visible discourse to *El Sur*'s final magical maternal atmosphere, the contemporary Spanish novel by woman seems to strain for this other "'grammar' of culture." Chapters 4 and 5, especially, voice increasingly bold expressions of maternal desire through their moves to recuperate and rewrite what might variously be labeled matriarchal, matrilinear, or maternal myth, archetype, and history, while the maternal in all the narratives read in this study in some way comes to stand for a metonymic alternative to the presence of patriarchal culture and its symbolic support—phallo(go)centric discourse.

And there are other, perhaps less prominent, though by no means insignificant, theoretical voices from France and elsewhere that have served to clarify the narrative voices that make themselves heard in this book. Annie Leclerc's call for laughter and ridicule characterizes the parodic and subversive tonal quality of the narratives by Paloma Díaz-Mas and Carmen Gómez Ojea read in chapter 6; American critic, Elizabeth Meese's call for a language of defiance certainly defines the strategy of Gómez Ojea and her protagonist, Tarsiana, in *Los perros de Hécate*, the second narrative read in chapter 6. Likewise American Rachel Blau DuPlessis's discovery of another discourse beyond the conventional ending of the romance plot helps reveal the difference in *Nada* and, to a degree, all the narratives read in this study that defer marriage as a convenient ending to their protagonists' plots (those by Carmen Martín Gaite, Carme Riera, Carmen Gómez Ojea and Adelaida García Morales).[38] Annis Pratt's explorations of archetypal patterns in women's fiction help delineate the exact contours of the alternate archetypal and mythic patterns proposed by Alós and Tusquets in the novels read in chapter 4.[39] And Rosemary Jackson's feminist perspectives on cultural meanings in the fantastic provide the grounding for chapter 7's reading of the narratives of García Morales.

Still, these theoretical voices are French and American and British. Have they anything to do with women in Spanish culture? Is it fair to import willy-nilly theories from abroad and force Spanish texts into their perhaps procrustean beds? Why not Spanish feminist theory? Here our North American Arimneste's response might be guarded but firm. Though one cannot point to as prolific nor as original positions in recent Spanish feminist theory, in Spain ideas from abroad have by no means gone unheeded. Since the late seventies, Spain's Arimnestes have been perking up their ears to catch these voices from across the Pyrenees. In 1983, at the Feria del Libro de Madrid, Carme Riera stated categorically that "'la literatura femenina' está de última moda en Europa y América" ("feminine literature" ["l'ecriture feminine"] is the latest trend in Europe and America). Going on to summarize the goals of such a writing enterprise, Riera located difference in two general directions: the raising of consciousness of women's marginal status, and the vindication of "una nueva palabra de mujer, conectada con el propio cuerpo para subvertir leyes, códigos y clasificaciones" (a new woman's word, connected to her own body to subvert laws, codes, and classifications).[40] It seems only logical to make connections between this sighting and citing of trans-Pyrenean feminist theory and the narrative strategies that Riera herself employs.

In 1980, in her essay "¿Por qué no ha habido mujeres genio?" Montserrat Roig sallied forth to consider the issue of "woman's word." She designated woman's archaeological explorations into her own condition as just one preliminary step toward the creation of "nuestro propio lenguaje" (our own language).[41] Almost echoing Irigaray, she describes woman's laborious progress as she moves from rejecting her role as a mirror for men to greater participation in a new dialogue, a dialogue with her own body, with silence, with prohibition. As a result, Roig maintains, the patriarchal figure is tottering; feminine masochism and the interiorized superiority of man are being dismantled. Though Roig cites French feminist, Annie Leclerc, as one who has succeeded in articulating her sexual condition, the Spanish writer opts for even greater heterogeneity, even greater freedom. Indeed, for Roig, woman's welcome loss of innocence has brought the fascinating and terrifying obligation to create, and for her that act of creation is theoretically limitless. It may include a language based on the female body, but it need not be circumscribed by a single dimension of female desire.

Carme Riera, in 1982, provided a thoughtful and balanced appraisal of the interrelationships between French and Anglo-American feminist theories and literature by women. Responding to several articles on the question of difference in women's writing, Riera offers the reasoned argument that though literature itself has no sex, women writers have most certainly entered a new era in which they have recovered their own word and have begun to speak for themselves.[42] This newly autonomous speech can take many forms, of course, and like Roig, Riera is reluctant to circumscribe the new freedom with a single set of ideas. Though she has read Leclerc, Cixous, and Clément, Chawaf, Duras, and Irigaray, and their ideas have exerted an influence on her writing, her curiosity and openness lead her to consider other theories as well: those of masochism in women's writing (Patricia Meyer Spacks), complicity between women writers and readers, orality in women's writing (Marta Traba), the marginality of women and their writing (Julia Kristeva), and the specific linguistic features of women's discourse (Robin Lakoff). Posing more questions than she answers, she leaves the door open for herself and other women writers to recuperate their silenced voices, to merge myth with reason, prophecy with logos, or as she metonymically sums up: "contribuyamos a un encuentro definitivo entre Casandra y Mme Curie" (let us contribute to a definitive meeting between Casandra and Madame Curie).[43] Other Hispanic voices emerging during the early eighties also inquire into many of the same issues. From New York to Barcelona the question of difference in women's writings engenders considerations of what may constitute woman's own language, and the proposals echo a common impulse: women insist on their own discourse, on the appropriation of their own self-defined modes of expression. This may include new visions of the mythical (Araújo), a marginal discourse based on oral tradition (Traba), or the ability to read silences and unveil a multiplicity heretofore shrouded by decrepit or worn out myths (García).[44] These critical, theoretical voices, which traverse the boundaries of Hispanic nationalism, clearly urge interested readers everywhere to perceive their convergence with contemporaneous narrative strategies of Spanish women.

As theories revealing multiplicity and multivocality in the narratives of contemporary Spanish women become more audible, the reader may increasingly perceive how, from the foremothers of the early postwar period to their more recent daughters, Spanish women novelists have struggled with ever-increasing boldness to free their discourse from the restrictive terms of the symbolic contract or the Father's Law. These gathering voices of "difference" are rendered especially audible if we follow Irigaray's musings on Plato a bit further. We then discover the hypothetical longing to imagine a "what if": what if people saw the father for what he is and demanded accountability? What if his "goods, his Good" were divided up?[45] Or, to shift metaphors, what if the father's mirror were taken apart, deconstructed as it were? What might it reveal? Irigaray imagines the following, almost self-evident, response: "two genders, at least, two kinds of resources and specularizations. Truth would lose its univocal and universal character. It could be doubled, for example."[46] What Irigaray really proposes is that woman, as reader and writer, should question the established hegemony of the masculine as universal, that she should uncover another reading to a story that has grounded itself thus far in a single legitimate exegesis. In the words of a Spanish critic who may well have followed Irigaray's lead, the woman writer who desires her own discursive reflection will seek that image: "replanteando el discurso dominante. Interrogando la dominación de los hombres. Hablando a las mujeres, entre mujeres" (by questioning dominant discourse. By interrogating the domination of man. By talking to women, among women).[47] Through this process both writer and reader assume the position of questioning subjects, drawing readings out of a text (as Gayatri Spivak has phrased such a gesture) that may be at odds with "received" readings.[48]

This is the position that I have chosen to assume throughout the following study. Such a posture, by remaining attentive to "difference" in each text and differences among all, draws out readings that may otherwise remain ignored. Each text is perceived in terms of its relationship to the prevailing discourses of its time. However, within their corresponding field, women insert themselves and respond through a variety of voices. The heterogeneity is impressive, ranging from the double-voicing of postwar adolescence to the silence of postwar aging (chapters 1 and 2); from the evolution of orality into textuality to destabilizations of patriarchal myth and proposals for an alternative mythopoesis (chapters 3 and 4); from interrogations to revisions of history (chapter 5); from parody and subversion to transgression and the fantastic (chapters 6 and 7). Though the voices may not be as neatly separate as they appear in the foregoing enumeration, each reading tends to privilege a particular strategy as dominant and characteristic within its particular intersection of historical-cultural and textual discourses. And though the study proposes no absolute or totalizing periodization or subperiodization of the general postwar period, the contours of the readings suggest an increasing boldness through time of the transgressive nature of these narrative voices. To highlight this evolution and draw, wherever possible, distinguishing links between culture and textuality, I have divided the study into the following tripartite structure: postwar (40s to 60s), subtitled "Preludes"; transition (70s), subtitled "In Sotto Voce"; and post-Franco (80s), subtitled "Gathering Chorus." Still, the nature of this confluence between theory and narrative encourages a final opting for a both/and of historical change and continuity.

The chorus is now assembled; the voices that span over forty years of articulation are gathered together in a harmonious blend of differences. Yet there are connections among the various members of this chorus: the desire to speak and create texts, each in her own way; the longing to base that articulation on reforged or recuperated links with mothers and maternal figures; the impulse to overcome silence and achieve, singly and in common, voices of their own. If I were asked to classify the voices or name this chorus in any way, then the matrilineal line from mother to daughter would probably best characterize the textual processes the following readings are about to unfold. The youthful and maturing voices of the first three decades of the postwar period—Laforet, Soriano, Quiroga, Matute—can be viewed as still tentative responses to the demands of a field of sanctioned phallogocentric discourses, hence their grouping in the section named "Preludes." Yet these "foremothers" in discursive struggle leave strong echoes that subsequent generations cannot ignore. As official discourse becomes somewhat less ominous and pervasive, more and more terrain for dialogue gradually emerges in the seventies; that is when the discursive strategies of "transitional" figures like Martín Gaite, Alós, and Tusquets find some space for their voicing—a voicing still somewhat tentative, articulated in a metaphorical "sotto voce." They, in their turn, prepare the terrain for the youngest daughters of a "gathering chorus"—Riera, Gómez Ojea, Ortiz, Díaz-Mas, García Morales—women who can now write with a certain confidence and boldness as women that largely eluded their foremothers during earlier decades.

So there emerge no rigid lines of demarcation nor easily fixed categories. The process of reading contemporary Spanish narrative by women advises us rather to abandon classifications that have failed to address the attributes of women's texts and invites us to engage, instead, in an alternative perception of maternal connections or continuities among women's voices. I realize that this position of "otherness," this ear for the supplemental differences of the maternal, is vulnerable to justifiable criticism. In fact, uneasiness with the positing of maternal difference as an effective escape from the demands of the paternal has been voiced by a number of critics.[49] Are we, then, inadvertently invoking here yet another essentialist binary opposition based on traditional biological distinctions we thought were by now discredited? No doubt such a danger does lurk at the extreme borders of polarized discourse, and Spanish essayist Empar Pineda has sensed its presence. Pineda fears, for instance, that this new feminism of maternal difference could fall once again into a trap of biological determinism, or essentialism, and that maternity could again be viewed through the lens of ahistoricism, idealization, and mystification.[50] But Domna Stanton's antidote to the regressive lure of falling back into traditional or essentialist assumptions about maternal creativity is suggestive in this context. She proposes replacing the maternal as metaphor with the maternal as metonymy, thus shifting the emphasis from "difference from" man to "differences within" and "among" women. This substitution of tropes would underscore "the desire for the other, for something/somewhere else," for an(other) discourse that would be capable of exposing "specific cultural values, prejudices, and limitations."[51] It would shift the plane of our vision to all women, to their heterogeneity, their multivocality.

The maternal would then be the beginning, not the end of our imaginings of something beyond the confines of the patriarchal, paternal, or phallocentric known. This assumption should render us as readers of texts from another culture more sensitive to the choices that each individual writer makes as a woman—indeed is able to make—from options that are historically or culturally available to her; that is, this position should enhance our sensitivity to how contemporary Spanish women novelists modulate their voices and those of their protagonists within the boundaries of their particular discursive position.[52] The position of the maternal other as metonymic trope is therefore never inalterably fixed; instead it points constantly to its own open indeterminacy and lack of finality. Indeed, the metonymic maternal chain establishes the very probability that each discursive position will be queried and ultimately transformed by the addition of another link in this infinitely diverse series. Or, to switch metaphors and resume the initial discursive position of these introductory remarks, each new voice may be expected to join and enhance the steadily swelling chorus to which it, and sundry others, belong. Though the result may be harmonious, there are no requisite demands for conformity to any a priori essentialist position. The maternal trope serves rather to nurture multivocality, diverse strategies of articulation both with and without the authorization of patriarchal, paternal, or phallocentric law.[53] And that is what Arimneste—I, we, all interested readers—are now prepared to discern and enjoy.

Part One
Preludes

1

The Double Voices of Youth
Writing Within and Beyond the Lines of Demarcation in Laforet's *Nada*

Who? Am I? Whom do I follow?
                    —Hélène Cixous, *Illa*

Something in the adolescent condition seeks to speak the as-yet-unspoken, or as Katherine Dalsimer has observed: "poetry is written, journals kept, music composed by individuals who will never again in their lives be creative in these ways."[1] Even tribal initiations of females seek to make the woman "more creative, more alive, more ontologically real."[2] The postwar Spanish narrative of female adolescence is similarly more than a vivid document of the conflictive status of young women in post-Civil War Spain. It also allows the reader an early glimpse of woman's desire as implied writer to achieve some measure of creative and cultural, as well as personal and social, authority. While the postwar narrative of female adolescence encodes how the culture insinuates itself into the beliefs and actions of the young woman and even, in certain ways, becomes the object of her desire, it also speaks in more muted tones of the young woman's reinscription of her cultural position into a text she may more fully claim her own.

The postwar narrative of female adolescence is thus especially revealing when considered within the framework of doubly coming of age as woman and as writer. Clearly the cultural restrictions of postwar Spanish society in many ways exaggerated the limitations usually associated with being an adult in contemporary society. For a young woman enclosed within a prison house of political as well as gender restrictions, coming of age as a writer could be no easy task. That is why Carmen Laforet's *Nada* (1944), as the first significant postwar Spanish novel of female adolescence—indeed as the first significant postwar novel by a woman—stands as such a formidable model of the ontological and creative challenges facing the young woman writer in the years immediately following the Spanish Civil War. This narrative metonymically inscribes the delicate social negotiations and textual renegotiations that the young woman writer's precarious positioning demanded at that time. These strategies here produce two voices: a more dominant conservative one telling of the young woman's ultimate insertion into socially sanctioned respectability; another, more muted one, that also dares to desire along the margins of (the Father's) patriarchal law.[3]

Nada's surface layer is structured to eventually give the impression of social conformity. After flirting with apparently disruptive social elements, the text seems to settle into a comfortable victory of dominant ideology. Yet beneath the level of a rather conventional, mimetic initiation into bourgeois patriarchy lies a more unsettling confrontation with other textual and cultural discourses. This results in a rewriting of the terms of Gothic and Freudian narratives in ways that subtly undercut the apparent escape into the dominant patriarchal order of the first level. As a result of this multivalence, *Nada* emerges as a web of textuality, not only as a tightly structured, socially overdetermined novel. We may perhaps attribute to this early textuality the novel's resonance in subsequent narratives of female adolescence, as well as throughout the development of postwar narrative by women.

Without doubt, *Nada* has left its mark upon a generation of writers and readers who have seen in this novel of youthful development an early mirror of their most intimate longing and desire, their anguish and uneasiness, and yet their eventual development as women and writers in spite of a mean and hostile environment. As contemporary writer, Carmen Kurtz, has voiced with precision: "Muchos años han transcurrido desde ese 1944 en que Carmen Laforet escribió *Nada*. Pero ahora, al releer ese libro, me he dado cuenta de que es un testimonio vivo, que no hay concesiones, ni palabras innecesarias, que Carmen no buscó trucos lingüísticos, ni trucos políticos, que se limitó a decir lo que vio y sintió haciéndonos ver y sentir como ella" (Many years have passed since that 1944 in which Carmen Laforet wrote *Nada*. Yet now, as I reread that book, I realize that it is a living testimony, that there are no concessions, nor unnecessary words, that Carmen did not seek linguistic tricks, nor political tricks, that she limited herself to saying what she saw and felt allowing us to see and feel as she did).[4] *Nada* immediately captured the attention and interest of the very young of its generation, as of Marta Portal, who read the novel on the sly with her companions in Catholic school: "Cuando salió *Nada* y alguna de las niñas mayores consiguió leerla, todo fueron cuchicheos e identificaciones más o menos aproximadas" (When *Nada* came out and one of the older girls managed to read it, everyone whispered and identified more or less with it).[5] Or as Rosa Romá confesses: "Me identifiqué con Andrea, testigo de unas vidas, unos sucesos que reflejaban bien aquellos años en los que yo todavía era una niña" (I identified with Andrea, witness of lives and events that reflected well those years during which I was still a little girl).[6]

Some writers encountered it later or reread it from a more mature perspective, but not with less emotion or appetite. As Marta Portal continues, "Después la leí vorazmente como incipiente escritora y me quedó muy grabado 'el clima' de la novela, la atmósfera de sordidez existencial en que se mueve la familia de la calle Aribau" (Afterwards I read it voraciously as a beginning writer and the "climate" of the novel etched itself upon me, the atmosphere of existential sordidness in which the family of Aribau Street moves).

For Susana March "el mayor bien que *Nada* aportó a las letras españolas fue su rotundo éxito de crítica y de lectores" (the best thing that *Nada* contributed to Spanish letters was its absolute success with the critics and readers).[7] Young Catalan writer, Carme Riera, acknowledges the profound influence on her own work of *Nada*'s theme of female friendship and its open ending.[8] Or, finally, as one of Spain's most prestigious editors and writers says with simplicity: "*Nada* es un libro que marcó un hito en la novelística española de la posguerra" (*Nada* is a book that marks a milestone in the Spanish postwar novel).[9]

As the personal testimony of these writers makes clear, *Nada* has echoed across the decades with a singular influence. This is not to say that *Nada* need be viewed narrowly as the only "Urtext" for all narratives by women that succeed it. However, it appears quite evident that somehow this seemingly naive product of a young woman's imagination helped open up latent wellsprings of female creativity. One might attribute its function as prototype to its presence as encouragement to other women writers—if this young woman could break into the powerfully entrenched publishing establishment, then others could too. But *Nada*'s status as model seems to rest upon a firmer base than its commercial success. Though it might be extravagant to force too many specific or direct influences—only Riera confessed such links to me—there is little doubt that *Nada*'s narrative strategies mark the beginning of a shift in textual responses to postwar culture for a generation of young women just beginning to write.

Yet *Nada* is not explicitly nor blatantly a self-conscious novel; its references to texts and their function are still oblique and infrequent. Still, as the mature narrative voice recollects the experiences of her immature self, the reader becomes more and more aware that the stories the young girl hears and the plots of the lives around her are the very threads that will be woven into her text. This becomes especially clear when the narrator reflects upon the departure of Andrea for Madrid: "De la casa de la calle de Aribau no me llevaba nada. Al menos, así creía yo entonces" (From the house on Aribau Street I carried nothing with me. At least, that is what I believed then).[10] The central irony of all her recollections—objectionable as they may be to her younger self—is precisely this: that without them, the text her older self has generated, and the one that has spun itself around us, would not exist.

Inherent, then, in the whole of *Nada* is an implicit and early search for a text adequate and appropriate for the young female writer. Facing a consecrated discursive heritage of institutionalized masculine authority, the young woman must struggle against the often alien voices of others to find those more in harmony with her own desires, her own gender. Wherever she might look, she finds disturbing models among her contemporaries—for example Cela's *La familia de Pascual Duarte*. If, as Robert Spires has observed, Cela portrays a protagonist in *La familia* for whom matricide was an existential necessity,[11] must a woman also turn against her mother and ultimately herself in the course of her own development? Or, conversely, if male writers need an absent woman to write (as Hélène Cixous has suggested), does a woman writer need to erase male presence to proceed analogously?[12] What might be at stake in the female creative process—at least in the youthful one that beckons a new generation of writers during the early years of the postwar period? What in this young woman writer's inventory is deemed suitable for appropriation? What seems to be revised or cast aside? How, even under the rigors of censorship, does this young woman insist upon a text more genuinely her own? The following reading of two levels of signification in *Nada* should at least suggest approximations to these and other questions about young female authorship in the years immediately following the Spanish Civil War.

On one level, perhaps its most obvious, *Nada* leaves this impression: it seems to gently nudge its protagonist in the direction of ideological safety and legitimacy. Its young protagonist, Andrea's, series of adventures and misadventures align themselves in such a way that she is temporarily inserted into a devalued form of the family (according to the bourgeois patriarchal discourse of her time), and then allowed to abandon that setting in order to move outward and into a privileged familial structure (again defined implicitly by the same reigning discourse).[13] Measured against the ideals of such discourse, Andrea's uncle Juan—mediocre painter and often brutal spouse—appears an ironic parody of the culture's ideal father-provider and husband. Clearly he possesses no real authority, dubious intelligence, a desperate impotence compensated for by violence and rage, and a nonexistent spirit of enterprise. The terms of that same discursive contract counterpoise against him his apparent opposite, Andrea's friend Ena's father, bourgeois entrepreneur and metonymic representative of the colorless backbone of Catalan enterprise and efficiency. It is between these two male figures that Andrea, in the broad course of her development, moves—from the spectral Juan, whom Andrea encounters upon her arrival in Barcelona, to the luminous father of Ena, with whom she finally embarks for a newly reordered existence in Madrid. Andrea's final initiation seems, then, entirely in keeping with the values of postwar patriarchal discourse, grounded themselves upon a perfectly functioning series of connections between the public paternal authority (El Caudillo) and the private familial sphere.[14]

Once positioned within this discursive framework we, as readers, tend to view Juan and his brother, Román—the sole surviving male members of a family in decay—as signs of an historical degeneration of patriarchal authority. Certainly they fail to measure up to their culture's privileged model for paternal behavior (authoritarian strength and protectiveness), and appear rather to represent the other side of the same discursive coin; that is, the ugly, degraded face of patriarchal power that manifests itself in an aggressive violation of female vulnerability. Juan's brutality and fury are consequences also of his pariah status within the bourgeois economy. Lacking even the resources of a working man, he enjoys no material basis upon which to erect his authority. Desperation with this positioning drives him to the dubious compensation of physical violence in order to impose his fragile will and assuage his unrelenting frustration. Measured by these same discursive terms, Román, too, appears as a man without economic consequence. Involved in some mysterious shady business ventures, he reflects the sordid side of postwar bourgeois patriarchy. Yet Román is more than an economic outcast. He may personify those aspects of the culture that, because of their unacknowledged unsavory characteristics, must project themselves upon a scapegoat, eliminate it, and thereby cleanse the collective conscience. Set up to perform this cultural function of scapegoat, Román is repeatedly portrayed as demonic and evil, as fascinating and overpowering young girls (Andrea and Ena), as having previously caused women to stray from the path of righteousness (Ena's mother), as attempting to seduce his brother's wife (Gloria), and as being more bestial than the beasts (the family dog is injured by Román's bite). The ethical preference of bourgeois patriarchal discourse seems to offer no place for such transgressors of its values, so Román is conveniently erased by self-immolation.

Layered onto this largely social and secular discourse of patriarchy are the additional unsettling implications of Catholic discourse, which names this troubled uncle Román, and thus casts him as a pariah in still another sense. Denominated heathen in a Christian world, Román's untamable and primitive sensuality must remain unauthorized by the rigid demands of Catholic discourse. Pierre Ullman has apparently caught these implications, postulating that "in a very broad sense, *Nada* could be called a Catholic novel. For one thing, certain notes and themes indicate the author's unconscious acceptance of her traditional education."[15] But we must be careful to identify this as only one of the discursive threads of the novel, and one that may indeed divert the reader's attention from an(other), less sanctioned story. Still, according to the terms of *this* reading, Román—as a dark and uncontrollable demonic force that requires sacrifice—surfaces as a manifestation of an unspoken Christian desire to cleanse the world of difference and dissent.

If this reading portrays Juan and Román as the embodiment of that that is odious and objectionable to the bourgeois patriarchal ideal, then the father of Ena eventually comes to inscribe "healthy" standards for the ideal patriarchal male. Whereas the uncles are bitter, sullen and possessed, Ena's father seems without malice, simple, open, sympathetic, and composed. And while Juan and Román are ineffectual and nonenterprising in business matters—remnants of a nonproductive, parasitic class—Ena's father is enterprising, active in the everyday struggles of the commercial world, and emblematic of a renewed vigor within the patriarchal bourgeoisie. The latter could even be called, quite aptly, a metonymic figure for the "one-dimensional man" who, according to Antoni Jutglar, "está empeñandose, cada día más, en no pensar" (is attempting, more and more each day, not to think).[16] Andrea describes Ena's father in just these terms and is seduced by their apparently unproblematic appeal: "era una de esas personas que no saben estar solas ni un momento con sus propios pensamientos. Que no tienen pensamientos quizá. Sin embargo, me era extraordinariamente simpático" (he was one of those people who don't know how to be alone with their own thoughts for even a moment. That perhaps don't even have thoughts. Nevertheless, I found him extraordinarily appealing) (272). It is not long until Andrea gravitates toward the security and order seemingly proffered by this positive side of patriarchy, and she seeks actively to associate herself with the familial group that enjoys privileges unknown to her more aberrant family: "me agregaba a la patriarcal familia" (I attached myself to the patriarchal family) (120).

While the male figures of *Nada* encode two sides of patriarchal discourse, one that ultimately appears privileged, the female figures also present—within the discursive terms of this reading—a contrastive polarity of adult female behavior in which one of the sides is again privileged. On the apparently devalued side stands Andrea's aunt, Gloria, never able to definitively transcend her status as a victim of patriarchal degradation. Constantly reaffirming that she is good and that she is pretty, Gloria pays lip service to the fact that she could make a better life for herself outside the insane asylum that is the house on Aribau Street. Yet unable to fully overcome her negative qualities of slovenliness, bestiality and reification, she remains an object of Juan's physical violence. Gloria does achieve the modest victory of learning to "take care" (characterized thusly by Patricia Spacks: "Woman's psychic triumph comes from responding to man's needs. . .").[17] But she remains so much in need of taking care that she is rendered utterly incapable of fleeing her oppression: "Pero a veces me acaricia, me pide perdón y se pone a llorar como un niño pequeño. . . . Y yo, ¿qué voy a hacer?" (But sometimes he caresses me, he asks for forgiveness and he starts crying like a small child. . . . And I, what am I going to do?) (291). In Gloria's case, "taking care" seems more a liability than a virtue.

Also, like many other Spanish women of the postwar period, Gloria finds herself forced to defy the terms of bourgeois, patriarchal discourse by engaging in secret work in order to allow her husband his illusion of economic importance.[18] Gloria's clandestine gambling is an essential source of family income. However, when Juan ventures into the red-light district of Barcelona and discovers his wife's employment, his blindfold is forcibly removed; he must confront the secret of his wife's gambling as a function of her taking care and the maintenance of his illusion. That is why the episode's closing image of Juan leaning upon his wife, though seemingly compassionate, could (within the terms of a privileged domestic economy) signal an undesirable reversal of authorized gender-specific roles. Therefore, from the perspective of dominant discourse regarding gender, this image of wife supporting husband might well be read as a metonymic figure signifying the perversion of traditional, consecrated familial structures (as described, for example, by Gomá) in which the husband and father is expected to provide the pillar of support for his wife and the mother of his children. Worst of all, according to these same discursive terms, Gloria's virtual abandonment of her ill baby while she goes out to gamble undermines the possible positive qualities of her conjugal caretaking and casts her still more censoriously as an incompetent and capricious mother.

It is therefore to Ena's family, and precisely to Ena's mother, whom Andrea eventually turns for a model of woman, wife, and mother apparently privileged by the traditional patriarchal economy. Ena's mother is a gracious complement rather than a threat or replacement for Ena's father and his role as provider. While he immerses himself in the hurly-burly of the business world, she busies herself with pregnancies and childbirths, all the while remaining a refuge of refinement and sensibility to which he can return after his hectic activities. If the husband and father is synonymous with activity, the wife and mother signifies repose. Her more obvious functions inscribe the ideal of a discourse of paternal "courtesy" relayed by Carlos Castilla del Pino from the words of Botella Llusiá, professor of obstetrics and gynecology: "Sería bello . . . que el hombre, cuando llega cansado a su casa, se encontrase no con una mujer también agotada, . . . sino con una mujer que tiene una cultura que a veces a él le falta, y que le sirve de complemento y reposo" (It would be lovely . . . if the man, when he returns tired to his home, would find not a woman who is also exhausted, . . . but a woman who has a refinement that at times he lacks, and who serves as his complement and his repose).[19]

Although Ena's mother seems to have been infantilized by marriage (her husband addresses her affectionately as "Mi niña" [my child]); although even her marriage was largely the result of paternal volition, and its fruits were bitter before they were sweet; although so many aspects of this bourgeois marriage were oppressive and stultifying, the magic wrought by becoming the mother of Ena seems to compensate fully for these tribulations. With the initially unwelcome birth of Ena, the mother seems to achieve the true "essence" of womanhood according to the reigning cultural discourse of her time. The baby's birth teaches the mother the meaning of renunciation, comprehension, and tenderness; the young mother learns that love is not only a blind passion between woman and man. In short, for Ena's mother, maternity functions as a door that opens unknown horizons of feeling—allowing the young mother to free herself from selfishness and the self-centeredness of youth—and it serves as an entry to one of the most respected roles for women within the dominant discursive contract of that particular historical moment.

On this level, the characterization of Ena's mother rests upon and integrates a complex of political and religious discourses about women during the time of the novel's writing. The linking of political and religious ideologies at that time grounded the idealized image of womanhood on such unselfish qualities as sacrificial love, passive acceptance of suffering, humility, and meekness. A German writing in the same year as the publication of *Nada*, and himself an official ideologue of the Nazi regime in praise of the Caudillo, expresses an idealizing praise of Spanish womanhood that echoes the Nazi glorification of "Kinder, Küche, Kirche": "La española ante todo, es madre, y sólo en segundo lugar esposa y amante" (The Spanish woman is, above all, a mother, and only in second place wife and lover).[20] Beinhauer goes on to say that because the Spanish woman sees maternity as her principal destiny, she is therefore worthy of greater respect. She is also accorded exclusive dominion over the family, the obligation of the father consisting in protecting his family and in providing them the means of existence.[21] This discourse of a gender-specific domestic economy casts Ena's mother—in her most visible aspects—as an amalgam responding to values iterated by the Christian and patriarchal discourses that prevailed during the early postwar period.

Eventually, the same bourgeois economy that defines and privileges Ena's mother's accommodation to the circumstances of her existence, pushes Andrea to come to terms with the relationship between her social status and her maturation into womanhood. An invitation to the party of her friend, Pons, elicits a wave of illusion and fantasy, a dream of unfettered horizons. Andrea fancies herself a Cinderella, a fairy princess, and articulates her embodiment of feminine qualities in a manner echoing Freud: "Al correr al espejo, contemplaba, temblorosa de emoción, mi transformación asombrosa en una rubia princesa . . . inmediatamente dotada, por gracia de la belleza, con los atributos de dulzura, encanto y bondad" (Rushing to the mirror, I contemplated, trembling with emotion, my amazing transformation into a blond princess . . . immediately blessed, through graceful beauty, with the attributes of sweetness, charm and goodness) (215).[22] Andrea's fairytale imagining thus encodes a strong libidinal urge to incorporate herself into the privileged bourgeoisie, but she is at that moment too possessed by her putative "instintos de mujer" (womanly instincts) (214) and too deluded by her desire to be an admired and praised object, to realize that her fantasies of femininity are ironically doomed by the very restrictions of the economy she desires. Wherever she goes, she seems fated to clash against barriers of class if not of gender.

Andrea is received coldly at Pons's party as she carries the stigma of her degraded family upon her: she literally wears its mark on her body in the form of old and inappropriate shoes. Unlike the legendary Cinderella, she does not receive the magical glass slipper enabling her to transcend her class; hers are worn shoes, insistent material manifestations of the gap between the world of childish fantasy and the cruel realities of social divisions. Neither does Andrea find glory at the ball, but instead rejection by another woman, Pons's mother, who represents and enforces the class barriers of her culture. Inversions of the Cinderella motif thus serve to instruct the protagonist that she cannot be as free as her youthful imagination had fancied. The demythification of Cinderella serves as a significant lesson on Andrea's path toward culturally acceptable womanhood; it stands as a painful reminder of the clash between desire and the culture's demands for woman's propriety in function as well as social positioning. However, just as Andrea returns to the house on Aribau Street with her hopes for escape dashed by her expulsion from this naive dream of paradise, Ena's mother coincidentally happens to be waiting for her to at least attenuate the class barriers of Andrea's position.

A heart-to-heart talk between Andrea and Ena's mother, strategically placed at the beginning of the third and final part of the novel, serves to round out this level of the protagonist's developmental trajectory and expose her to a privileged and seemingly definitive model of womanhood—the self-sacrificial mother of patriarchal discourse. When the conversation between Andrea and Ena's mother begins, Andrea is still an unhappy child suffering from her recent disappointment. But as this mother reveals her innermost feelings, Andrea begins to forget about herself, transcend her adolescent self-centeredness, and find peace and compassion in a total identification with the thoughts and feelings of her friend's mother. Like Andrea, Ena's mother was once caught in a trap of fantasies and literary deceptions that mediated between herself and reality. Parallel to Andrea's Cinderella fantasy was the mother's fantasy of herself as heroine of a romantic novel, and this fantasy caused her mistaken youthful attraction to Román. The older and younger women also parallel each other in their early misinterpretations about the nature of femininity, and their self-deception as women deluded by overactive imaginations. So, as Ena's mother recounts the vicissitudes and joys of her life, Andrea is movingly exposed to a defense of maternity and a reaffirmation of woman's role of "taking care."

From the point of view of dominant patriarchal discourse, Andrea's identification with Ena's mother positions her solidly between the roles of adopted bourgeois daughter and future self-sacrificing mother, conceding to her more stability and satisfaction within the ambience of that desired social class than any roles she had essayed before. The novel ends with Andrea in the company of Ena's father as the two depart for Madrid. She has been invited to live with this family and to work in the father's business. From this perspective, Andrea "retires to a comfortable position after an exciting venture," as Sherman Eoff has observed.[23] Andrea views her final opportunity as an opening of "los horizontes de la salvación" (the horizons of salvation) (293), not those of adventure, uncertain changes, or freedom. She appears increasingly sobered as she grows out of adolescence, more and more interested in the values of light, order, and security. Although she manifested a certain fascination with the eccentricities of the family on Aribau Street, Andrea's sympathies were often directed toward material well-being, and even more toward the stability of "the patriarchal family" (20).

Thus it is that the ending of *Nada* is both a new beginning and a potential ending. From this perspective, the novel ends ideologically—going away with Ena's father forms a sharp contrast to Andrea's accompanying and aiding Juan in his journey through the red-light district. But even within the framework of this socially overdetermined reading, there is no way to say that the novel ends with absolute closure. There is, instead, a kind of calculated openness—the neatness of the symbol of a new dawn, the setting out on a journey—while, at the same time, the selection of character and circumstance are such that the journey becomes a little less risky, the projected outcome a little more secure. This time the cards seem stacked in Andrea's favor, at least from the perspective of the dominant discourses of her culture. As Andrea makes her journey toward the horizons of social salvation, her quest appears rounded off into patriarchy's image of safety and security: the sanctioned bourgeois familial order.

Another story exists alongside, or below the surface of the reassuringly conservative one with which *Nada* apparently ends. The novel's coincidentally irreverent look at postwar society shocked and even angered cultural authorities. Somehow, even if their readings were to ultimately reveal values not unlike their own, censors were quick to reprove a world that apparently clashed with the regime's official ideology. The novel's often degraded environment and characters clearly subverted the ideology of optimism that the victors' discourse wished to promote. A horrified spokesman for the Instituto Nacional del Libro Español (INLE) decried in 1945 what he called an "Asiatic" menace threatening occidental culture and luring writers to "abatir toda la construcción conceptual y estética creada por la civilización cristiana. De ellos es Carmen Laforet" (demolish the whole conceptual and esthetic structure created by Christian civilization. Among them is Carmen Laforet).[24] Curiously, this representative of the regime's cultural discourse sensed that *Nada* was also "deconstructing" certain established ideological and esthetic conventions that were officially sanctioned at the end of the Civil War.

Nada's ending and apparent privileging of one side of a sociocultural antinomy was apparently not enough to quell the uneasiness of officialdom. This text was also engaging in a more subtle destabilization of generic expectations (and therefore indirectly of ideology).[25] Its engagement with a rewriting of Gothic and Freudian narrative paradigms insinuated that something less cozy lurked beyond the apparently clear resolution of undesirable and desirable oppositions that we have just observed. *Nada*'s veiled challenges to these generic contracts instead intimate subtle transgressions of intertextual paradigms, thus serving to interrogate the apparently conservative implications of its binary surface structure.

It is widely known that many readers have detected in *Nada* resonances of the Gothic novel, specifically *Wuthering Heights*.[26]

David William Foster and others have pointed out the affinity of the tenebrous house on Aribau street and its phantasmal, degenerate inhabitants with the stock setting and characters of the Gothic tradition. Yet, until this poststructuralist era, we were largely unprepared to conjecture how this intertextual echo might transgress the categories of dominant discourse. In *Nada* the Gothic intertext is exploited, no doubt, for its thematic and esthetic potential, but the demands of another historical moment also push this generic borrowing beyond the strictest bounds of traditional convention.

By weaving itself, at least in part, from the Gothic tradition, *Nada* is able to evoke the deepest fears and desires of its readership. The house becomes a shrunken version of every child's castle, and as such, it establishes what Leona Sherman has called an "axis of fear and desire."[27] From that location, the reader tends to fit other elements into their customary slots and react accordingly: s/he wishes to fear and admire characters lined up neatly into good and bad; s/he awaits the revelation of a shocking family secret; s/he fears woman's victimization and then longs for her eventual salvation. (These are perhaps the very literary conventions that unconsciously inspire the terms of our first reading.) A titillating nightmarish region of mystery and potential danger beckons us not only to enter the narrative, but to eventually seek repose. Using this narrative ruse, *Nada* pulls its reader into its world, yet as it seduces its readership with resonances of the Gothic mode, it moves subtly out and beyond toward a revised text of its own.

People and events in *Nada* are finally not as starkly polarized as they might be in traditional Gothic narrative (or in the discourses of postwar patriarchy). The reader ultimately finds that the gratifying option of choosing between clearly delincated polarities is withheld. Moving beyond the Gothic narrative contract, *Nada* disallows the foisting of our fears or loathing upon an evil villain; our desires can find no satisfaction in untainted goodness. Something enters the Gothic device to break it down from within, and various characters suggest obliquely how this occurs. Román, for example, who appears as the novel's closest approximation to a villain (involved as he is with shady dealings and seductions of females outside the cramped moral space he claims as his own), is actually introduced early on as agreeable, affectionate, and jolly (28). Though later he *does* appear demonic, his ultimate permutation is to become, after his death, the object of the narrator's desire: "me acometía una nostalgia de Román, un deseo de su

presencia" (a nostalgia for Román hit me, a desire for his presence) (286). In his absence she realizes her loss, especially her
longing for his esthetic presence, his hands caressing passionate
sounds from the strings of his violin or the weathered keys of his
old piano. Thus neither simply bad nor good, Román transcends
traditional Gothic moral polarities (and by extension dominant
patriarchal discourse) to become for the narrator a figure encoding ambivalence, indeed a difference grounded in desire.

At once inside and outside the dominant culture—as a man who
is also political outsider and worshipper of pagan idols—Román
creates as would a woman; that is, he submerges himself in waves
of fervent artistic expression, defying the boundaries of legitimacy that frame his separate little world. His obsessive and defiant immersion in his art provides a more suggestive model for
the narrator than does his more readily apparent malevolent
disposition. In the course of his downfall, as he sheds the role of
Gothic villain to don the attributes of misunderstood and doomed
romantic artist, it is this role as creative outsider that kindles the
fires of Andrea's final longing for him. In this way he is something
akin to the Heathcliff that Sandra Gilbert and Susan Gubar read
in *Wuthering Heights:* Román's dark, brooding qualities as an artist
seem to escape in some way the civilizing strictures of patriarchal
discourse.[28] Representing an artist on the margins of officially
sanctioned culture, Román cannot be easily written off by the
liminal would-be author. Instead, as he insinuates himself into her
unconscious imagination, the compelling image that finally remains is that of his hands—hands, which analogous to the words
of the emergent writer, "sabían dar la elocuencia justa de un
momento" (knew how to express the precise eloquence of a moment) (287). She, too, implicitly seeks precise, incisive expression
from the elusive, slippery medium of literary discourse.

The problem of expression or lack thereof is a central legacy
that finds its way from Gothic narrative to its rewriting in *Nada.*
Nada seems to structure itself around that aspect of the Gothic
that Holland and Sherman have called the "topos of the mysterious family secret," with the castle as the all-encompassing structural symbol for concealment.[29] In the house on Aribau Street,
Andrea seems party to similar hidden aspects concerning the
interrelationships of the house's strange inhabitants. As does the
heroine of the Gothic, she overhears "los susurros de la casa" (the
murmurs of the house) (208), mysterious sounds that hide the
secrets of adult lives from her. Yet the secrets turn out to be the
rather banal rantings of the frustrated threesome—Juan, Román,

and Gloria—and Román's relentless impulse to seduce his sister-in-law.

Through its desire to disclose, *Nada* moves to a kind of counter-Gothic, insisting on the revelation of more sordid aspects of post-war urban life. The "mystery" of Gloria's nocturnal disappearances is witnessed by the narrator as activities for economic survival; the "mystery" of Gloria's nonrelationship with Román is revealed through a conversation between them overheard by the narrator. *Nada*'s counter-Gothic thus bares multiple sources of female entrapment and opens the castle doors to reveal that woman is entrapped as much by words and actions as by heavy stone walls. To this effect, when Gloria attempts to tell her version of her own life to Andrea, the young writer woman is thereby situated as receiver of another text that leaps across the boundaries of the traditional Gothic moat.

Gloria proves, in a very real sense, to be trapped in somebody else's text rather than in a concrete castle/house. During the war, she is actually sheltered with Juan and Román in a "marvelous castle" (50), but there and elsewhere it turns out that castle walls were not the menacing enclosures of the Gothic. In fact, quite taken with the amenities of her castle lodging, Gloria was trapped instead within unintelligibility—a more portable kind of enclosure. The words of male discourse entrapped her, words that were exchanged in secrecy, behind closed doors: "Juan y Román se encerraban para hablar. Creía que hablaban de mí. Estaba segura de que hablaban de mí" (Juan and Román locked themselves up to talk. I thought they were talking about me. I was sure that they were talking about me) (48). She internalizes a fear of the brothers' power to script her movements, to write her into their text—dispositions that she can neither accept nor understand. Furthermore, the exclusively male preoccupations of wartime provided the context of their "writing" of her life, thus rendering that context as unfathomable to Gloria as their words. Her place in their text was always as marginal creature, even as pariah. Only when Andrea appears as interlocutor or implied reader, does Gloria attempt, as narrator, to give form to her experience and name her longing for another text, one with a happier ending, or even more, one in which she might be the author of her own plot.

When Gloria describes the sweetness of Juan's affectionate return from the front as like "el final de una novela" (the end of a novel) or "el final de una película" (the end of a movie) (53, 54), she expresses her desire for the happy ending that she craved but that the realities of a harsh existence could not allow. Hers was to

be a text that continued, one in which the happy ending was
paradoxically just the beginning, and the worst was yet to come.
Still, in the face of such depressing turns in the plot, Gloria's wild
spirit prevails. As she struggles to move beyond her subjugation to
an increasingly violent male text, she provides another of what the
narrator has called the "complete and dark stories" of the house of
Aribau Street (43), weaving with her unsentimental narrative yet
another strand in the narrator's post-Gothic text.

Gloria's narrative also ultimately discloses to Andrea that the
contemporary narrative text (which more closely follows the
shape of life itself) can no longer expect the beautiful closure of a
circle (251). Beyond the predictable resolution of Gothic and
other popular narrative for women will have to lie a different text,
one that embraces the messiness, openness, and ongoing travails
of experience. Though Andrea does not explicitly articulate as
much, we, as readers, finally discover what is perhaps the most
important theoretical implication of Gloria's narrative: Gloria's
existential condition, her desire to set the record straight, and the
peculiar situation of the contemporary female writer emerge as
striking analogues. This character and the woman who takes up a
pen are similarly caught within a largely male-authored, even
bellicose text and culture. Such a textual or discursive enclosure
compels them to seek an outlet from their uneasiness, which they
do on occasion by brazenly seizing the word and telling their own
side of a largely untold or unheeded story. Certainly, in this role
of woman attempting to flee the forced encirclement of the
Other's words, Gloria breaks out from the prison house of overwhelming negativity where our first, more socially overdetermined reading seems to have finally consigned her.

If Gloria's uneasiness with the male "text" discloses female desires for alternatives to imprisoning discourse, and if Román's
compelling expression provides a model of wild esthetic passion,
then Juan's contrasting artistic aridity provides one more model
of artistic creation that the young woman, as implied writer, will
inventory and implicitly challenge. As the narrator describes:
"Juan pintaba trabajosamente y sin talento, intentando re-
producir pincelada a pincelada aquel fino y elástico cuerpo. En el
lienzo iba apareciendo un acartonado muñeco" (Juan painted
with effort and without talent, attempting to reproduce stroke by
stroke that fine and elastic body. On the canvas there began to
appear a pasteboardlike mannequin) (36). In contrast to Juan's
stiff and sterile images, Gloria is redrawn by the narrator's words
into an incredibly beautiful and miraculous creature. Juan can

only rage against his subject, but he cannot truly see her. Though her body holds the answers to his artistic expression, something separates this would-be artist from woman's vital potential; he paints but a deadened representation of her body, not her living corporeality. And yet, Juan's esthetic blindness is not without significance: the metonymy of one unseeing male eye and one unyielding brush suggests the need for difference if the "body" of woman's creation is to avoid confinement in the Other's rules of representation.

Temporarily, however, Andrea was also prey to another kind of blindness as she dreamed of escaping the meanness of Aribau Street by playing at Cinderella. But, as we have seen, that fairy-tale plot is ironically deconstructed in the world of social-class restrictions, and with its rupture, Andrea's dream of a possible Freudian conclusion to her narrative evaporates. That is, the heterosexual bond with Pons that might have provided an escape route from her undesirable home failed to materialize.[30] This turn in the plot is another mark of difference significant to the reader, who by this point in the narrative (having observed the text's shifts and turns vis-à-vis the Gothic contract) now suspects, and more than likely desires, that Freud's narrative of feminine development will also be revised or reversed. So when Ena's mother appears on the scene to narrate the story of her youth and marriage, less visible layers of the plot begin to surface. While Ena's mother talks of her symbiotic bond with her daughter, and as she affirms this intimacy, she not only reaffirms official patriarchal discourse regulating women, ironically she also signals a virtual rewriting of Freud's narrative resolution for women.

By stressing the essential continuity of the mother-daughter relation—the dyadic matrix of two generations of women—Ena's mother comes to represent the maternal side of a Demeter-Kore relationship, first to her daughter, then, from the moment of their conversation onward, with Andrea.[31] The mother, rather than the lover, becomes the bearer of meaning, the "writer" of a different discourse. When Andrea finds it easy to understand the mother's language of creation ("este idioma de creación," 240), she not only identifies with her future sociobiological role as mother, she also begins to encode the discourse of future texts by women. The foregoing realization enunciates an implicit affirmation of what Hélène Cixous has called a "langue maternelle," a maternal tongue or "a language that searches for and comes from the other(-mother)."[32] Though, as we shall see in subsequent chapters, Cixous's idea of such a language will reach its fullest flower after years of postwar female authorship have passed, it is not without significance that *Nada* already sows the seeds for such sources of female authorship; it writes the prologue for (or voices the prelude to) future strategies of supplementarity. As Conley reminds us, the image of two women giving and receiving functions as a metaphor for the poetic process.[33] Even if the exchange between Ena's mother and Andrea is initially read as a conservative affirmation of woman's proper biological and cultural role, underlying this more apparent reading lurks always the more destabilizing implications of such female bonding and sources of inspiration. This becomes especially possible when reread by subsequent generations of readers from the perspective of an(other) field of sociocultural discourses. Then the mother-daughter dyad provides a potential source for alternative narrative strategies, standing initially as metaphor, later as metonymic means for evading the absolute encirclement of patriarchal (or phallocentric) discourse.

In *Nada* the maternal bond soon spills over into analogous bonds of female friendship as Andrea seeks to protect her friend, Ena, from the possible advances of her uncle, Román. Until this occurs, the friendship between Ena and Andrea is sporadic, infected by Ena's apparent thralldom to Román's malefic powers. Sometimes Ena is exceedingly affectionate and communicative; on other occasions, she seems cool and aloof to her friend. But after the intimate exchange between Ena's mother and Andrea, the latter is better equipped to "read" her friend's actions and attitudes with greater acumen. Another intimate conversation, this time between the two friends, contains more surprising revelations that actually begin Andrea's own revised reading of the motivations of her friend ("empecé a mirar a mi amiga, viéndola por primera vez tal como realmente era" [I began to regard my friend, seeing her for the first time as she really was]) (267). Even incoherences seem charged with meaning.

Though Ena was indeed fascinated by Román's magnetism, she also had a curious ulterior motive for her actions. Indeed, there was always some method to her madness. She knew about her mother's youthful infatuation with Andrea's uncle, and she also knew about her mother's humiliation by this eccentric manipulator. Part of her apparently mesmerized adherence to this older man was for no other reason than to effect some form of daughterly vengeance for her mother. Instead of a case of romantic thralldom pure and simple, Ena's apparent seduction is reshaped, at least in part, into a practical and loving consequence of the mother-daughter dyad. This bond, a compelling reason for Ena's desire to humiliate Román, drives Ena to exact a punishment that her mother was powerless to do. As Ena rewrites her mother's plot, and Andrea and Ena resolidify the bonds of their friendship, *Nada* takes one more final swerve from more traditional (Gothic or Freudian) narratives.

Instead of tying off into a modernized myth of Cinderella, Andrea's final affirmation of her bonds with Ena and her friend's mother signals the narrative transgression that Rachel Blau Du-Plessis has found recurrent in the writings of modern women, and that Virginia Woolf discovered through earlier readings of Mary Carmichael: "Chloe liked Olivia."[34] Opting to close with a strong affirmation of female bonding and only the shadowy possibility of heterosexual pairing, *Nada* insists on the preeminence of women's friendship as a more positive and self-affirming ending to the narrative of feminine development than romantic pairing or marriage. In this light, Andrea's going off to Madrid with Ena's father proves more than an integration into *his* patriarchal world. His world is but a stepping stone to a room of Andrea's own: "podrás escoger a tu gusto tu domicilio" (you may choose your dwelling as you like) (293–94). Thus what appears, at least on the surface, to be a safe and conservative ending headed for social conformity, is then charged with other, more disruptive possibilities for the young emergent female writer. Faced at once with a social and literary culture that would seek to organize her life and her text according to the demands of alien discourses, she explores the implications of the lives around her to posit—at least tentatively—alternative modes of thought, action, and writing. Above all, the young woman draws from maternal sources of inspiration, with all the metaphoric and metonymic power they may bestow on her gender, so that she may eventually become the mother of her own self-modulated voice and author of her revised cultural positioning.

Nada thus ends with two eventualities, the possibilities of conventional textual and cultural closure or continued openness. By opting for both voices or implications, this text could pass the political censors and indirectly subvert the very underpinnings of their hesitations. Even more importantly, this early narrative of female adolescence could provide a textual model for numerous descendants, proving that one could render unto Caesar with a "correctly" coded text on one level, while at the same time, with sleight and artifice, one could insinuate a subtext with the elusive magic of Cassandra. *Nada*'s closing motif of the journey is therefore not unparadoxically rich and resonant with the promise of openness. Its road beckons others, luring future generations of questing women writers toward horizons where their lives and texts may become more increasingly their own.

2

Feminine Plots and Their Undertow
Aging, Ambivalence, and Silence in Narratives by Soriano, Quiroga, and Matute

"The times are not ripe for us," the times are "not yet."
—Tillie Olsen, *Silences*

In contrast to the postwar narrative of female adolescence, which moves toward a greater degree of existential and textual openness and revision, the novel of female aging from the fifties and sixties appears to move in an opposite direction toward increasing existential and textual closure and dispossession. The funnelled structure of narratives such as those that occupy our attention in this chapter—Elena Soriano's *La playa de los locos (The Beach of the Mad)* (1955), Elena Quiroga's *La enferma (The Madwoman)* (1955), and Ana María Matute's *La trampa (The Trap)* (1969)—seem to parallel the narrowing self-assessments of their protagonists, positioned as they are at that juncture in their lives that Lacanians have called the "mirror stage" of aging. Kathleen Woodward's application of Lacan's term for childhood development to its opposite, aging, describes the inverse of the pleasures of the mirror image of youthful Narcissus as the horror engendered by the mirror image of the aging body, and that theoretical framework seems especially appropriate as an approximation to our three protagonists.[1] The maturing protagonist of *La playa* describes the transformation of her image into something similarly horrifying and even less than human: "Voy a convertirme en un ser híbrido, asexuado, sin objeto ni fin entre mis semejantes" (I am going to transform into a hybrid, asexual being, without objective or goal among my fellow creatures).[2] She attempts to deny the reality of her own aging image by averting her gaze from the mirror of youth that confirmed it: "nueva constatación del tiempo huído,

53

aquel espejo vivo e insultante del presente" (a new confirmation of
fleeting time, that living and insulting mirror of the present) (38).
The narrator of *La enferma* also has occasion to reflect upon the
image of her biological loss: "Un hondo pozo en mí" (a deep well
in me).[3] And Matía, of *La trampa*, attempts to deny aging by
averting her eyes from her mirror image and removing herself
from temporality: "la mujer que contemplo, cuando cierro los
ojos, es intemporal" (the woman that I regard, when I close my
eyes, is atemporal).[4]

One might rightfully argue that the mirror stage of aging is not
confined to women alone. As Woodward points out, even Freud
attempted to repress the reflection of his own aging.[5] Yet for
woman, whose identity has traditionally been molded at least in
part by the degree of her youthful physical appeal, the mirror
stage may be doubly threatening. If she has seen in that reflection
only an image of the Other's desire rather than the outlines of her
own, then the passing of that alienating image leaves her vacuous,
largely unprepared to supplement her loss with anything but
despair. Over half a century ago, Karen Horney already recognized the power of the Other and woman's dependence upon it
for her self-image: "Since for such a long time woman's only
attainable fulfillments—whether they involved love, sex, home or
children—were obtained through men, it necessarily became of
paramount importance to please men . . . such a concentration on
the importance of erotic attractiveness implies an anxiety for the
time when it might eventually diminish in value."[6]

Still, if the aging woman could always reflect back on fulfillment—even through the Other—as Horney implies, perhaps the
"mirror stage" would hold less terror, but along with anxieties
about the narrowing of future options come regrets about the loss
of something that never really was. Years of dependence on the
discourses of the Other often leave the maturing woman not only
lacking identity, but unfulfilled and with a skewed perception of
her own worth. As Howard A. Novell has written: at middle-age
"a woman suddenly has the mirror of life thrust at her and she
takes a long, agonizing look and begins a period of marked
introspection and usually faulty reappraisal of herself."[7] In this
way, aging for the nameless narrator of *La playa* has as much to do
with remorse about the past and ambivalent attempts to come to
terms with an unfulfilled youthful passion as it does with the
bleakness of future emptiness. The similarly unidentified narrator of *La enferma* attempts to delay and deny aging while she
contemplates the disillusionment of dashed hopes and delimiting

compromises wrought by time. In the village where she goes to dispose of family property, she encounters a catatonic woman and listens—in implied identification with her—as villagers tell about the woman's tragically unconsummated youthful love affair and her consequent submergence into madness. Finally, the maturing narrator of *La trampa,* as she returns to Spain for her grandmother's centenary birthday celebration, recalls her unfulfillment as daughter, wife, mother, and Spanish citizen. She furthermore charts the ultimate of unfulfillment and loss—the silencing and loss of her voice.

One might also argue, however, that these stories of unfulfillment and loss issue from a common discourse at mid-century—that of existentialism. Given the particular conditions of post-Civil War Spain—social disruption, poverty, and a desperation tempered only by the most fragile of hopes for speedy amelioration—existentialist discourse became a favored vehicle for recording a variety of responses to the grim circumstances of postwar malaise. In *La playa* and *La enferma* final closure is effected with what seem to be direct borrowings from the existentialist intertext in general and Camus in particular. One of the final sentences of *La playa* bears an uncanny similarity to Meursault's ruminations at the end of *The Stranger:* consider *La playa*'s "es inútil enfrentarse con la ininteligible risa de la eternidad: ni siquiera es risa de burla, sino de sobrehumana indiferencia" (it is useless to confront the unintelligible laughter of eternity: it is not even a laugh of ridicule, but instead of superhuman indifference) (193) alongside *The Stranger*'s "I laid my heart open to the benign indifference of the universe."[8] For *La enferma*'s protagonist, a return home to isolation and existential imprisonment is rendered in terms that also resonate with reminiscences of Camus, this time of his absurd man who suffers from the "clear vision . . . of the walls enclosing him":[9] "El muro crecía ante mis ojos, no me atrevía a saltarle" (The wall grew before my eyes, I did not dare to scale it) (243). And Matia's loss of voice ("como el protagonista de un cuento infantil, perdí mi voz" [like the protagonist of a children's story, I lost my voice]) (30) can be traced to the influence of existentialist discourse that associated the child's loss of voice with a loss of innocence and Paradise, a passage marking the beginning of that great and inexorable solitude and silence characteristic of the adult condition.

Nevertheless, though existentialist discourse was common currency during the period that interests us here, for the woman writer its use must constitute at least in part a concession to the

Other, another adaptation to the dominant discursive practices of her time. The result of such inevitable complicity was to experience ambivalence or even voicelessness as alien discourses were at once incorporated and endured. The mature woman around mid-century thus experiences a double loss of youth slipping away and of self-defined enunciation eluding her. Or, in her disillusionment with the course of her former life and the state of her decline into maturity, she reveals how disastrously little she has shaped her destiny, how much her life and the definitions that have guided it have emanated from the Other.

All three of our protagonists, in their virtual and reflected voicelessness, not only embody the consequences of unrelenting social repression at mid-century but also the double bind that has characterized so much of woman's existential and creative positioning: woman, in order to speak, must submit to the structures of phallogocentrism, must sacrifice herself to the Symbolic Order, or contract, as Lacan, Kristeva, and others have described such a predicament.[10] As objects of a cultural order often indifferent to their desire, our protagonists hover between their uneasiness with the demands of the Other and their longing to submit to those demands for the sake of their serenity and cultural conformity. The aging woman at mid-century thus configures in a most painful and extreme way the plight of woman immured within the structures of phallocentrism or—as Elizabeth Meese has described such a paradoxical positioning—situated in "the site of struggle between contradiction and repression."[11] Because these aging protagonists speak or grow mute for reasons often beyond biology, the present chapter will explore how the problem of aging serves to bare sites where alienating signifiers have defined woman before she could define herself. Well before the aging process exacerbates her "Angst," discourses of the Other have already inscribed themselves into the text of the mature woman's life. Aging simply underscores her confusion and ambivalence as the voices of others echo from her lips.

In *La playa* imagery of beach and sea is revelative of the protagonist's feelings and perceptions about herself, yet her choice of descriptive discourse tellingly reveals just how much, in Lacanian terms, "the unconscious of the subject is the discourse of the other."[12] The narrator-protagonist's description of the beach at La playa de los locos is a remarkable example of how the phallogocentric vision of the world insinuates itself into the female psyche and then is unconsciously projected by her as a "natural truth":

la playa, pequeña y recatada, en la repentina, imprevista curva del acantilado, que se alza treinta metros en torno de ella y parece guardarla, esconderla, abrazarla virilmente, como un padre celoso o como un raptor brutal; la playa, en forma semilunar, blanquísima, de aspecto virginal, como si nadie, jamás, hubiese tocado su tierno cuerpo de arena; la playa, desnuda y sola, extendida voluptuosa y confiadamente al sol, dejándose caldear hasta el menor recodo, como una nereida descuidada en su ignorado abrigo; la playa dulce, secreta, fascinante, como inaccesible. . . . Allí estaba, a treinta metros bajo mis pies, ofreciéndose irresistiblemente, negándose provocadoramente, llena de misterio, invitando a su conquista temeraria, a la locura, a la muerte. . . (77). La arena era pálida y fina, como lavada y cribada, y sin ninguna huella de ser vivo, y parecía brindarme su desfloración deleitosa (80).

(the beach, small and demure, in the sudden, unforeseen curve of the cliff that rises up thirty meters around her and seems to guard her, hide her, embrace her virilely, like a jealous father or a brutal abductor; the beach, in a half-moon form, brilliantly white, of virginal aspect, as if no one, ever, had touched her tender body of sand; the beach, nude and alone, stretched out voluptuously and confidently in the sun, letting herself warm up even the slightest curve, like a careless nereid heedless of her coat; sweet beach, secret, fascinating, as if inaccessible. . . . There she was, thirty meters below my feet, offering herself irresistibly, denying herself provocatively, full of mystery, inviting her fearless conquest, unto madness, unto death. . . [77]. The sand was pale and fine, as if washed and sifted, and without the single trace of a living soul, she seemed to beckon me to her delicious defloration [80]).

Let us consider the above description from *La playa* as the result of a series of discursive choices. The narrator observes a presumably pristine natural site—a small isolated beach surrounded by steep, coastal cliffs. She romantically projects her feelings onto this natural phenomenon, thus rendering it a metaphor. Apparently, she wishes to emphasize size and shape, solitude and isolation, mystery, inaccessibility, and even the potentially dangerous and threatening attributes of the site, so she chooses to personify nature, a common romantic and postromantic literary convention. But because "woman has always functioned 'within' the discourse of man" (as Hélène Cixous has proposed),[13] the narrator speaks her own feelings and desires through the discourse of phallocentric desire. Her metaphoric signifiers speak, thus, from the phallic position, spreading the beach in a provocative posture that displays a series of seductive gestures beckoning conquest and penetration.

It could no doubt be argued that the narrator's personification of nature reflects her own longing to be the one possessed, that it speaks indirectly of her lifetime of erotic unfulfillment. Still, it is no less ironic that the very conception of sexuality underlying her image of nature (and implicitly of herself) is the same one that contributed to the initial and lingering frustration of her desires: her longing to somehow fit herself upon the procrustean bed of passive, expectant, and ultimately dependent femininity. She was herself that beach waiting to be deflowered, that tragic paradox which denied at the same time that it desired possession.[14] It could also be said that the aging woman projects her own physical and psychic ambivalence onto the beach that alternately beckons and denies; and as a small creature dwarfed by the untamed wildness of nature, she expectedly expresses the frailty of her human condition when she portrays the beach as an invitation to risk death.

But these possible interpretative angles notwithstanding, the overwhelming power of the description resides in its evocation of well-known feminine gestures of seduction before a male gaze signifying likewise active male desire. The female narrator's assumption of the male position as her own at least indicates just how pervasive are those narrative metaphors and tropes that issue from the culture's phallocentric structuring of desire. They provide a ready-made lexicon for expressing, and even more, structuring sexuality from a position outside the borders of woman's self-inscribed desire.

The protagonist of *La playa* perceptively locates her ambivalence within a precise historical matrix, characterizing her youthful self as a true daughter of the times. Describing herself as "un complejo producto de transición, de crisis humana en todos los órdenes" (a complex product of transition, of human crisis in all its orders) (115), she bitterly recognizes that she was "envenenada de errores y contradicciones" (poisoned with errors and contradictions) (115–16). After recollecting her inability to surrender sexually to her lover, she works through a penetrating analysis of her ambivalent and confused imprisonment between alienating ideologies and possibly liberating alternatives. She recognizes her dogmatic, narrow, and puritanical moral and sexual information on the one hand and her free-thinking education on the other. Exposed to fascinating theories about primitive and pagan pleasures, she was forbidden to apply those theories to practice. Yet, though conditioned by the immanence of parental morality, she experienced the strain of her generation to touch a transcendent future painted with paradisiacal colors. Thus victimized by contradictions characteristic of women of her class and historical moment, she experienced the troublesome conflict described unequivocally by Laurel Limpus: "even when you consciously reject the morality of your parents, you often find that your body will not obey the dictates of your mind."[15] There seemed to be no outlet from such contradiction except repression.

The consciousness that she was the product of historical crisis leads *La playa*'s protagonist to a growing awareness of how she was caught up in alienating texts that mediated between her and the resolution of her quest for fulfillment. Cognizant that she was the victim of "la clásica organización de la vida, y la vigencia de la imagen petrarquista de la mujer ideal" (the classical organization of life, and the prevalence of the Petrarchan image of ideal womanhood) (115), she was nevertheless unable to break the hold of that text and give way to spontaneity. The stiff and alienating image of Renaissance female perfection held sway to such a degree that, ironically, she might have welcomed the role of cheap and phony Laura.[16] Though she seems keenly conscious of the pitfalls of woman's sacrificial position, the protagonist repeatedly expressed a weakness for just such roles. She would have cast herself as the heroine of sentimental fiction or as a fearful Gretel directed by her Hansel ("la niña perdida en el bosque azaroso de la vida, que avanza agarrada temerosamente de la mano del varón omnipotente" [the little girl lost in the hazardous forest of life, who advances fearfully clutching the hand of an omnipotent male]) (118). Had her young lover met her quixotic literary criteria and expectations, she would have acceded to these sacrificial textualizations of her desire, but he did not meet such criteria, and the possibly risible and reprehensible role of the queen Calafia with Esplandián was entirely objectionable to her. It might have signaled an overturning of the phallocentric textual and sexual economy to which she ultimately remained faithful and thus able only to conceive of herself as love object or passive infantile accomplice. Somehow her internalization of traditional texts, with their culturally authorized categories of proper gendered behavior, prevented her from subverting those sacrificial discursive requirements and breaking free from her painful ambivalence.

Freudian discourse (especially from *Civilization and Its Discontents*) also seems to have influenced the ways in which the narrator voices her uneasiness before the inhibiting restrictions of her culture. The narrator's anguished "¡debiste . . . tomarme! Pero existe la civilización" (you should have . . . taken me! But civilization exists) (85) corresponds quite strikingly to Freud's more reasoned lament "it is impossible to overlook the extent to which civilization is built up upon a renunciation of instinct."[17] Yet in *Civilization and its Discontents,* Freud is surprisingly more generous and open to unknown sexual possibilities. The human animal that might emerge was, for him, still a matter of conjecture insofar as its psychosexual characteristics were concerned: "For psychology the contrast between the sexes fades away into one between activity and passivity, in which we far too readily identify activity with maleness and passivity with femaleness, a view which is by no means universally confirmed in the animal kingdom" (53). The narrator-protagonist of *La playa,* on the other hand, recollects the youthful thrill of polarization, and dismissing its affectation, she prefers to remember it as powerfully inevitable and even gender specific. For this reason, her young lover initially appears as strong, wise, and dominant, and she remembers her response to his pose as ignorant, helpless, and dominated.

This inclination of *La playa*'s protagonist to view character traits as sharply polarized into civilized-cerebral and natural-instinctual is instrumental in her attempt to mask and shrink and diminish her youthful self in order to fit the role of her culture's idea of the "natural" woman. She internalized the phallocentric fear that to love a cultured and talented woman is a form of homosexuality. Apparently devoid of self-irony, she expresses gratitude to her lover for having instilled in her a desire to diminish her intellect: "¡Toda mi vida te agradeceré aquel afán que me infundiste de empequeñecerme, de aniñarme, de reducirme a la instrucción mediocre y a la frivolidad de las mujeres corrientes, para resultarte más accesible y atractiva!" (All my life I shall be grateful to you for instilling in me that desire to belittle myself, to infantilize myself, to reduce myself to mediocre learning and to the frivolity of ordinary women, in order to become more accessible and attractive!) (95). Ironically, she was too intelligent not to be aware of her self-deception, and yet she persisted in assuming this alien desire to hide her intellect, to repress her literary culture, to surround herself with a false aureole of frivolity and coquetry. From this same perspective, she assesses her reading activities as a barrier separating her sensibility from the "normal" stimuli of life, thereby echoing, in this self-deprecating appraisal of her cultural gifts, the position of Freud's disciple, psychologist Helene Deutsch: "Woman's intellectuality is to a large extent paid for by the loss of valuable feminine qualities: it feeds on the sap of the affective life and results in impoverishment of this life either as a whole or in specific emotional qualities."[18] Coinciding thus with prevailing post-Freudian discourse that sought to bridle the female intellect, *La playa*'s protagonist similarly sought to adjust herself to intellectual and erotic "castration," to becoming a figure characterized by lack and passivity and a position outside the economy of her own autonomous desire.

Yet, in spite of her captivity within the polarity of masculine-feminine, active-passive, the narrator-protagonist of *La playa* intermittently offers acute observations of the restrictive cultural codes that underlie her choices. One recalled conversation between the young woman and her lover expresses her consciousness of the paternal law that underwrites female existence. The pair was exploring a ruined manor house when they discovered an antique carving of a pregnant Virgin. With the sharp perceptivity we have come to expect from her, the narrator decodes the icon as a statement of patriarchal paternity and possession: "contemplamos absortos aquella extraña y deforme imagen—quizá realizada por encargo de algunos antiguos propietarios obsesos de paternidad—" (we contemplated with absorption that strange and deformed image—perhaps commissioned by some ancient landowners obsessed with paternity) (121). At this point she seems to echo Engels's linking of private property with man's discovery of his paternity and the establishment of the patriarchal family. Though the narrator does not articulate a consciousness of the historicity of patriarchal paternal authority, the reader can here discern the unspoken dimension of the observation: a disclosure of woman's authority as absence in this historical contract, with the inevitable consequence of female contradiction, ambivalence, and even despair.[19]

As the conversation turns to aging, the narrator, nevertheless, shows herself fully aware of the relationship between woman's fear of aging and her particular reified ontology within patriarchal culture: "Las mujeres diríamos sin reserva nuestra edad y llevaríamos el rostro sin afeites, si a vosotros no os importase tanto nuestra cronología y nuestra apariencia, si no fuesen factores ridículamente decisivos, no ya para vuestro amor, sino para vuestro simple aprecio" (we women would tell our age without reserve and we would go without make-up if our chronology and our appearance weren't so important to you, if they weren't ridiculously decisive factors, not only for your love, but for your simple appreciation) (123). She contrasts the masculine admiration for architectural or stone ruins to man's repulsion before the "living ruin" or the "feminine ruin." And as she reflects upon her youthful critique of the male view of female aging, she includes a defense of older women by praising herself in her present mature condition: "Sin embargo, intrínsicamente, ahora soy mucho más interesante que entonces" (Nevertheless, intrinsically, now I am much more interesting than I was then) (124).

The narrator's ambivalence between her longing to adjust to the demands of phallocentric discourse and her tenuous desire to express her own, rendered her finally incapable of allowing herself the luxury of being directed by the young man. Still, while she realizes how she might have capitulated to mediocrity and provinciality, her criticism is directed ironically not so much against the dangers of gender-role polarization as against her lover's hesitation to act out those polarities:

> Tú debiste ser más fuerte, más brutal. Tú debiste forzarme. Yo era de esas mujeres que necesitan ser perseguidas, atrapadas, violentadas, atropelladas por el varón primario, anterior a toda civilización. Tú debiste arrastrarme por los cabellos hasta tu caverna y destruir a zarpazos toda mi fría capa de cultura.

> (You should have been stronger, more brutal. You should have forced me. I was one of those women who had to be pursued, trapped, forced, overwhelmed by the primitive male, anterior to all civilization. You should have dragged me by the hair to your cave and destroyed with blows my whole cold mantle of culture) (134).

This image of the dominated and raped female reveals what Irigaray might call "a certain misprision" of primitive instinct (perhaps derived from popularized, even movie versions of early human society).[20] The greatest tragedy of the narrator's dependence on such imagery for the representation of her sexual longing is that such fantasies ensnare her within a trap of eternally unsatisfied erotic hunger. Such primordial eroticism, even if it were desirable, is largely unattainable in contemporary culture. In her desire to be pinned down, as it were, by the primitive male phallus, the fulfillment of her desire is doomed from the start. In making her needs wholly dependent on an imagined Other, who then becomes the projected signifier of her desire, this woman has left herself exposed to the inevitability of her own perpetually frustrated desire.

Never learning to articulate unambivalently a desire outside phallocentric boundaries, the narrator of *La playa* finally accepts the role of passive female patient with her lover as medical authority in an analogue of the relationship between male psychoanalyst and female analysand. In spite of earlier realizations of her young lover's shortcomings, when he declares "con una voz grave, helada, irrefutable, como en un diagnóstico clínico— 'Seguramente eres una frígida' "—(with a grave, icy, irrefutable voice, as in a clinical diagnosis, "Surely you are frigid") (142), she accepts his harsh diagnosis without protest or reproach. Not alone in her acceptance of this dictum, the protagonist shares with other women her fate of suppression, repression, and the obscuring of her desire and pleasure under the term "frigid."[21] She desired accession to the demands of the Other in order to assume a piece of his masculine authority, but circumstances did not allow her to effect such a transference.

She remained governed by her supposed lack, her female corporeality:

> me avergoncé de ser mujer, de ser pedazo de carne débil y lujuriosa . . . (146) . . . en nosotras hay una servidumbre irredenta a nuestro físico. Por mucho que alcemos las ramas hacia el cielo, nuestra raíz siempre queda hundida en la tierra, en el barro bíblico (148). Esta es la triste y gloriosa condición de nuestro ser: la servidumbre de nuestro cuerpo (149).

> (I was ashamed of being a woman, of being a piece of weak and lustful flesh . . . [146] . . . in us there is an irredeemable servitude to our bodies. As much as we might raise branches toward the heavens, our roots are always buried in the earth, in Biblical mud [148]. This is the sad and glorious condition of our being: the servitude to our bodies [149]).

This paradoxical self-analysis, at once paean and depreciatory lament, is best understood within the tradition of Judeo-Christian religious discourse and popularized Freudian theory. It exposes an interiorization of patriarchal religious discourses, as Simone de Beauvoir has clarified: "the flesh is sin. And of course, since woman remains always the Other, it is not held that reciprocally male and female are both flesh: the flesh that is for the Christian the hostile Other is precisely woman. In her the Christian finds incarnated the temptations of the world, the flesh, and the devil."[22] Furthermore, if we add to the narrator's Christian devaluation of female corporeality Freud's popularized statement, "After all, the anatomical distinction [between the sexes] must express itself in psychical consequences," the body as a source of joy and pleasure is denied, the female body is characterized as a lack, and woman's potential for self-defined gender identity and desire is silenced.[23]

Overcome by her ambivalence and entrapment within discourses of her alien Other, the protagonist of *La playa* is rendered diminished and hollow when her lover disappears, ostensibly to the war. Since her attempt to invest her libido in him failed, she is left with nothing in its stead, nothing but despair. The end of that unconsummated love affair signifies the end of her text; her life thereafter is summated in some twenty pages, a life of indifferent acts, mechanical and meaningless words, historical unconsciousness. Little wonder that her aging is frightening; it threatens to impose a second closure upon a constantly narrowing range of possibilities. Nevertheless, a text like *La playa*, about a bright and educated woman whose life figuratively ends when her fleeting first love evanesces before its consummation, stands as poignant testimony to the misspent power of unnamed female desire. Attempting to enclose within the vehicle of phallocentric discourse her undefined longing, the narrator has groped for something that could never be found: "¿qué quería yo? ¿Qué buscaba?" (what did I want? What was I looking for?) (192). The story of this agonizingly ambivalent and doomed search for fulfillment through the Other bares the intertext of woman's ultimate silence, if not yet the sounds of her reply.[24]

In *La enferma* the absence of woman's own voice is centered on Liberata, the maturing village woman who slipped out of verbal intercourse and into mutism when her beloved, Telmo, failed to return to her many years before. The visiting protagonist becomes a listener of varied tales told about Liberata, of contrasting points of view representing the particular positions of various citizens of the village. As critic Juan Luis Alborg has observed: "Los hechos se repiten, a veces, como si un mismo cuerpo se nos mostrara desde distintos ángulos, pero al final hemos recorrido toda su piel" (the facts repeat themselves, at times as if the same body were to reveal itself from different angles, but in the end we have traversed its entire skin).[25] Those perspectives or points of view differ one from the other in their details, but all constitute articulations external to the subject and imposed upon her by others. Liberata, in this situation, embodies the Lacanian subject who "is spoken rather than speaking."[26] And as the aging protagonist of *La enferma* ultimately identifies with the mute woman, she, too, comes to signify woman who is spoken—inherently with error and distortion—rather than able to speak herself. As another villager wisely comments apropos Liberata: "¿Quién sabe la verdad si ella no la dice?" (Who knows the truth if she herself does not tell it?) (196).

It is telling that don Simón Pedro, the village priest, is the first of these narrators. As a prototypical member of the provincial Spanish clergy at mid-century, he is situated at a confluence of prevailing conservative religious and political discourses. The "name of the father" or the "Father's Law" certainly seems to speak through him, establishing its preeminence before other speakers contribute their narratives. Consequently, the priest's portrayal of Liberata as a sensual, mysterious, inexplicable force is colored by his internalization of religious discourse, his own repressed erotic fantasies, and by his articulation of more general phallo(go)centric assumptions about women. Spontaneously calling Liberata "aquella niña ardiente y desequilibrada" (that fiery and unbalanced girl) (117), he then reflects upon his choice of adjectives. It seems strange to him that he should have chosen just those words to describe her, so he immediately retracts them and amends his description with "reservada y fría" (reserved and cold) (117). Obviously, she appears to him as either one or the other of binary oppositions (hot or cold), and either choice, because of its tropological uncertainty, is ambiguously unreliable ("aunque quizá la verdad sea la que acabo de decirle" (although perhaps the truth is that which I have just told you) (117). This fluctuating antinomy articulates, in the words of de Beauvoir, a "Manichaeism . . . introduced in the heart of womankind," by Western culture, and such a structuring of woman's identity reveals its ultimate grounding in the binary oppositions of phallogocentric discourse.[27]

Silent Liberata is therefore recreated by Simón Pedro. As a result, she is portrayed as dark and unfathomable, an unknown region awaiting his act of creative penetration. She is also feared, again in the words of de Beauvoir, as "the night of immanence":[28] "le atraía lo mismo que a muchos el abismo, o la noche, o la mar" (she attracted him [Telmo] in the same way that the abyss, or the night, or the sea attracts others) (123). And Liberata's gaze obsesses the priest, for it seemed to threaten the young Telmo with "posesión, deseo y odio" (possession, desire, and hatred) (132); that is, with a reversal of phallocentric privilege for which the male gaze is signifier. Though Simón Pedro hastened to protect that privilege by attempting to dissipate the girl's visual power, young Liberata ignored the priest's directives to engage in more frivolous activities, remaining for him a siren of the sort described by Esther Harding: "They conquer men not for love, but for a craving to gain power ['posesión']. They cannot love, they can only desire ['deseo']. They are cold-blooded, without human feeling or compassion ['fría']."[29]

Liberata is thus invested with magical and dangerous qualities—the fearful side of the phallogocentric opposition—as "un desván oscuro, o como un túnel donde todo podría sucederle" (like a dark garret, or a tunnel where anything could happen to him [Telmo]) (117). While the priestly description of woman as threatening force may express the unconscious fears and desires of one sworn to chastity, or a cultural tendency to choose one or the other side of a polarity to describe woman, these unconscious projections also display certain characteristics of man's creative activity. As de Beauvoir has again described, woman is likened to objects that may be suffused with male consciousness: "grotto, temple, sanctuary, secret garden—man, like the child, is fascinated by enclosed and shadowy places not yet animated by any consciousness, which wait to be given a soul: what he alone is to take and to penetrate seems to be in truth created by him."[30] By casting Liberata as a menacingly dark and subterranean force, Simón Pedro can infuse raw material with his own powers of creation. A shadowy tabula rasa, Liberata's reemergence is utterly dependent on the strokes of the priest's metaphorical stylus.

As Simón Pedro concludes his narration by describing Telmo's bondage to his beloved ("y él volvía a ella, fatalmente, como quien va a la muerte o al peligro" [and he returned to her, fatally, like someone who goes to his death or to danger]) (132), he links love and death, thus amplifying his recreation of Liberata by casting her as "femme fatale" through an act of symbolic generation we might call "magical misogyny."[31] Though Simón Pedro insists that Liberata was unique ("era única"), as he articulates her qualities that assertion becomes more and more problematical. Unwittingly, he has shaped a phallo(go)centric archetypal figure of woman as the essentially unknowable and mysterious Other, who, without a voice of her own, remains confined to the mystifying words of Simón Pedro, *her* unknown Other.

It would be a mistake, however, to implicate only male narrators as the perpetrators of Liberata's distorted identity. As all the narrators attempting to describe the speechless woman must function according to the same symbolic contract, the fate of their object remains equally subjected to alien impositions, regardless of the gender of the speaker. Alida, childless yet obsessively and excessively maternal, is Liberata's caretaker. We soon learn from the narrator-protagonist that Alida represents a perversion and deformation of maternal behavior: "Ella también se había deformado, convenciéndose de que aquella mujer enferma era su niña, su criatura" (she, too, had been deformed, convincing herself that that sick woman was her child, her baby) (55). In an attempt to reinforce her own sense of self-importance and identity in a culture that values highly the qualities of self-sacrificing mother, Alida insists upon her charge's absolute helplessness, infantilism, and submission. This results in a characterization of the voiceless woman as all that she was not for the priest. In a complete turnabout, her character transforms from darkness and danger into lightness and peace: "estrella, paloma, la niña de mis ojos" (star, dove, the apple of my eye) (161). Instead of appearing as a sign signifying fatality and death, Liberata reappears for Alida as a giver of life: "no quisiera cortarle la respiración, quisiera dársela" (she didn't want to cut off his breath, but rather bestow it upon him) (168). Although Alida's perception of the madwoman is colored by more positive hues, it is still externally imposed by means of conventional poetic tropes while its object remains hollow, intrinsically undefined, and silent.

Angustias, the mature unmarried sister of Telmo, offers another point of view, claiming that hers is the truth: "sin inventar nada, contando sencillamente la verdad" (without inventing anything, simply telling the truth) (199). Yet it is not long until she discredits her own assessments of the mysterious creature, admitting: "¿Entonces, cuál era la realidad?" (then, what was reality) (206). Thus she, herself, signals that her perspectives will be as unreliable as all the others. Similarly to Alida's, Angustias's position is influenced by protective, maternal feelings; these, however, are reserved for Telmo, her brother, not the abandoned Liberata. Liberata, as seen by Angustias, corresponds to the images of her provided by other representatives of the phallocentric order. She reappears as wielder of maleficent, possessive powers: "le royó la tranquilidad. Adiviné que le sería dañina, y lo fue" (she gnawed away at his tranquility. I guessed that she would be harmful to him, and she was) (204). Liberata supposedly exercised "aquella posesión que . . . le restaba libertad" (that possession that . . . took away his freedom) (213).

While Angustias reiterates myths of negative female power, nothing is said of how her brother's treachery or perhaps even cowardice led him to choose conventionality over passion and thus plunge his childhood sweetheart into madness. Angustias can only see her brother as a kind of aimless vessel that found itself with an unwelcome passenger aboard: Liberata "negra y altiva" (dark and proud) (213). Represented once again as a kind of siren, Liberata is categorized by Angustias as the conventional "dark lady," which, as Leslie Fiedler has shown, represents the threat of both sex and death as a figuration of the "ingrained European habit of identifying evil with blackness."[32] Once more, Liberata is unable to escape the fascination that the townspeople have with myths and images associated with feminine evil and the frightening aspects of their own projected desire.

And so Liberata is that which the Other chooses to make of her. Nothing in herself, she is doubly fictional: ontologically and textually. To Simón Pedro she possesses a fascinating negativity; to Angustias her negative traits are more annoying and directly threatening. Lucía, the housemaid, echoes the assessments of her "novio" (sweetheart) and thus shares the prevalent unkind views of the madwoman. Justa, the telephone operator, transmits the opinions of her father; and Dámaso, Alida's husband, is indifferent to women's concerns, distanced as he is in his male world of maritime activities. Only Alida, whose whole life and spirit have been dedicated to solicitous care of "la enferma," creates a positive portrait of the creature she helped reduce to a state of utter helplessness.

Somehow the problems of aging, madness (or psychological alienation), and self-definition or its lack are all mirrored in Liberata for *La enferma*'s protagonist. In fact, the mirroring technique is multiple, for the narrator, in her passive reception of the villagers' stories about Liberata, reflects back upon herself the loss and lack of the madwoman. Both are dispossessed of youth, passion, psychic equilibrium, and most importantly, the opportunity to voice the content of their own desire. Caught in a metaphorical hall of distorting mirrors, the mature woman sees images that forebode little more than narrowing options and possibilities; the mirrors cloud up and darken, and around the refracted images there rises a wall of diminished possibility. *La enferma*'s narrator can only conclude with an obsessive image recollected from the past: a wall rising up and encircling her with fear and solitude. Others, too, seem to construct walls of words around her, making the way out—if any—seem more and more remote. So encircled, the protagonist of *La enferma* drowns out her ephemeral words with tears. Like *La playa*'s narrator, who concludes her narrative epistle with the knowledge of her former lover's death, thereupon tossing her useless words into the sea, this second maturing narrator also withdraws into voicelessness. From ambivalence to anguish, the ontological and discursive options of these two narrators dissipate into reluctant resignation and silence.

Solitude and silence circumscribe the mature lives of all our protagonists. Matia, of *La trampa*, lost her voice at an earlier age, but at maturity she becomes even more painfully aware of the "ultimate solitude," which, like an archipelago, makes of each individual an island entirely separate from others. The diary she is writing is analogously ruptured and jumbled, as is the overall narrative that encloses her. Matia is disturbed by this chaos, unprepared for the discursive subversiveness that it might portend: "Lo leo, lo tomo, escribo otra vez: y lo que leo, lo que escribo, me parece indescifrable. Lo releo, y no entiendo una sola de estas líneas. Como si estuviera escrito en un desconocido idioma" (I read it, I take it, and I write once more: and what I read, what I write, seems indecipherable to me. I reread it, and I don't understand even one of these lines. It's as if I were writing a foreign language) (276). Clearly, this despair signifies more than individual anguish before the blank page; it says something about our contemporary distrust of language and our hopelessness before the elusiveness of meaningful communication. For a woman, it is even more compelling, suggesting also and again the double bind that requires woman's submission to an alien contract if she is to speak at all. At the risk of repetition, we must emphasize that this imposition, founded upon cultural definitions of the speaker's (or writer's) lack, forces her to speak in a tongue figuratively foreign to her and outside the context of her own desire.

Matia's recollections as a maturing woman—like those of *La playa*'s protagonist and the narratives surrounding Liberata—reveal just how much she has lived her life inserted within the folds of alien discourse. Estranged early on from her father, long-suffering aunt, and manipulative, authoritarian grandmother, she grows up to become subsequently estranged from cousin, husband, son, and mother-in-law. As a sign of her ultimate alienation from other people, surroundings, and events, she is positioned as doubly estranged through exile to the United States. There she not only loses her language of childhood innocence, she loses her national tongue as well. Anywhere she might turn, then, she is surrounded by the echoes of her own silence—as much in her condition of internal exile as in her uneasy existence as an American.

Matia's American experience inserts her into an alienating and noncommunicative marriage with David, a man who goes off to war and returns broken and an alcoholic. Degenerating into a state of drunken nonbeing, David is most vividly recalled by Matia as a rat-like creature devoid of human qualities. Not without nostalgia she also recalls how with him she attempted to construct "un idioma" (a language) (229), only to later lose it forever. Both wife and husband finally capitulated to the sensible language of David's mother, Beverly, as this efficient American matron dispatched her broken son to a sanatorium and the young couple's son, Bear, to her own care. Matia is thus left without links to husband or child, floating in a sea of "estúpidas palabras" (stupid words) (276) without the power to reconstruct those severed connections. She blames herself for her predicament, though she is also lucidly aware as a writing woman that at least part of her problem originates in her role as naive reader: "Nadie tenía la culpa sino yo, tan sólo yo, que había creído infinidad de frases que había leído, y creído, que el mundo estaba repleto de bondad" (No one was at fault but I, only I, who had believed an infinity of phrases I had read, and believed, that the world was filled with goodness) (229). Now, in spite of her desperate cynicism, her diary becomes an anguished attempt to supplement the deceptive texts of her past.

At least one of the justifications for the existence of Matia's disordered diary is to provide her with a medium through which to explore her perplexing difficulties as a mother. The theme of motherhood, and the alien discourses defining it, recur with obsessive frequency; each entry of the diary in some way confronts and mulls over the problem. Matia, herself a motherless child ("cuando mi padre me envió al campo con la vieja Mauricia, yo no tenía madre, ni apenas su recuerdo" [when my father sent me to the country with old Mauricia, I had no mother, nor hardly a memory of her]) (27), is emblematic for the prevailing absence of the mother-daughter dyad in her culture.[33] Matia has always been marginal to the mother-child bond, and since she had never experienced positive models of the maternal function during childhood, as an adult she seemed unable to establish a mode of maternal behavior for herself. Though this allowed her a measure of flexibility impossible within the confines of traditional expectations concerning motherhood, it also left her disoriented and unsure of herself; that is, she ends up lacking a maternal voice of her own.

On several separate occasions, Matia reflects upon her inability to function according to established patterns of maternity or according to the demands of prevailing discourses defining the role of mother: "Bear sabe que no puedo comportarme como una madre al uso. (No diré una buena madre, esa definición me resulta demasiado comprometida.)" (Bear knows that I cannot behave like an ordinary mother. [I don't say good mother, that definition seems too compromised to me]) (75–76). Later she is unable to avoid the value judgment she rejected earlier: "Sí, hijo, no soy una madre buena, al uso; ya lo sé" (Yes, son, I am not a good mother, an ordinary one; I know that already) (127). Consequently, Matia becomes increasingly self-critical, more compelled to entertain feelings of guilt for having allowed her estrangement from her son. Though no one can know exactly whose fault it was, or if it was anyone's fault at all, Matia's tendency to lapse into feelings of self-blame may be but an example of how the internalization of dominant discourses defining motherhood cast women into yet another double bind. As Mary Ellmann observed at about the same time that Matia agonized in her diary: "obviously, it is impossible for women either to give or to withhold attention without risking the injury of their children. The eagerness with which mothers are chosen as the cause of regrettable effects is a psychological fact in itself, an independent fixation, predictable in the discussion of all social problems."[34]

To understand Matia's ambivalence before the discourses governing motherhood, we might view her dilemma within the framework of Julia Kristeva's distinction between "motherhood" and the "Mother." To Kristeva, motherhood signifies the phallic attempt to reach the Mother and place her firmly within the social and biological matrix of the symbolic contract; that is, while the Mother may signify a slipping "away from the discursive hold," motherhood urges women "to maintain the ensuing order."[35] Seen within this contrastive framework, Matia's uneasiness with the terms of motherhood causes her to unwittingly lose also her powers and pleasures as Mother. Sadly, she throws the maternal baby out with the phallic bathwater, and herein lies a major source of her discomfort. In her desire to elude the requirements of motherhood, Matia shrinks from showing tenderness toward her son: "Dudé si coger una de esas solitarias, lacias y conmovedoras manos; pero casi en seguida desistí" (I hesitated to grasp one of those solitary, languid and touching hands; but almost immediately I desisted) (128). In her attempt to escape the smothering desperation of overbearing motherhood, Matia prescribes niggardly terms for parental love: "Nadie debería amar a los hijos con amor posesivo y destructor. . . . Deberíamos racionar el amor, como se raciona la morfina a los enfermos graves" (No one should love their children with a possessive and destructive love. . . . We ought to ration love, as one rations morphine to the gravely ill) (77). Attempting to avoid the possessive and destructive side of phallocentric "motherhood," Matia is left without the fulfillment of an(other) "Mother." Such a conflictive discursive positioning is revealing as an indicator of Matia's likewise ambivalent attitude toward writing.

Ending her narrative with an agonized query: "Y Bear, ¿dónde estás, ahora? ¿Adónde vas?" (And Bear, where are you now? Where are you going?) (277), Matia occupies the double function of mother and maturing writer who searches desperately for a self-defined maternal intimacy and verbal expression. Or to invoke Kristeva once again, Matia, in her conjoining of the maternal and artistic functions, serves as "a locus of vulnerability, of calling into question of oneself and of languages."[36] By confronting the difficulties of maternity in the vast upheaval of her postwar environment, Matia discloses the almost unresolvable conflicts that internalized discourses forced her to face in that respect. And by textualizing those recollections as a woman thrust into the disappointments of maturity, Matia signs her disordered diary with the vulnerability of both maternal and verbal dispossession.

In many ways the particular situation of Matia—and the general condition of other dispossessed and displaced women like herself—is symbolized by the maternal condition itself, which Diana Hume George has named "exile." Matia, as both literal and figurative exile—as well as mother—is a "double site of loss" (to borrow once again from George).[37] And as writer in search of her lost language, the poignancy of her condition sums up the particular wasteland that the mature Spanish woman writer often came to occupy at mid-century. So although a mother, Matia finally comes to maturity with the same sense of loss, solitude, and silence as her childless predecessors, the protagonists of *La playa* and *La enferma*. Having internalized alien discourses on aging, femininity, motherhood—in a word, on women—the lives of all three are inscribed into a similarly constricted plot of shrinking possibilities and loss of voice.

Yet, though these three mature women, unlike their younger counterparts, end up without voices they might claim as their own, they have exposed the Derridean double bind: spoken or silent they have disclosed the contradictions or repression inherent in phallogocentrism.[38] They have related an important tale, a story of great significance in its time: from them we have heard of inhibiting and even maddening intertexts and of the prison house of internalized dispossessing discourse. Their anguish and ambivalence may have rendered us sad or angry; certainly it has sharpened our perception as readers. We are now prepared to more acutely discern difference in the voices of "transition," voices from the seventies that will articulate with a determination to speak their own minds. That which social and existential "Angst" often silenced during the previous decades will reemerge, gesturing provisionally toward a discourse of transformative supplementarity.

Part Two
In Sotto Voce

3

Talking Herself Out
Articulating the Quest for Other Texts in Two Narratives by Carmen Martín Gaite

> Cuando vivimos, las cosas nos pasan; pero cuando contamos, las hacemos pasar. (When we live, things happen to us; but when we tell [stories] we make things happen.)
> —Carmen Martín Gaite, "La búsqueda de interlocutor"

> Los libros . . . hay que atreverse a leerlos uno mismo. Es la única forma de inventar o de descubrir algo inédito. (Books . . . one must dare to read them oneself. It is the only way to invent or to discover something new.)
> —Carmen Martín Gaite, "Los malos espejos"

During the seventies, silence is broken with the sounds of voices speaking their orality into textuality. This narrative strategy, which draws from articulation more archaic than writing, finds an insistent proponent in Carmen Martín Gaite. Martín Gaite's call for the approximation of spoken and written discourse complements and underscores similar positions in the contemporaneous theoretical writings of Barthes and Todorov, and it even seems to hearken back to Saussure's earlier nostalgia for speech uncorrupted by writing.[1] When Martín Gaite posits conversation as a most satisfactory realization of narrative skill,[2] she intersects with Barthes's earlier notion of a "zero" or spoken level of writing and his later blissful "writing aloud."[3] Her acclaim of dialogical narrative's power to make things happen seems to echo Todorov's "las palabras crean las cosas en lugar de ser un pálido reflejo de ellas" (words create things rather than being a pale reflection of them).[4] Certainly Carmen Martín Gaite's narrative mark of identity has been her unrelenting quest to foreground "parole" in her texts. And accordingly, interest in the dialogical aspect of Martín Gaite's narrative has been prolific and distinguished.[5]

Still, the conversations of Martín Gaite's narrative texts are not heard but read. Though texts like *Retahílas* and *El cuarto de atrás* may appear to be spoken, they are not unmediated speech. (This playful deception is undermined in *El cuarto* when pages of a manuscript multiply simultaneously with the interlocutors' spoken discourse.) The unique power of these later narratives by Martín Gaite is their dynamic blend of orality and textuality, their refusal to opt for the either-or of "langue" or "parole." They exemplify most distinctively, among narratives by women at this time, the creation of text as play and production (theorized most clearly by Barthes)[6] and writing as a process of opening meaning, a maneuver described by Derrida as inherent in writing.[7] The ludic nature of Martín Gaite's later narratives, especially *El cuarto*, consists thus in a playing with the strategies of both speech and writing while opting for neither as mutually exclusive. In this way, *Retahílas* and *El cuarto,* by performing the Derridean move of putting into doubt a system of oppositions, break the boundaries of those oppositional structures that have underwritten logocentric texts and culture, thus opening the way to meanings outside them.[8]

This impulse to write beyond the boundaries of a mutually exclusive orality and textuality is paralleled in Martín Gaite's work by an analogous desire to break through oppositions governing cultural definitions of gender. Yet, though critical attention to Martín Gaite's contribution as a social critic has also been extensive, her importance as a vanguard figure in the transformation of narrative strategies specific to the interplay of gender and textuality has not been as widely documented.[9] It is this aspect of Martín Gaite's work, the one that is most crucial for the establishment of theoretical links with preceding and succeeding narrative strategies by other women writers, that I shall stress in this chapter.

Retahílas intrigued readers as soon as it appeared in 1974. It was different in so many ways from the earlier decade's preferred text—social realism—, and its unabashed insistence on the pleasure of the text appeared almost self-indulgent to readers schooled in the didacticism of "committed art." Yet, though this was a narrative that dared to revel in the pleasure of its finely wrought medium, it did not sacrifice its message. It simply insisted on playfully escaping the circle of existent narrative conventions.

The verbal medium of *Retahílas* is capacious enough to function on several levels: it is a vindication of language itself, of the intrinsic worth and power of the word, especially the spoken word

as it provides the source of writing; on another level, the medium
functions in the familiar mode of coding system for the relaying
of messages; and on yet another level, it serves as a self-conscious
device whereby the writer explores the potentials and limitations
of her craft. On the first level, telling or speech creates enthusiasm
in the speaker, and to feel enthusiasm is to feel ecstasy or divine
inspiration. Transcendence is to be found in the word rather than
through it, spoken or shared language providing a kind of verbal
apotheosis that inscribes itself into the written text. Language thus
ceases to be merely a system of signification for something beyond
itself, achieving rather a fullness in and of itself. On a second
level, *Retahílas* is preoccupied with the sending and receiving of
messages, thus incorporating not only the author's own concerns
with interlocution as expressed in *La búsqueda de interlocutor,* but
prevailing structuralist theory surrounding the speech act as
well.[10] Playfully experimenting with structuralism's attentiveness
to the functions of code and context in the relaying of messages,
Retahílas expands those notions to effect implicit transformations
of codes governing gender within a specific cultural context. And
still beyond this level, but ultimately inseparable from it, the novel
speaks more or less indirectly of the woman writer's struggle for
creative authority. Its preoccupation with language becomes both
medium and message for the story of the woman who, in wresting
words to shape them according to her pleasure, positions herself
as an adversary of what Elaine Showalter has called the "ghosts of
repressed language."[11]

In *Retahílas* we find two speakers—a woman and a man—who
are temporarily isolated in their own world of words, who spend
an entire night immured "en su castillo inexpugnable de palabras"
(in their impregnable castle of words).[12] The conversation between Eulalia (aunt) and Germán (nephew) takes place in a mysterious and decrepit Galician "pazo" as the two await the death of
Eulalia's grandmother.[13] Against such a backdrop of decay, of
objects as well as of human life, the two interlocutors carry out, in
part, what Enrique Sordo has identified as the double function of
self-knowledge and intercommunication.[14] Thus what is said
serves as much to define each individual as a self as it does to
construct a bridge between the two individuals. Crucial to the
process of self-definition is the confrontation of each speaker with
prevailing gender expectations in the culture. And, as the female
and male speakers forge unexpected interpersonal links between
themselves, they further break through the bonds of prevailing
cultural codes governing gender.

What Sordo and I (in an earlier analysis of this novel) did not see as clearly in the seventies, however, was that through the "rereading" of texts and culture that the speakers' interlocution entails, they not only deconstruct delimiting cultural conventions but textual ones as well.[15] As Eulalia and German's conversation considers the influences of internalized textual oppositions on the formation of their gender identity, they implicitly "engender" not only new codes for the expression of gender, but an(other), non-polarized space in which future texts may continue to reshape textual codes and conventions. The pair's attempt to talk their way out of confining antinomies offers them and the reader of their text a brief glimpse of a better code, a "third code" as it were, of spontaneity, joy, and refined communication capacious enough to incorporate corresponding modifications of existent narrative oppositions.

In the course of the dialogue, Eulalia mentions that her grandmother was a "feminist in the old style" (199), and now this old-fashioned feminist is dying. This comment is not without significance as a sign that orients both character and reader toward an awareness of the need for new concepts of gender in the culture and its texts. Eulalia tells how she herself passed through a period of "feminismo furibundo" (furious feminism) (145), but she admits that that stance brought her little authentic satisfaction.[16] Paradoxically, Eulalia also admired and identified with a certain heroine of sentimental novellas, but was likewise unable to find satisfaction or authenticity in that role. In a similar fashion, Germán expresses a dissatisfaction with the role options that his culture concedes to the masculine gender, and his discourse displays with all the poignancy of such self-revelation the limited options available to men and women alike in the gender system of the speakers' culture. What is gradually revealed throughout the course of the narrative is that the disappointments of this woman and this man go beyond the level of the individual; the speech of these two individuals metonymically encodes descriptions and analyses of the unhappy polar alternatives of woman and man in a particular cultural milieu (the materially comfortable, but spiritually and psychologically alienated Spanish bourgeoisie). And while this uneasiness voices desires for the reinscription of gender in a specific cultural context, it implies a simultaneous desire to rewrite those texts grounded in the same cultural particularity.

The course of Eulalia's life has been characterized by a continual vacillation between the binary roles represented by the literary protagonists/Adriana and Madame de Merteuil: "Aquel campo de batalla oculto donde madame de Merteuil perseguía sin descanso la sombra evanescente de Adriana" (that concealed battlefield where Madame de Merteuil tirelessly pursued the evanescent shadow of Adriana) (200). From Eulalia's perspective, two textual models stand face to face and neither is apt as a model for her life or text. Yet as she "rereads" or reconsiders these texts of her youth, Eulalia negotiates between their confining binary oppositions, attempting to discover a way out of their alternatives. In this way, her dilemma doubles as that of the woman who writes, similarly faced with an intertextual inventory of narratives that seem to invite her sacrificial conformity to their either-or of gender identities.

On one side stands Madame de Merteuil, the notorious and infamous heroine of Laclos's novel, *Les Liaisons dangereuses*. Though the Madame was victimized by the constrictions of her society, she was, in turn, victimizer of others who came into contact with her. Madame de Merteuil is thus an ambiguous figure—complex and perplexing—at once a sign for liberation and degradation. She is too negative for comfort, and yet strangely appealing for her strength, her daring, and her cunning. On the opposite end of Eulalia's intertextual polarity is the image of Adriana—the beautiful Sicilian heroine of an oft-read sentimental novel who is about to be carried off in the moonlight by an ardent suitor. Adriana obsesses Eulalia for seven summers with her significations of love, passion, and the mysterious sinfulness of night. Both characters are inscribed with a sinful sexuality, but Adriana embodies the woman capable of surrendering totally to the abducting lover, while Madame de Merteuil encodes the woman capable of making man surrender to her. In this sense primarily sexual beings, the two literary models represent opposing or polarized models of female sexual behavior, and as such, leave woman as reader and writer with an unshakable uneasiness before this unsatisfying either-or.

As behavioral and textual paradigm of femininity, Madame de Merteuil has too much of the masculine in her to be unproblematic and appealing to Eulalia. Laclos's protagonist dared to upset the discourses of sexual politics ordering her culture, and for reversing their codes of behavior, she was duly punished. Standing in opposition to the social mores of her time, she had to pay for her transgression and ultimately suffer rejection. So Eulalia, though a one-time fervent admirer of the cynical Madame, is not entirely comfortable with the French rebel's example.[17] But at the same time, though Eulalia cannot resist the fascinating pull of

Adriana—the romantic and sentimental model for female gender identity—she is too strong to regress to the passivity of adolescent fantasy that Adriana revives. These troubling inadequacies in behavioral and textual options pose some disquieting questions: did Eulalia ever have an alternative to this unhappy choice between unsatisfactory binary oppositions? And what might the implications of her alternative say about the woman writer's desire for a voice of her own?

For a very brief time Eulalia experienced, or at least glimpsed, intimations of a liberative code of behavior for women. Analogously, this insight locates a potential site of regenerative codes for the texts of women. As an adolescent, Eulalia read her sentimental novels at night by the light of the moon: "bandera de la noche, diosa desafiante" (flag of the night, defiant goddess) (35). The moon became her accomplice in youthful transgression, and she soon identified with it and abandoned herself to it. At the same time, her mother became another sympathetic accomplice, the two sharing a bond as "luneras" (moon people) with the "defiant goddess" of the night.[18] To this nocturnal, maternal moon space, the girl took books she had stolen away from the study or paternal space of her father and Uncle Ramón. Thus by stealing or transferring paternal texts to an alternative maternal location, the young girl conferred upon her reading activities a clearly subversive, transformative, though always tenuous quality ("leer era acceder a un terreno . . . amenazado y siempre a conquistar, a reinventar y defender" [to read was to accede to a terrain . . . threatened and always in need of conquering, reinventing and defending]) (34–35). Her gesture was, in Derridean terms, "exorbitant," out of bounds, inside an(other) terrain.[19]

⌒ This contiguous placement of old texts within a context signifying feminine, maternal bonding and defiance marks alternate spatial boundaries signifying the transcendence of behavioral and textual polarities. It is underscored by Eulalia's youthful dismissal of binary oppositions ("fugas contra la insolayable separación entre alma y cuerpo que las normas mandaban respetar" [flights from the unavoidable separation between soul and body that the norms demanded be respected]) and her discovery that her reading habits constituted a silent rebellion against the cultural grain ("una rebeldía contra leyes y horarios y un marcado placer por lo prohibido" [a rebellion against laws and timetables and a marked pleasure for the prohibited]) (37). Thus Eulalia's later spoken recollections of this youthful rebellion conjure up the idea of an(other) dark, maternal space for woman as reader and writer, and they implicitly reclaim the right to relocate therein those paternal texts that might thereby be reinscribed with a voice of woman's own.

Eulalia's remembrances also reveal how the maternal principle was soon subject to paternal distortion when the girl's words were decoded by clerical authority. Young Eulalia's spontaneous honesty and candor about her feelings, her freely expressed joy in her body and her femaleness, soon suffered misinterpretation and distortion by her confessor. Her spontaneous text reemerged from his consciousness in "palabras distintas y mucho más vulgares" (different and much more vulgar words), and her joy was rewritten as "una atribución tan tergiversada y burda" (a very distorted and coarse attribute) (38). Thus entirely misreading the girl's "text," the priest defines himself as a metonymic representative of how patriarchal discourse often distorts the messages of females who seek to claim the power and freedom of maternal symbols. This particular clash of discourses thereby relegates the girl—and later woman—to a duplicitous existence, a contradictory and unresolved vacillation between gender polarities. It seems that until the night of spontaneity, which constitutes the plot of *Retahílas*, Eulalia had to show one face to the world and feel something else inside. Like the creatures of her childhood books, she felt herself another "ser de ficción" (fictional being) caught up in the alienating texts of others.

Even as a feminist, Eulalia was rendered incapable of conceiving options beyond unsatisfactory binary oppositions. She still opted for one of her literary models, Madame de Merteuil, who "destronó a las mujeres de la raza de Adriana" (dethroned the women of Adriana's breed) (148), and it took a dialogue with Lucía, Germán's more traditional mother, to reveal the contours of Eulalia's trap. Their conversation reveals that Eulalia could then conceive only of the polarized roles of mother or person. But Lucía was scandalized by such a dogmatic alternative: "le parecía una clasificación de libro de texto malo; se podía inventar algo distinto de lo que veíamos a nuestro alrededor" (it seemed to her a classification from a bad textbook; one could invent something different from what we saw around us) (146). If Lucía's insistence on something other than the obvious or apparent can be read in terms of language or textuality, as well as behavior, then her desire to transcend the limited oppositions of extant gender codes is not unlike a speaker's desire to transcend the limitations of language or a writer's to transcend textual conventions: "because there is always on the level of language, something which is beyond consciousness . . . it is there that the function of desire is to be located."[20] Lucía's Lacanian desire will settle for nothing less than flight beyond the boundaries of known binary polarities and invention as a strategy for evading the confines of Eulalia's "bad text."

Eulalia did attempt to find another text of spontaneous communication with her estranged husband, Andrés, but because she lacked the inventive spark of someone like Lucía, that attempt eventually met with failure. Still, at first she seemed to hit upon a textual model that would prove more satisfactory and promising. Wife and husband meet after a period of separation and attempt to reforge a link between them through language. Her goal is to make him stay with her until daybreak; her means of doing so is to hold him with the power of words. Envisioning herself in the role of Scheherazade, Eulalia views telling as the very substance of life: "Vivir es disponer de la palabra, recuperarla, cuando se detiene su curso se interrumpe la vida y se instala la muerte" (to live is to make use of the word, to recuperate it; when its course is halted life is interrupted and death is established) (187).[21] The use of language can form or dissolve a relationship, for it is the very substance of the interpersonal bond: "el lenguaje es la relación misma" (language is relationship itself) (195). The inherent potential of language and the narrative strategy of Scheherazade seemed to offer, at that juncture, a textual viability that previous models could not. The very fluidity of Eulalia–Scheherazade's voice seemed to resist the more rigid contours of the other, more polarized, narratives.

Yet what Eulalia did not realize during that encounter with Andrés was that any language or any word would not do. Andrés signaled to her through word and gesture that the linguistic code between them was false, and that this in itself signified the inauthenticity of their attempt to revive a dead relationship. Scheherazade may not herself have been dead, but the language of her desperate attempt to salvage her relationship most unhappily was: "esa palabra muerta . . . era una aparición macabra, desvinculada de nuestra relación actual" (that dead word . . . was a macabre apparition, disjointed from our present relationship) (195). Eulalia learns a painful lesson indeed: that her rather excessive literary borrowings from the past were of dubious consequence in her attempt to repair a ruptured relationship in the present. All she could do was rail at her husband in the language of novels of passion; feel the venomous spite of pulp fiction; crave vengeance like movie heroines; write letters like pale romantic heroines; and evoke the wronged wives of the classical theater, Russian novel, film, and confessional. She was then rather victimized than liberated by those textual resonances that insinuated themselves deeply into her emotions and seemed to inhibit rather than elicit originality or invention.

If the disappointing dialogue between the estranged spouses is at least in part attributable to Eulalia's mistaken regression to tired patterns of speech or textuality—"Eulalia-la-de-antes" (she of before)—then the changelessness of her spouse—"Andrés-el-mismo-de-siempre" (the same one as always)—occupies the other side of dialogical failure. While Eulalia looked to the past for her models, Andrés remained firmly positioned in a changeless present. One perspective is tellingly absent from this polarized, ill-fated dialogical exchange: that of the future. And here is where the novel's clever inclusion of Germán's voice serves to supplement this discursive lack of the older generation. Germán's half of the dialogue reveals tensions and conflicts felt by a young man sensitive to the pressures of contemporary bourgeois Spanish society. Germán is thus a metonymic foil to Eulalia's traditional girlhood confessor, articulating the dissatisfaction of today's male with the dominant texts of his culture. By speaking out from the past and into the future, Germán articulates through his anxieties a voice often stilled by the polarized gender system of traditional phallogocentric discourse.

Germán, as youthful interlocutor, seeks to push beyond the confines of his culture's oppressive "código de virilidad" (code of virility). He chafes under the weight of that "sack of stones" that has been his to bear, and now in the spontaneity of his verbal exchange with Eulalia, he revives and momentarily seeks to lay down that burden of gender polarities. In the silky threads of speech that spin themselves between nephew and aunt, the everyday world of young men in the consumer society—a world of alcohol, drugs, sex, travel, telephones, motorcycles, cars, and discotheques with which Germán has established an uneasy truce—is held in abeyance. Germán articulates the desires of the man who also longs for something different. He verbally affirms that "no tienen por qué existir bandos ni esa distribución de papeles tan tajante . . . esas diferencias que nos meten de pequeños y que nos embarullan la capacidad de ser nosotros mismos como queríamos ser" (there is no reason why factions and such sharp distinctions need exist . . . those differences that they fill us with when we're small and that spoil our capacity to be the selves that we want to be) (166). As his mother did before him, Germán expresses a desire beyond the level of language, beyond what is commonly known and accepted, and seeks an(other) text free from the restrictions of enemy bands and the distribution of gender roles in unsatisfactory polarities.

The nature of the narrative exchange between Germán and Eulalia—that between a man and a woman rather than between two men—is a first step on the road to an(other) discourse among men.[22] It certainly reveals how restrictions in gender coding for men have expressed themselves in analogous restrictions in male communication or in the generation and reception of texts between men. As Germán relates to Eulalia, when one friend of Germán's father intimated that another friend, Harry, might be a homosexual, the father was quick to deny his friendship with Harry. Frightened and threatened, Germán's father could not conceive of a relationship between men that might transcend the homophobic boundaries of his culture. But when the other men laugh about Harry, Germán avoids confrontation with them, and defense of his friend, in a similar attack of homophobia: "me pareció grotesco tenerlo que defender allí en aquel círculo de gente que él no habría podido aguantar, lo dejé a todos riéndose como oligofrénicos y me fui a bañar. Y por la noche le estuve escribiendo a Harry una carta que luego rompí" (it seemed grotesque to have to defend him in that circle of people that he would not have been able to stand, I left them all laughing like oligophrenics and went to take a bath. And at night I was writing Harry a letter that I later tore up) (129). Perhaps Germán's reluctance to defend his friend before a group Harry himself would have shunned was an act of wisdom; perhaps his own desire to wash his hands of an uncomfortable situation was an escape from commitment. Certainly his inability to write to his friend reveals a poignant lack of communication between men that Germán seeks to explain by his inability to evoke Harry as interlocutor.

The question of Harry's function as interlocutor or recipient of letters, and as letter writer himself, poses questions about male roles and the male text that Germán's passing commentary to Eulalia introduces but never resolves. If Germán's communication with Harry was brusquely severed before it could materialize, the son was unable to resolve the same contradiction that plagued his father. The father, torn between the homophobic pressures of the group and his dependence on Harry's texts ("le necesita . . . le pide que no deje nunca de escribir" [he needs him . . . he asks him to never stop writing]) (129), is unable to reconcile his need for the text with his fear of its author's sexuality. The desire to effect

communication, indeed to write, seems at odds with the pressures
to maintain firmly delineated boundaries of sexual behavior. The
ruptured generation and reception of texts parallels the separation between men imposed by the demands of their social conditioning. Again, the problematic of interlocution is inescapably
linked to formulations of gender identity and sexual practice, and
any resolution on one front would likely effect parallel transformations on the other. In the meantime, the men live in an uneasy
truce with their contradictions, articulating them only with an
interlocutor of the opposite sex, as Germán does with Eulalia.
Through Germán's confessions, we take leave of the father in a
duplicitous position between rejection and desire; and similarly,
Germán admits his desire yet his inability to fully escape the
pressures of social conditioning that stymie his interlocution with
other men. His voice speaks of a desire to which the future may
better be able to respond.

Still, *Retahílas* draws to a close with an encomium by Eulalia and
Germán on the power and pleasures of well-wrought language.
The novel does invoke solace and temporary fulfillment in the
wellsprings of verbal art, specifically in the medium of oral communication. On another level, the spontaneous and articulate
communication exchanged by the interlocutors engenders a code
for a new openness between woman and man. As the protagonists
recollect their past, they also reevaluate their behavior as objects of
imposed gender identities. They express nostalgia for a future
when woman and man might be freer from the repressive injunc-
tions of internalized texts and social conditioning. And through
this talk of desire, the two—woman and man—both give voice to a
textual process that itself embodies and articulates the quest for
discourses beyond the binary either-or.

In the language of *Retahílas*'s contemporaneous structuralism,
this narrative proposes a new grammar of coding through its
internal verbal or syntagmatic structure. That is, within the narrative process of the novel itself, a "third," an(other), or a non-
polarized code of gender roles and textuality is glimpsed. This
preview is created by the proper structuring and expression of
spoken language and its effects on the interlocutors. Eulalia's
name in Greek means "to speak well," and this ability has the
power to transform her into a protean creature free from the
bonds of restrictive either-or gender classifications. Germán observes her unlimited possibility thusly: "te miro mientras hablas y
te veo una cara increíble, de joven, de niña, de bruja, cambia a
rachas, a la luz de las palabras que vas echando al fuego" (I watch

you while you speak and I observe an incredible face, of a young woman, a child, a witch, it changes in fits and starts, by the light of the words that you toss to the flames) (222). However, coming to bear upon this freedom of language, and analogous gender definitions in the syntagmatic narrative, are limitations inherent in the paradigmatic structures of contemporaneous culture. In the extended cultural context there functions an extant grammar of often unsatisfactory gender polarities, one that hovers about threatening to limit the behavioral options available to woman and man, and to dispose correspondingly limited textual paradigms or structures for those who write. *Retahílas* can be appreciated as a sincere challenge to these verbal and nonverbal restraints, and as a textual apotheosis that at least temporarily transcends them. Through orality and a complex weave of intertexts, Eulalia and Germán implicate what the writing of other texts for woman and man might turn out to be.

El cuarto de atrás goes farther in the directions charted by *Retahílas,* and it does so with spectacular cunning. The same preoccupations with interlocution and the text inform both novels, but the later work moves beyond *Retahílas*'s central insistence on the rupturing of binary oppositions to an even greater multiplicity or heterogeneity. The layering of its textual elements is more playful and complex, and the blending of texts read, spoken, and rewritten is more richly concocted. Cultural, historical, and imaginative texts are woven and rewoven into a narrative web that always exceeds the sum total of its separate threads.

The initial scene of *El cuarto* plunges the reader into this discursive abandonment through the skillful device of a woman struggling with the demons of insomnia. Caught thus between sleep and wakefulness, she waits, impatient for the visitation of words that dance before her but elude her grasp. Suspended between these two states of consciousness, she begins to sketch her way to memories of the past, evoking languid heroines reclining on Turkish couches and her own childhood room, its decor inspired by the same ladies' magazines that published stories of dreamy heroines awaiting mysterious nocturnal phone calls. The woman's eyes fix upon piles of books surrounding her bed, upon an etching of Luther in conference with a demonic being likewise perched on piles of books at his interlocutor's bedside. She rediscovers a sewing basket filled with precious trivia, including a mysterious letter recalling fragments of other trifles strewn about a deserted beach. In a scene reminiscent of Buster Keaton comedy, she trips on a copy of Todorov's study of the fantastic in literature and further superimposes bits and pieces from book, film, epistle, and her life experiences. Like a Russian doll, each encounter with a fragment from the past reveals another and yet another in a time and space in which memories of experience, dreaming, and texts coincide, indeed, overlap.

The semidream state evoking the preceding jumble of implicitly experienced and clearly fictional elements is reflective of a lifetime devoted to reading and the internalization of texts. It draws its inspiration from multiple forms of cultural and literary discourse, thus establishing at the outset of the novel the impossibility of life unmediated by texts. If the introductory chapter, and, in fact, the entire narrative of *El cuarto*, is made up of a dream state, then the dream is of a particular nature: it is a dream of texts in which, as Foucault has observed, "the imaginary resides between the book and the lamp."[23] It is a dream "no longer summoned with closed eyes, but in reading" and in a field of multiple cultural discourses that shape experience.[24] Recollections of experience throughout *El cuarto* are often associated with the reading of specific texts or the consumption of specific cultural discourses (such as film, songs, or political propaganda), thus making this narrative truly a book about books, a text about texts, a newly spun web of reformulated cultural discourses.

Yet, as we have been observing, experience and even reading—as creative and inventive as the latter might be—are not, for Martín Gaite, sufficient for the creation of a text. As the two introductory quotations by the author suggest, daring, independent reading and telling as aspects of a complementary process are necessary for the production of inventive texts. Life just happens to us, but when we tell, then and then only do we make things happen. By extension, by narrating events, we make things real. Along with the groundwork of creative reading, then, must go the shaping process of telling—of giving voice—if the recollected fragments of past texts and other forms of discourse are not to remain just that—fragments. As we have witnessed in *Retahílas,* or the debut of this process, telling saves things from oblivion, but even more importantly, it engenders the transformative process of the written narrative text itself.

Thus we revisit once again the author's theory of the interlocutor, so central to the existence of *El cuarto* as it was to *Retahílas.* Without the entrance of an interlocutor figure, the text would remain frozen at the end of the introductory chapter; the fragments would remain dangling with nowhere to go. But just as the first chapter ends with an implicit plea for an interlocutor ("no sé a quién se lo digo" [I don't know to whom I can tell it]),[25] the night is punctuated, at the beginning of the second chapter, with a phone call. The caller is a mysterious man who turns out to incorporate many of the discursive threads that weave the novel's introductory scene. His arrival makes possible the continuation and further development of the textual process, and what is more, his collaboration in its genesis makes it appear spontaneous and potentially infinite.

The visitor's presence as interlocutor, interviewer, confidant, and companion "propicia los derroteros del relato" (establishes the course of the narrative), as Luis Suñén has observed,[26] literally making possible a story that might otherwise remain truncated in silence. This is not to say that the entire text of *El cuarto* is dialogical; the interlocutor serves rather as a stimulus and a receiver for a broadly conceived form of telling that includes solitary recollection as well as dialogue: "lo importante es seguir hablando, con los demás o una sola" (the important thing is to keep on talking, with others or to oneself) (89). The third chapter takes place entirely in the narrator's consciousness, as she goes into the kitchen to fetch a thermos of tea for herself and her visitor. Still, she never forgets about the man waiting for her in the living room, nor about his function as the ultimate recipient of her narrative: "Me tengo que acordar de contarle lo del cuarto de atrás" (I have to remember to tell him about the room at the back) (97).

A principal textual thread that winds itself from the narrator's reading through her telling to the newly generated text is that of popular romance. In ways that *Retahílas* foretells, the original texts pass through the narrator's filter of uneasiness and desire, emerging in their new textual environment as codes that have shifted well beyond their point of origin. This process in *El cuarto* plays even more directly with the borrowed codes, and presents itself more openly as a "subversive force with regard to old classifications," as Roland Barthes has defined such workings of the text.[27] If, for example, Martín Gaite recognizes the promise of the encounter—one of the stock codes of the "novela rosa" (sentimental novel)—as an essential ingredient of any novel,[28] she uses it in *El cuarto* as the initial and underlying code of her text, but not as its determinant according to original convention.

Unlike the encounter of "la novela rosa," which insistently ends in love and marriage, the analogous code structuring *El cuarto* conspicuously and self-consciously deviates from its source.

Though a degree of subtle and subdued sensuality from "la novela rosa" may pervade this encounter, there are limits to the degree of borrowing. And even though the narrator is aware of how much her responses have been influenced by the internalized literary codes of her youth—"es difícil escapar a los esquemas literarios de la primera juventud, por mucho que más tarde se reniegue de ellos" (it is difficult to escape the literary schemes of early youth, in spite of how much one may later deny them) (141)—the patterns of those early codes are questioned and ultimately reinvented and rewritten. As the narrator queries: "¿por qué tenían que acabar todas las novelas cuando se casa la gente?" (why did all the novels have to end when the people got married?) (92). Obviously there is no fixed rule that legislates literary practice, which requires the predictable and unimaginative use of the "happy ending" code in narrative. So, as if in response to the query posed by her narrative voice, the author swerves from the demands of this convention by incorporating the encounter into *El cuarto* with objectives radically different from those of its conventional forebears. In *El cuarto* the encounter simply serves as a coming together of two reader/speakers for the purpose of sharing responses to textual and cultural discourses; it is no longer a thinly veiled ploy for the inevitable sexual pairing of two individuals.

While the narrator associates her own fears and the comforting presence of the interlocutor with memories of analogous scenes from "la novela rosa" ("Oh, Raimundo—exclamó Esperanza, mientras brotaban las lágrimas de sus párpados cerrados—contigo nunca tengo miedo" ["Oh, Raymond," Hope exclaimed, while tears welled up from her closed lids, "I'm never afraid when I'm with you"]) (38), Martín Gaite's textual coding here rejects the stock solution of sentimental novels such as the woman's reclining of her head on the man's shoulder. This protagonist is thus uncomfortably, though exhilaratingly, outside predictability. On the one hand, she engages in something akin to what Barthes has called "plaisir" or the pleasure of the text (a homely fireside feeling: "Sería bonito que hubiera una chimenea" [it would be nice if there were a fireplace]) (40); on the other, she experiences a kind of Barthean "jouissance" or bliss (paradoxically producing a disconcerting, discomforting feeling: "Mi languidez placentera se ha convertido en tensión, en algo incómodo" [My pleasant languor has become tension, something uncomfortable]) (39).[29] The narrator's conflicting feelings vis-à-vis the mysterious interlocutor, their shifting uncertainty at the outset and at certain other junctures of the dialogue, constitute a metonymic sign for the very evolution of a text that will, simultaneously, preserve and nurture the pleasurable and known, and disquietingly strain toward the disconcerting and unknown ("la incertidumbre" [uncertainty]) (55).

In many ways, *El cuarto* represents a successful attempt to at once preserve attractive aspects of a traditional female literary culture and to break out of bondage from its more restrictive features. As Linda Levine has pointed out, Martín Gaite has created in *El cuarto* a novel employing intertextual resonances of "la novela rosa" in a manner similiar to Cervantes's use of the chivalric novel in the *Quijote* or Juan Goytisolo's use of Golden Age drama in *Reivindicación del Conde don Julián*.[30] But unlike the mature Cervantes's mocking irony or Goytisolo's mordant wit, Martín Gaite's attitude toward the codes of "la novela rosa" is more lovingly selective. Rather than resorting to an irony that destroys the old in order to create the new (Goytisolo), she turns to constructive synthesis as a means of transcending the limitations of convention.[31] Given the fluid or spiraling nature of the text of *El cuarto*, the author can juxtapose, for example, the narrator's pleasure in a recollection from the "novela rosa" ("Cuánto me gustaban las novelas rosa" [How I liked sentimental novels]) (39), with the interlocutor's entreaty to talk about mystery literature, thereby meshing both codes through contiguity and opening them to functions they could not otherwise have in their original closed, conventional environments.

The interlocutor, too, is much more than an avatar of the heroes of "la novela rosa." Derived, as well, from tales of mystery and the fantastic, from the detective genre, from the unidentified correspondent evoked by the sewing basket letter, from the interlocutor of Luther's engraving, even from the author's own academic research into the customs of the eighteenth century (the ladies' companion of the "cortejo" custom),[32] the visitor/interlocutor constitutes yet another sign for the symphonic nature of this text. He, as does the narrator, metonymically inscribes into it a network of reading experiences and confrontations with cultural discourses that will be reconsidered and intricately interwoven (or told) into the written text.

The woman reader/writer characterizes her visitor as an informed, even superior reader when she declares: "Entiende usted mucho de literatura, efectivamente" (You really know a lot about literature) (198). Likewise, he defines himself as an original and perceptive reader: "entiendo de literatura y sé leer entre líneas" (I

understand literature and I know how to read between the lines)
(196). From the beginning to the end of the encounter, he reinforces the literary tone of the entire text. For example, when
cockroaches appear, he immediately asks the woman if she likes
mystery literature. Almost uncannily, in his role as literary critic,
he knows that she has not cultivated the mystery mode in her
work, so their discussion soon leads to his brief assessment of
"aquella [novela] que ocurría en un balneario" (that novel which
took place at a spa) (48) as an abortive attempt to write mystery
fiction. In the Cervantine tradition of authorial self-criticism of an
earlier work in a later one, the man may also be a personification
of an aspect of the writer's self, as Julian Palley has pointed out.[33]
But most importantly, the reactions of the man as a reader of texts
generated by the narrator are illuminating for their theoretical
insights and their dialectical effects on the narrator as a teller of
tales or writer in evolution.

The narrator's reading of those texts relying heavily on the
hermeneutic code for their effect on the reader—that is, the
fantastic, mystery, suspense, detective fiction—can be seen to have
been profoundly influenced by her contact with Todorov's theories of the fantastic. All around her resonate projections of her
own experience with the fantastic or mystery text: cockroaches
reminiscent of Kafka, the interlocutor's telling her not to bite her
nails as does Max de Winter to the girl in *Rebecca,* the visitor's
propensity to search for clues, his diabolical appearance. But,
although the woman makes repeated and obviously pointed references to Todorov's study and its implied influence upon her, it is
the man, the mysterious interlocutor as a sophisticated, critical
reader, who unrelentingly directs her attention to the theoretical
significance of mystery or the fantastic as genre and who coaxes
her to accept its full implications for her work.

Very early in their encounter, the roles of the two readers seem
to be polarized. The narrator interprets and generates texts
through a seemingly intuitive process, carried along by the thread
of her tale, reluctant to break the spell of her telling with interruptions. On the other hand, the man as interpreter of texts is
more apt to break the flow of the narrator's discourse with his
theoretical explanations. Though his observations may be correct,
even incisive, they are annoying to the narrator as she is more
intent upon submerging them both into the spell of her story. As
she recounts the events inspiring her novel of the spa, the man
alights on the word "ambiguity," insisting upon interjecting a
theoretical observation: "La ambigüedad es la clave de la literatura

de misterio" (Ambiguity is the key to mystery literature) (53).
Indeed at this point the interlocutor fairly echoes Todorov. Yet the
narrator, so impressed at other instances by Todorov, here agrees
"sin ganas" (grudgingly) (53), unable to be enthusiastic about this
inopportune interruption. Significantly, the man's interruption is
analogous to a similar occurrence experienced by the narrator at
the spa. Then the girl, intent upon delivering a love letter to the
young object of her desire, is interrupted by news of Hitler. Thus
suddenly finding her spell of enchantment rudely broken, she is
driven into a rage at her miscarried attempt to communicate. The
narrator consistently displays a marked preference—then and
now—for the spontaneous flow of discourse, rather than for any
theoretical interruptions about the same.[34]

Though the male reader/interlocutor bears a marked resemblance to Todorov as he comments upon the fantastic genre,
there nevertheless exists a fruitful ambiguity as to which aspects of
Todorov's theories he finally comes to embody. As we have seen,
he tends to return with insistence to his affirmation of the need
for ambiguity and uncertainty in literature, concepts also stressed
by Todorov. These observations are generally well taken by the
narrator, who respects her visitor's insights and judgments: "siempre da en el clavo" (he always hits the mark) (55), but another
aspect central to Todorov's interpretation of the themes of the
fantastic is incorporated into El cuarto—the theme of the Other—
and that aspect is embodied more by the narrator herself. The
theme of the Other with its emphasis on the "themes of discourse"
or language as structuring agent of man's or woman's relation
with others, parallels the author's own views on language. For just
as Todorov has observed: "all life comes back to the question of
our speech."[35]

If the male critic's reading seems more focused upon the theoretical definitions and conditions of the fantastic text, then the
woman writer's reading and generation of texts seems more influenced by the theme of the Other, by the discursive relationship
between persons, also characteristic of the fantastic text. In the
dialogical play between the interlocutors of El cuarto, Martín Gaite
seems to hint at possible gender-links in patterns of reader/writer
responses. The narrator's anxieties and impatience with her interlocutor's propensity toward theory and her own preference for
unimpeded dialogue recall a similar pronouncement by Anaïs
Nin: "woman was born to represent union, communion, communication between abstract ideas and the personal pattern which

creates them . . . woman has to create within the mystery, storms, terrors, against abstractions."[36] Though we might argue with Nin's sexual determinism ("woman was born"), her words are nevertheless remarkably appropriate as a conceptualization of what takes place during the fearfully stormy night that serves as backdrop for *El cuarto,* and they serve as analogue to Martín Gaite's personal views on the differences between male and female writers.[37]

Still, beyond the notions of Nin's essentialist woman writer and similar ideas expressed by Julia Kristeva on the textualization of female desire, *El cuarto,* like its predecessor *Retahílas,* gestures forcefully toward synthesis and away from what Derrida might call "this system of oppositions." Though the male interlocutor may initially appear an imposition, during the course of the narrative he becomes markedly influenced by the woman's experiences with literary texts and other cultural discourses. He becomes more feminized, more sensitive to the pleasures of communication and the details of female history and culture: he appears genuinely interested in the narrator's observations of popular female film stars and political figures, in how girls curled their hair during the postwar period, and later he is visibly moved by the narrator's disclosure of how her childhood experiences became the source for her tale of the imaginary Island of Bergai. Our final image of the man is as an essentially encouraging and supportive figure, even as a solicitous and maternal figure, as he helps the narrator lie down, arranges a pillow beneath her head, and gently caresses her forehead.

While the narrator rests, the man engages himself in the ordering of her manuscript—after asking her permission to do so. Thus, after participating with the narrator in her spontaneous process of telling, he becomes a reader actively engaged in a collaborative shaping of her written text; she, in contrast, becomes a writer presumably more aware of the theoretical implications of her work. At the novel's close, as the narrator kisses her sleeping daughter, her eyes fix upon the daughter's copy of Dashiell Hammett's *The Thin Man.* As she reads the jacket—". . . indicios contradictorios, pistas falsas, sorpresa final" (. . . contradictory signs, false clues, final surprise) (210)—we cannot but remember the presence of the enigmatic interlocutor, his acute observations on the mystery text, and we suspect neither can she. The two have undoubtedly influenced each other by their mutually fruitful exchange. The novel's ending as implied beginning suggests the desirability of a composite, androgynous reader and writer, one who is able to recodify literary texts and other discourses of the culture through a synthesis of abstract theory with personal experience.

Not every reader in *El cuarto* is as sensitive or as perspicacious as the writer and her interlocutor. Carola, the unexpected and inexplicable phone caller—a character derived from the "rival" of sentimental fiction—interrupts the interlocution of the narrator and the man. As a reader Carola is naive, less taken by the pleasures and the complexities of texts, often unconscious of their effects on behavior and discourse. In this way she represents and sheds light on the conventions of an average reading public, especially those of the average female reader.

That Carola is a lightweight in literary competence is revealed when she compares her literary tastes with those of Alejandro (apparently the male interlocutor): "a él siempre le han gustado mucho los libros que se entienden mal, tenemos gustos muy distintos en eso . . ." (he has always liked books that are hard to understand, we have very different tastes in that . . .) (161). Nor is she overly enthused about the narrator's writings: "desde luego escribe usted en plan follón, se saca poco en limpio" (after all you write in a presumptuous way, one can hardly make sense of it) (164). Those ambiguous qualities of the text that impassion the informed, sophisticated (and perhaps male) reader—like Alejandro—are greeted with indifference or dislike by the average (female) reader like Carola. Yet, as does her male counterpart, during the course of her telephone encounter with the narrator, Carola seems to display the potential for change as she grows more aware of the challenges of the text. She finally becomes less the rival figure and more the inquisitive reader as she wishes, for apparently esthetic reasons, that the narrator were the author of those old letters she has secretly read against the wishes of Alejandro.

Carola soon launches into a rambling discourse about her plight as the victim of her consort. As she explains her predicament, her own voice echoes with cultural and literary discursive fragments she has heard, seen, read, and assimilated and that now provide the patterns of speech that express her character. In this way, as Luis Suñén has pointed out, Carola is "un personaje antológico" (an anthological character).[38] Playing the role of a more experienced and conscious reader, the narrator acts as an intermediary to Carola's multiplicitous utterances, thus filling in the gaps of unconsciousness with her own skill as a highly perceptive reader. In this role as reader, as well as writer, the narrator also serves as an interpretive guide to a hypothetical reading public, especially an uninformed female one, which may be unconscious of less visible discursive strategies in seemingly banal or popular literary and cultural texts.

Initially seeming but a jealous suburban housewife, Carola acquires added dimensions through her use of literary allusions that are, in turn, interpreted by the narrator. When she exclaims, for example, "¡Qué sabrá usted lo que es una pasión!" (How would you know what a passion is?) (151), the narrator, as a more studied reader and decoder of her culture, remembers the couplets of singer Conchita Piquer. Acknowledging a tendency in dominant cultural discourse to underrate and disparage these popular songs, she counters that position by admitting being moved by their capacity to affirm passion in "el mundo de anestesia de la postguerra" (in the anesthetized world of the postwar period) (151). She values precisely what official culture disparaged—the songs' crudeness that served to challenge the false optimism of "los propagandistas de la esperanza" (the propagandists of hope) (152). Through a complementary process of unconscious and conscious reading and interpretive telling about particular forms of cultural discourse—in this instance, certain popular songs— Carola and the narrator together generate a text identified by its positive resistance to the repressive insipidity of official discourses defining women.

Carola is aware of some analogies between her relationship with Alejandro and conventions from the police novel, "Blue Beard," and gypsy couplets (respectively, the hiding of the letters, the man's cruel and judgmental stare upon discovering Carola with the letters, the preoccupation with love and money). Yet, as she proceeds to tell of her early days with Alejandro, she unconsciously utters a phrase lifted directly from a gypsy couplet, "maldito parné" (damned dough) (158), for which the narrator again provides an intertextual gloss comparing the irreconcilability of love and wealth in the gypsy couplet and the sentimental novel. Similarly, Carola laments the wall of silence and mystery between herself and her man that the narrator elucidates through an analogy in the film version of Rebecca. Thus Carola enunciates specific sites of discursive practice that, upon their transference to the orbit of the narrator's interpretive process, are disclosed in ways that would not have been possible had they remained restricted to either their original locations or to Carola's unconscious utterances. The narrator's dynamic text thus renders them newly "exorbitant."

Carola and the narrator inhabit the same literary and overall culture, the same historical moment; that is, their texts and sociohistorical contexts are shared. Yet Carola is more a prisoner of convention than is the narrator. The former's capacity to engage in Barthean "jouissance" or disturbingly original interpretations of texts is limited. However, inclusion of Carola in the narrative of *El cuarto*—though not restricted to the exploration of her role as a conventional reader of texts and culture—is felicitous nevertheless for this same reason. It adds another perspective to the novel's consideration of discursive strategies, shedding light on the frequently unconscious absorption of discourses taking place in contemporary culture, and posing the acute necessity of questioning the origins of our tropisms, the nature of the banal (the assignation of banality or freshness of meaning so often depending on our interpretive strategies). The inclusion of Carola as reader thus links up with those areas of literature and culture that often insinuate themselves into the average or uninformed readers' unconscious and, until interrogated by the informed and subversive reader, remain there largely unquestioned.

The narrator's telling and transformation of her rich and broad reading experiences constitute, then, the central thread of *El cuarto*. She has also read fairy tales with originality and the creativity to recodify through retelling: for example, Little Red Riding Hood becomes a visual sign for the female adventurer, and the acts of Perrault's "Pulgarcito" (Little Thumb) become a metonymic model for the play and surprises of the improvisational text. *Alice in Wonderland* and the whole of Lewis Carroll's marvelously upside-down universe also serve as models for the narrator's own inversion or subversion of conventional textual expectations.

The protagonist of *El cuarto* thus repeatedly characterizes herself as a reader and narrator for whom literature has come to mean "brechas en la costumbre" (gaps in custom) (76)—in Barthes's terms "jouissance" or bliss. From the early days of her girlhood, she tirelessly subverted old textual codes and synthesized them to suit new circumstances, as she did with Esmeralda. Esmeralda, a heroine whose name echoes the sentimental novel, nevertheless "despreciaba la riqueza y se escapaba de su casa en una noche de tormenta" (despised wealth and escaped from her house on a stormy night) (183). Thus an inversion of the heroine of sentimental novels (the stereotype who inevitably becomes integrated into the wealth and comfort of an idealized domestic sphere), the protagonist of the girl's literary experiment is a sort of female Robinson, a strong individual who flees comfort and domestication.

If *El cuarto*'s protagonist, as self-conscious narrator, has consistently rejected the "happy ending" convention of popular women's fiction—mainly because it imposes closure and leaves no more to tell—she is still reluctant to dump the entire sentimental genre. In fact, during the specific historical moment of her youth, when society placed a far higher value on the end of courtship than it did on thê means, an acceptance of the play of courtship and the sensual pleasures of popular romance as ends in themselves may have constituted a genuine form of cultural subversion. What is most at stake here, then, is independence: of reading, telling, interpretation, and reinscription of traditional texts through their recombination in new environments. The wild and permissive order-in-disorder of "el cuarto de atrás" (the room at the back), "una habitación donde cada cosa está en su sitio precisamente al haberse salido de su sitio" (a room where everything is in its place precisely for having left its place) (104), is obviously the central metaphor for the text of this novel by the same name. Displacement and replacement through independent reading, interlocution, and recombination in new textual environments is the process whereby *El cuarto* shapes itself as a site where everything has its new and unexpected place precisely because it has left its fixed place of origin.

This fluid and delightfully reordered text also, and not insignificantly, provides a forceful commentary on what constitutes a successful text by and about a woman, especially a woman in the process of generating her own text. In this final, and perhaps overriding sense, *El cuarto*, like its predecessor *Retahílas*, affirms a proud acceptance and vindication of the female, maternal or communicative principle in life and art; it welcomes abstract theory with the reservation that it never predominate over spontaneous communication; and it admits, even celebrates, a guiltless joy before the undeniable pleasures and sensuality of popular female romance. Above all, *El cuarto* continues and reinforces the sweeping gesture advanced by *Retahílas*. It maintains an unswerving faith and confidence in the transformative power of the word—written, read, told and rewritten in an endless spiral of recreative potential.

Talking and telling are in *Retahílas* and *El cuarto de atrás* thus absorbed into a writing process that is satisfied with nothing less than the rupturing of discursive contracts that authorize logo-centric binary oppositions or trap readers and writers into senti-mental closure, misunderstood feminism, or an uncritical consumption of the banal. By reshaping their intertexts through reclamation and revision, these two later narratives by Carmen Martín Gaite employ a synthesis of voice and pen determined to "make things happen" and "invent something new."

4

In Search of Her Mother's House
Matrilinear Myths and Archetypes in Alós's *Os Habla Electra* and Tusquets's *El mismo mar de todos los veranos*

> The loss of the daughter to the mother, the mother to the daughter, is the essential female tragedy.
> —Adrienne Rich, *Of Woman Born*

As the previous chapter has revealed, Carmen Martín Gaite's playful heterogeneity constitutes a distinctive contribution to discursive practices among women writers during the seventies: by affirming her joyful interest in the readerly and writerly pleasures of the text, Martín Gaite was able to simultaneously break through the restrictive boundaries of text and culture. Another significant voice during this same period can be heard in Catalan writers Concha Alós and Esther Tusquets who, in 1975 and 1978 respectively, fix their attention on the discourses of myth and archetype as structuring devices for their new novels. Alós's and Tusquets's choice of myth and archetype and their focus on the those aspects of the feminine that transcend the exigencies of the local and immediate are not unrelated to the cultural circumstances of their work. During that period the two are involved in personal, professional, and political ideas and activities that draw them beyond the boundaries of their specific culture. Among other interests, Alós had read and been influenced by nonwestern philosophy and spirituality; Tusquets, as publisher, had been involved in promoting and publishing the works of non-Hispanic women writers, among them Italian feminist tales for children. Feminists from abroad were welcomed by these writers who sought to discover, wherever possible, the links that women share across the frontiers of cultural particularity.

Alós's *Os habla Electra* and Tusquets's *El mismo mar de todos los veranos* emerge in the seventies as part of Spanish narrative's overall tendency to deviate from the totalizing tendencies of social realism and engage in greater experimentation.[1] In this way, *Os habla* moves to a resolution of social realism's putative dichotomy between realism and imagination. By conceding to the imagined its undeniable legitimacy, the author is able to explore what lies beyond, below, or on the margins of the apparent. This shift in focus is even defined by the narrator at the outset of the novel: "Y, casi siempre, lo real, lo que entonces creíamos real—a veces por la sola y flaca razón de existir otro testigo—se mezcla íntima y totalmente con lo imaginado, echando raíces en el pasado como una planta carnívora de crecimiento perenne" (And, almost always, the real, that which we believed real—sometimes for the sole and flimsy reason that another witness existed—mixes itself intimately and totally with the imagined, sinking its roots in the past like a perennial carnivorous plant).[2] One finishes the reading of *Os habla* with the feeling that one has just awoken from a disturbing, compelling, and often perplexing dream, a dream brimming with stunning and powerful archetypes. *El mismo mar* is also striking and uncommonly rich in its use of archetypal structures and mythical allusions. As Luis Suñen has observed: "toda la novela es una continua alegorización de lo real a través de la utilización del mito o del arquetipo como base de comparación" (the whole novel is a continuous allegorization of the real through the utilization of myth or archetype as a basis of comparison).[3] Both these novels, then, engage in the exploration of the dark side of the moon—those archetypal and mythical levels of discourse that previously narrower conceptions of the real often hid (or prohibited) from view.

Concurrent with the fictional creativity of these writers, literary theory was also engaged in problematizing and historicizing myth and archetype. In fact, it might be helpful to view the process that informs the narrative discourse of Alós and Tusquets as part of poststructuralism's breaking up of unified or totalizing conceptions of myth and archetype. While narrative was busy eluding the demands of what Fredric Jameson has called the "fatally reductive" imposition of a period style, it was also rediscovering Jameson's concurrent claim that the romance archetype does not escape from reality but rather contains it.[4] Still, growing numbers of writers from the periphery—regional and women writers, for example—could not settle for a mere shift from social realism to myth. Along with moves to decenter the imposition of style came interrogations of tendencies to totalize patterns of myth and archetype. The result was a feminist decentering of patriarchal/paternal myth and archetype that yielded revelations not unlike Derrida's upon reading Levi-Strauss: that "there is no absolute source of myth."[5] Feminist theory and women's writing of myth and archetype thus engage in a process of Derridean "supplementarity" through which the now relativized patriarchal or paternal source of myth and archetype is shifted, displaced, and replaced with a gender-specific alternative.

Among these theoretical perspectives, the work of Annis Pratt emerges as a useful key to the perception and assessment of myth and archetype in narrative by women. Pratt, uneasy with the difficulty of forcing quest patterns by and about women into archetypal paradigms proposed by critics such as Northrop Frye or Joseph Campbell, proposed—upon her observations of difference in texts by women—a contrasting (or supplementary) tripartite structure for the female quest. Its general outlines consist of a search for links with the maternal (or matrilineal roots), a straining toward transformation or metamorphosis, and a forcible reintegration into patriarchal society. This schema differs from that of male heroes most importantly because woman is not being initiated as a central figure in the society, patriarchal society considering her as marginal. Thus for every aspect in woman's quest (called matrilinear by Pratt), there is a strong counteraspect (patriarchal).[6] Woman is finally forced to return to the patriarchal society she has temporarily eluded. In the interim of the quest, however, as the female hero searches for her links with a lost maternal past, the elixir of androgyny is glimpsed and the potential for revisionary female mythopoesis emerges, even if the individual quester is forcibly reintegrated into the patriarchy.

Because the hero of *Os habla* is female, and her integration as a free subject into patriarchal culture is problematical at best and impossible at worst, the "phases" of the quest romance outlined by Frye are often absent from the experiences of this female hero. Pratt's theories of archetypal patterns in women's fiction provide, however, illuminating, supplemental schema for conceptualizing the dialectical oppositions present in *Os habla* and a means of identifying archetypes unique to the female quest pattern. A comparison of Pratt's paradigm of the inner journey with Frye's phases of the quest-romance thus provides a revealing theoretical framework for discerning the difference in *Os habla*'s configuration of the quest pattern. Such theory also facilitates the reader's reception of how this novel voices its transformations of myth and archetype.[7] It is precisely this supplemental archetypal discourse, produced through reinscription, that marks Alós's novel as an important transformation in the overall poststructuralist narrative project of the seventies.

Another quest—that for reconciliation and union between mother and daughter through the recuperation of matrilineal roots—is central to Tusquets's *El mismo mar*. The narrator-protagonist of this novel, a middle-aged woman separated and estranged from husband, mother, and daughter, and abandoned in her youth by her Green World lover, is an unmothered and unmothering woman. Entering into a lesbian relationship with one of her literature students, a girl from the New World, she attempts through this intimacy to reforge the severed links of her own maternal-filial relationships. Again, archetypal patterns that inform this quest are feminized, made gender-specific, not because they emanate from any absolute source or totalized mythical pattern, but rather because the difference of their historical and cultural positioning demands an analogous difference in their writing. The archetypal patterns of Tusquets's *El mismo mar* shape a supplemental discourse of utopian female desire within a dystopia of bourgeois patriarchal mediocrity.

The title of *Os habla Electra* alerts the reader that this novel has referents in the world of myth and archetype. It resonates with a variety of patriarchal Greek and biblical myths, recalls pre-patriarchal myths and archetypes originating in Mother Right and matriarchal power, all the while weaving both these mythical heritages into a subtle fabric of lost matrilineal power, the quest for female identity, brief glimpses of a better social order, chaos and apocalypse in a world without gods, and possible rebirth. In many ways the novel's jumbled and oneiric images suggest a structure that recalls Frye's archetypal romance paradigm, the quest myth.[8] This is especially true in the novel's overall thematic struggle between fertility and the threat of its destruction by the wasteland. Yet though the story is familiar, it is at once strangely new, for the old paradigms fail to elucidate just how the collective archetypes are imaginatively reinterpreted and recombined to tell of the quest and struggle of Electra: mother, daughter, woman.

At the outset of the novel, the Green World remembered (identified by Pratt) replaces the myth of the Birth of the Hero (identified by Frye) as phase one, and the Green World lover recalled (Pratt) takes the place of the male hero's pastoral, Arcadian version of innocence (Frye) in phase two. These contrasts open the text to interrogation: why should the female's quest focus initially on the Green World instead of on the origins of her birth; how might the Green Worlds of male and female heroes differ; and if the female hero does come to dwell upon her origins, what are the consequences of that search on the total quest pattern? *Os habla* begins to suggest cultural answers to questions of archetypal difference by following its initial recollection of the lost Green World with a search for the real father; that is, for legitimate patriarchal or paternal identity. But the father remains elusive; paternal authorizaton is absent (hence the myth of origin is displaced). The female hero instead replaces paternal power to concede legitimacy with an alternate maternal multiplicity and her own recuperation of matrilineal identity. *Os habla* thus reconsiders the Green World in the female quest pattern not as the thing *left* behind to be superseded by subsequent stages of more mature development, but as the thing *lost* behind to be recuperated and reintegrated into the matriliner identity of the female, personal and collective. In patriarchal culture, this boon is often unstable and temporary, hence the often tragic dimension of the female quest in general and *Os habla*'s insistence, in particular, on this difference.

Without delay, *Os habla* lamentingly recollects a fertile Green World subsequently destroyed by fire, development, pollution: "el bosque impenetrable, donde yo me adentraba con Electra en busca de la mandrágora silvestre, única hierba capaz de aliviar su insomnio" (the impenetrable forest, into which Electra and I went in search of the wild mandrake, the only herb capable of alleviating her insomnia) (9–10). Not only is the flora of the Green World remembered, but the herbal lore of both mother and daughter Electra, their capacity to function in harmony with nature for the purposes of healing and the alleviation of suffering is conjured up with evocative desire. Even the nature of the plant initially recalled—mandrake, an herb of fertility—serves to implicitly set up a continuing dialectic between fertility and the wasteland, between mother Electra and her role as matrilinear Great Mother and her usurper, Madame la baronne, "terrible patriarchal mother" and agent of death and destruction in her relentless drive to speculate and develop the land of Salt des Ca.

The novel's concentrated opening imagery, in its haunting delineation of this dialectic between matrilinear archetypal patterns and patriarchal responses, articulates an archetypal structure recentered on an axis of female desire and disgust. Even more, associations between Green World space and the powers and attributes of women linked to it suggest very early that a temporally distant matrilineal culture may be woman's collective as well as personal loss, and that the quest of this female hero may be recalling an important historical shift that official culture has conspired to repress—the shift from maternal to paternal hegemony in the culture as a whole. That may be why the Green World is presented here as something more than the loss of personal innocence or youth; its gender inflection refuses to defer the tragic implications of otherness in patriarchal cultural discourse.

Consequently, after the novel's initial recollections of the lost Green World, Electra engages in the historically inevitable task of searching for her real father. As a woman in patriarchal culture, Electra discovers early in her life that she is illegitimate. To compensate for this fact, in an attempt to bestow upon herself an enviable (or culturally legitimate) identity, she creates images of her father that are modeled on myths and archetypes from the patriarchal textual tradition. Her fantasy casts her father as a biblical Noah, a romantic sea captain, a pirate, or Zeus. She imagines him alternately engaged in constructing an ark for the salvation of the chosen or impregnating Electra mother with the invisible seed of his divinity. These patriarchal myths prove ironically ineffectual, however, for when Electra is unable to incarnate her father outside her imagination, she remains abandoned by these heroes of the patriarchal intertext.

In a sense, this ultimate abandonment by a biblical savior figure and a classical god can be seen as emblematic of the condition Electra shares with other women of her culture: she comes to symbolize the eventual illegitimacy of patriarchy's daughters, dependent on man the father for their legitimate identity, yet dispossessed of that same identity and legacy by the abandonment inherent in patriarchy's structures of paternal lineage. Unlike the male hero, this patriarchal daughter finds herself bereft of birthright and is unable to acquire it a posteriori. Neither is Alós's Electra, unlike her namesake of the Oresteia, blessed with a rescuing male who comes to restore order, meaning, or legitimacy to her existence. Finally undelivered by her true father, this Electra is instead imprisoned and deprived by her false father, Kant, a zookeeper who cages his women as he does his animals. Thus she is denied any semblance of the patriarchal identity usually conceded male heroes and is instead enclosed within the confines of a paternal imposter.[9]

Nevertheless, in Electra's fruitless search for a dream, perhaps impossible within the context of her patriarchal enclosure, she does encounter moments of joy with those rare male figures associated by their values and actions with matrilinear, Green World patterns of behavior and imagery. Ali Tucuman, that panther-like Arab who is unlike other men Electra has known, schemes with her to free the animals in Kant's zoo from captivity and does succeed in reintegrating a dolphin back into its natural habitat. Ali comes to be characterized as accomplice and companion to Electra, as worthy of inhabiting Green World space with her. His unity with animals, freedom, and the unrestricted life force cuts across strict lines of gender and associates him more with matrilinear archetypal patterns of existence than with their oppressive patriarchal responses.

Similarly, the Green World lover is recalled in Electra's memory with matrilinear imagery. Electra daughter's memories coalesce with her mother's writings, thus resulting in a textualization of joyful sexuality that doubles as both the mother's and daugher's recollection/inscription of her/their Green World lover. The women praise the lover's body, rendering him in an imagery that links him to the realm of nature in its totality: to ripened fruit, to moist, tender greenery, and to voluptuous animal life (93). But at the moment of remembering and writing, all is sadly relegated to a distant past in the lives of both women. Electra daughter retains but a symbolic remnant of her vanished Green World lover: a dehydrated modified sprig of mint along with the words that evoke him.

The recollections of betrayal and abandonment by patriarchal male figures, and of vanished Green World space and lovers, lead notwithstanding to a discovery of the multiplicity of the mother figure in the third and central phase of this novel's supplemental quest paradigm. In this stage, the power of matrilinear patterns becomes most crucial to Electra's quest, and the differences between the male and female quest pattern become most evident and significant. The richness and potency of the mother's image is transformed from the individual into the archetypal; the inauthentic and impotent image of the father fades away and is abandoned; and Electra comes to realize the indissoluble matrilineal identity between herself and her mother, among all daughters and mothers, among all females already born and still to be born. Stage three of the journey thus spills over into a sustained image of power in the face of repeated disappointments and deprivation.

The totalizing tendencies of patriarchal discourse would prob-

ably encircle Electra mother within the double-sided fence of
censure and moral regeneration, first by casting her as a common
prostitute, then as a conventional, redeemed wife who was for-
merly, mistakenly evil, immoral, and licentious. In view of the
historical effects of such discourse on the daughter, she has no
alternative but to push their boundaries aside by appropriating
an(other) discourse outside this paternal either-or. As she does,
Electra daughter recreates her mother as a once powerful and
free creature who was divested of her potency by patriarchal
enclosure.

First, the daughter-narrator raises her mother to the level of
protean, mythical, and even divine creature: "Mi madre era múlti-
ple. Dos y noventa y nueve, como los nombres de Dios" (My
mother was multiple. Two and ninety nine, like the names of God)
(23). She lifts her mother from the figure of common prostitute to
that of mythical matriarch—strong, self-sufficient, and indifferent
to the moral strictures of patriarchal discourse:

> Simbólicamente, me la imagino con la cabellera suelta, y como era,
> corta de talla, ancha de cadera y sólida la mano, sosteniendo una
> paleta de albañil, untando cada ladrillo con el cemento justo y levan-
> tando, sin ayuda de nadie, el muro que construía a nuestro alrededor
> y que nos envolvía, obligándonos a ella, a todos nosotros, sus "seres
> queridos." Ella sola—altiva la barbilla gordezuela—había construido
> un matriarcado, con aquella despreocupación, indiferencia o valentía
> para despreciar, una vez hubieran cumplido su misión de semental, a
> los padres de sus hijos. Abeja reina.

> (Symbolically, I imagine her with her hair loose, and as she was,
> short-waisted, wide-hipped and steady-handed, balancing a mason's
> trowel, spreading just the right amount of cement on each brick and
> raising, without the help of anyone, the wall that she constructed
> around us and that contained us, obliging us to her, all of us, her
> "loved ones." She alone—her chubby chin held high—had con-
> structed a matriarchy, with that nonchalance, indifference, or courage
> to scorn, once their mission as stud was completed, the fathers of her
> children. Queen bee (160).

From this matrilinear, or as the narrator expresses it, matriarchal
perspective, patriarchal identity or discourse ceases to have importance, and correspondingly, patriarchal power is dismissed as
immaterial.[10]

Not only are the mother's procreative powers transformed by
the daughter's matrilinear discourse, but her overall sexuality is

conceived within the framework of the Green World archetype as well. The same recollection, which doubles as the memory of the Green World lover for mother and daughter, functions as an image in which sexuality is restored its matrilineal or matriarchal power. The women's articulation of their sexual experience recalls the phallus cult and worship of male youth identified by Helen Diner as common in a female-dominated society: "Tu falo a mi medida . . . macho joven. . . . Esta es una danza antigua que tú y yo sabemos" (Your phallus is my size . . . young male. . . . This is an ancient dance that you and I know) (93–94).[11] This particular expression of erotic imagery further serves to characterize Electra as a creature outside the boundaries of patriarchal discourse and possessed of a sexual potency only later repressed by patriarchal enclosure.

Electra also recalls the symbiotic relationship that her mother had to everything that meant life ("recuerdo la naturalidad con que aceptaba todo lo que significaba vida" [I remember the naturalness with which she accepted everything that meant life]) (116), thus contributing another aspect to the mother's matrilinear character. As Bachofen reminds us: "matriarchal peoples feel the unity of all life,"[12] and mother Electra is no exception. Her "green thumb" is more than a knack for gardening; it is portrayed as that intimate link with natural forces characteristic of the Green World woman: "tenía la mano 'verde' y bastaba que la impusiera sobre un esqueje moribundo y lo cubriera con un palmo de tierra para que se convirtiera en un árbol o en una clavellinera" (she had a "green thumb" and it sufficed that she touch a dying cutting and cover it with a bit of dirt for it to become a tree or a carnation) (182).

Mother Electra's link with nature acquires its greatest potency when she is able to control the weather through magic and witchcraft. Often as an act of vengeance against the "terrible mother" or against "policing" women, Electra would entone mysterious sounds, sacrifice rats, and never fail to bring rain.[13] Her acts of witchcraft are not fearful for the female hero, for the latter views them from the perspective of matrilinear mythical discourse as acts of self-defense and self-preservation in which the mother assumes the greatest measure of power available to her. Witchcraft in this archetypal context thus differs radically from its function in the archetypal male quest. Whereas the male hero must struggle against witches as part of his agon, the female hero confronts her mother's witchcraft as a positive expression of lost female power. The witch mother functions as awe-inspiring accomplice—or at least exemplar—for the female, rather than as adversary, as she often does within the context of patriarchal mythical discourse.

After repeated confrontations with varied and powerful aspects of the mother, the image of the father fades and is abandoned. The daughter recuperates her mother, which is to say herself and her matrilineal identity: "Porque Electra, entonces, no era Electra, sino un símbolo. Ella era yo y mis hijas y las hijas de mis hijas y todas las muchachas que nacerán un día . . ." (Because Electra, then, was not Electra, but a symbol. She was I and my daughters and the daughters of my daughters and all the girls that would be born someday . . ." (215). This identification with the mother is underscored most boldly when the daughter goes into the forest to bear her own child with Amazonian strength and independence.

Electra daughter remembers the birth of her child and their brief sojourn in the Green World as the best time of her life. Never again was she closer to Nature; that is, to life, to love, to herself: "La Naturaleza y yo éramos una misma cosa y aprendimos a respetarnos. Nada me era hostil" (Nature and I were the same thing and we learned to respect each other. Nothing was hostile to me) (136–37). Content in the warm little cave where she established residence, she would not have traded it for all the rooms of a palace. She was able to provide for herself ("recogía bellotas, higos, moras" [I collected acorns, figs, berries] (133) and for her child ("Yo tenía leche . . . Yo tenía leche y Caín mamba. Feliz, me abracé a mi pequeño" [I had milk . . . I had milk and Cain nursed. Happily, I embraced my little one]) (132).

Electra daughter names her child Caín, a decision she explains in the following manner: "Caín era un nombre que me había gustado siempre. Además, admiraba la rebeldía de este hijo de Adán. Me parecía injusto su castigo ya que su pecado fue sólo una consecuencia del comportamiento de Yavé, arbitrario y caprichoso" (Cain was a name that I had always liked. Besides, I admired the rebellion of this son of Adam. His punishment seemed unjust to me since his sin was only a consequence of Yaweh's behavior, arbitrary and capricious) (132). Electra's interpretation of the Cain figure is suggestive in terms of the ongoing struggle between matrilinear archetypal patterns and patriarchal responses that pervades her quest. Cain, as a tiller of the soil, was associated with the Canaanites, the farmers who preceded the Hebrews or keepers of sheep in the same territory. The Hebrew deity prefers Abel, the shepherd, over his brother, the agriculturalist; hence originates Yaweh's supposed arbitrary and ca-

pricious behavior. Actually he is taking sides with the Hebrews
against the Canaanites, and Cain's marginalization is a consequence of two cultural systems struggling for survival. Cain,
whose matrilinear trade was preferred by pre-Hebrew goddesses,
suffers displacement by those "patriarchal desert nomads" (as
Joseph Campbell ironically labels the Hebrews),[14] in much the
same way that Electra daughter is forceably reintegrated into the
enclosure of patriarchy and her mother—Great Mother, witch,
and herbalist—suffers displacement by Madame la baronne—
"terrible mother," speculator, and land developer. Even as matrilinear Electra of Salt de Ca is displaced by patriarchal Electra of
"la calle de las Gárgolas."

"La calle de las Gárgolas" and "la ciudad de las Gárgolas" (the
street and city of the Gargoyles) are two sites that symbolize the
other side of the dialectic between matrilinear and patriarchal
archetypes. They are the places characterized by "duros límites"
(rigid limits) (67) and "ritos bárbaros, patriarcales e incomprensi-
bles" (barbarian rites, patriarchal and incomprehensible) (98); and
though one is called street and the other city, they are part of the
same archetype for patriarchal enclosure (limits) that underlies
the agon of Electra's quest. In this space people worship Isis and
Osiris (102), a divine pair who symbolize the transition from
matrilineal clan to patriarchal family.[15] Here, in the patriarchal
enclosure, the wondrous powers of Electra mother are lost, and
the daughter repeatedly laments such a loss: "Electra había
olvidado todos sus poderes" (Electra had forgotten all her powers)
(69); "Como si un bebedizo la hubiera despojado de su identidad.
De sus poderes (As if a potion had divested her of her identity. Of
her powers (181); "¿Dónde estaban los poderes de Electra?"
(Where were the powers of Electra?) (201). The final query is part
of an extended "ubi sunt" on the lost matrilinear powers and
freedoms of the mother: her numerous bastard progeny, her
open bedroom, her erotic freedom ("alegre promiscuidad" (joyful
promiscuity) (200). Thus it is in this site, the place of the
Gargoyles, that patriarchy imposes its stifling response to matrilinear patterns of existence.

The protagonist's agon with seemingly ubiquitous patriarchal
responses to a fleeting Green World is not confined, however, to
the street or city of the Gargoyles. The takeover begins early in
Salt des Ca when the "terrible mother" arrives to begin her ultimately victorious struggle with Electra. It is also initiated with
the authentic father's abandonment of his daugher; continues
with the transformation and desertion of the once Green World

lover, Mal; and it culminates in the memory of rape trauma
resulting from the false father Kant's attempt to possess and
objectify Electra: "Yo no soy tu papá. Y tú me gustas" (I am not
your dad. And I like you) (211). The eventual victory of patriarchal responses are visible everywhere and in almost everyone.
As the world approaches destruction, the onetime Green World
lover of Electra mother, Macía, is overcome by violent jealousy
when Electra exercises her erotic freedom; "policing women" hurl
stones at Electra, attempting to repress the erotic freedom of the
matriarch; Fosca, the narrator's sister, becomes accomplice to the
dreaded Madame in her mistaken interpretation of liberation as
simply woman's economic independence. Even Electra mother
becomes a "policing woman," taking Cain away from her daughter
and subsequently abandoning the young mother to an asylum
where she is drugged and "hombres de blanco, severísimos, me
interrogaban. Creo que me reñían por haber huído" (men in
white, very severe, interrogated me. I think they scolded me for
having fled) (139). This image of the mental institution as a place
where women are controlled by severe men who impose stern
punishments for flights from patriarchal enclosure is yet another
manifestation of the female hero's agon in an increasingly restrictive society.[16]

Finally the agon is over. The world is destroyed, leaving only
four survivors: Sofía, Lidia, the narrator, and a man named
Marcel. It seems as though man and woman have been given
another chance to begin life anew (suggesting here Frye's culmi-
nation of the quest). The small tribe celebrates a ritual renaming
ceremony in which Electra reaffirms her matrilineal name, this
time giving rebirth to herself with a shout of pride: "Me llamo
Electra" (I call myself Electra) (177). Sofía acts as leader of the
group, concerning herself with its nutrition and survival. The
women grind corn and feed the greater part of the resulting corn
cakes to Lidia, who is in the eighth month of pregnancy. Though
the group desires a boy from Sofía, they hope Lidia's child will be
a girl, thus linking corn with procreation in a manner reminiscent
of ancient, matrilinear corn mother and daughter myths (for
example, Demeter and Kore).

Of most significance, though, is the archetypal reaffirmation of
rebirth and fertility in the women's pregnancies and the earth's
restoration of its natural cycles after the holocaust. As in the
parable of the fig tree ("When her branch is yet tender, and
putteth forth leaves, ye know that summer is near," Mark 13:28),
so the survivors are heartened by the hope of fertility symbolized

by the rebirth of that same tree: "Las ramas de la higuera se están hinchando. Sofía bromea, dice que están preñadas como ella. A todos—a Marcel también—nos esperanza que brote el árbol" (the branches of the fig tree are swelling. Sofía jokes, says that they are pregnant like she is. All of us—even Marcel—are made hopeful by the sprouting of the tree) (202). An apocalyptic vision offers the reader a glimpse of what might be the elixir of a more androgynous society. Here woman could exercise wisdom (as Sofía's name, of course, signifies), guidance, and a unity with natural forces; man could be progenitor of a reborn race, working in cooperation with woman rather than assuming the superiority of hierarchical authority: "Marcel nos será muy útil: hay que enterrar a los muertos, sembrar las espigas que hemos encontrado . . . puede, también, fecundarnos a las tres. Y todo comenzará de nuevo" (Marcel will be very useful: the dead have to be buried, the grains we found have to be planted . . . he can also impregnate the three of us. And everything will begin anew) (183). Marcel was to be useful and equal, perhaps more useful because of his greater physical strength, but not more powerful simply because of his gender.

But what the small band of survivors did not foresee was the tenacious survivability of their sociocultural conditioning. Though Sofía is superior in many ways to Marcel, the latter "se preocupa demasiado de su papel de macho de la comunidad" (is too preoccupied with his role as the male of the community) (206). Jealousies between Sofía and the other women also erupt. Though they thought they could recreate culture, they are overcome by "una educación que había sembrado en nosotros monstruos que al crecer tenían que devorarnos" (an education that had sown monsters in us that once grown would devour us) (218). While everything else seems to resume the rhythm of fertility, "sólo los hombres y las mujeres no nos entendemos" (only the men and the women do not understand each other) (206). Sofía and Lidia kill each other and the man with the only knife they have, unable to survive the conditioning of a competitive, individualistic, patriarchal economy. Something goes dreadfully wrong between Frye's sixth phase or "cosy" renewal and the impossibility of renewal that we find in *Os habla*. Pratt's concept of patriarchal backlash discloses the tragic difference between patriarchal and matrilinear archetypal quests within the context of patriarchal culture. Man's preoccupation with his virility, the rivalry between women awakened by man's presence, and woman's deeply inculcated modes of reacting vis-à-vis the male are all problems inher-

ent in patriarchal culture that the supplemental discursive strategy
of this text's matrilinear quest pattern so shockingly reveals.

Thus it is that the narrator, daughter Electra, comes to be the
sole survivor on earth, but even as she is encircled by vultures, she
stubbornly refuses to relinquish all hope. Hers is the resistance
and resilience from which culture heroes are made, and the figure
that she cuts of lone survivor on the beach of total human destruction only reinforces the reader's feeling that there can be hope in
ambiguity. We can only echo the narrator's final question: "¿Y
ahora, qué?" (And now, what?) (218). She has pointed out our loss.
It is for us, as readers and implicit questers, to decide.

Os habla Electra presents a rewriting of the quest in which the
opposite of what is most desired is finally encountered. And yet
we are able to glimpse briefly the mirror reflection of utopia—
foggy, cracked, but still not totally destroyed. The novel is an
omen, a prophecy, a nightmare that reminds us that there still is
time—albeit precious little to be sure—for us to wake up to the
usurpers and actively reconstruct our world. As we have seen, *Os
habla* reveals how the quest of the female hero, given the per-
vasiveness of patriarchal discourse with its limitations and contradictions, is more problematical than that of her male counterpart.
The culture into which she must integrate herself simply is not
structured to enable the female hero to possess her elixir. A
society that blindly follows and integrates "terrible mothers" of
greed or harbingers of death and destruction—such as Madame la
baronne and Kant—has no room for people whose power derives
from erotic freedom, magical arts, and most importantly, links
with life and nature. Thus at a crucial juncture in the history of
Western culture, *Os habla Electra* implies, via the protagonist's
tragic quest, that a collective recuperation of matrilinear archetypal patterns may be necessary not only for a fruitful resolution
of the female quest. Indeed, if a blindness to difference and a
fanatical attachment to patriarchal myths prevails, the very survival of the culture and the lives of its citizens appear at stake.

In *El mismo mar*, the unmothered narrator's struggle with the
memory of her mother informs her quest at regular and crucial
junctures. While the mythical male hero also encounters mother
figures along his road of trials, they often incarnate nostalgia for a
lost childhood, a longing for the bliss of tender innocence and
sensual permissiveness, a "benign, protecting power," as Joseph
Campbell has described such a figure.[17] In sharp contrast, this
protagonist's encounter with contradictory images of her mother

represents the struggle of every daughter to understand, forgive, and achieve atonement with a mother figure made hostile by her compliance with the discourses of patriarchal culture. Too willing to play compromising games, the narrator's mother sought to please and appease the father rather than establish communicational or affective links with the daughter. As a result, the narrator's memories of her mother reflect the painful push and pull of matrilinear and patriarchal archetypal oppositions, as suggested by Pratt's theoretical perspective. Or as Luis Suñen has described in more general terms: "La figura de la madre pasa de ser algo verdaderamente adorable en su comportamiento ajena a toda convención, a convertirse en la figura que encarna la personificación de todas las ataduras que han ido atenazando la libertad nunca estrenada de la protagonista" (The figure of the mother goes from being something truly adorable in its behavior beyond all convention to become a figure that incarnates the personification of all the bonds that have tormented the never-used freedom of the protagonist).[18]

Initially, we see the mother figure as a spirited and playful creature who reveled in shocking and challenging the repressive morality of three spinster neighbors. She insolently removed and hid the fig leaf from a nude statue guarding her threshold; the three older women frantically searched for and replaced it. This joyful provocation was repeated as a nightly ritual. Thus, at the outset of the novel, the mother recalled seems—like the early Electra mother—an inhabitant of a Green World of matriarchal erotic freedom, an adherent of a playful phallic cult. Recalled as always surrounded by "hombres hermosos, hombres jóvenes, elegantes muchachos" (beautiful men, young men, elegant boys),[19] the very structure of this enumeration indicates that she seemed to move in "a women's realm [where] male youth is the ideal of beauty," as Helen Diner has described.[20] The protagonist's mother seems, at first, to represent the lost Green World of matrilinear archetypal roots.

But this mother figure is subsequently revealed as a paradox. Again much like Electra mother, her matrilinear aspects are soon counterpoised to her cold, forbidding, and distant patriarchal counteraspects. Compared to the rational, male-oriented, and even threatening goddess, Athena ("la diosa de la luz, Atenea tonante" (the goddess of light, thundering Athena) (26), she is finally recalled in the opening section of the novel as "la diosa que aniquila a su paso los cultos de Demeter, que ignora para siempre y desde siempre los secretos festejos dionisíacos" (the goddess who annihilates along the way the cults of Demeter, who forever has been and will be unaware of secret Dionysian feasts) (34). Her games were thus deceptive, inauthentic, or at best—like Electra's—merely temporary. Yet, significantly and again like Electra, her evolution as an individual parallels the collective evolution of woman in Western culture: she moves from the annihilation of prepatriarchal Demeter cults to an ignorance of Dionysian religion and its agon between the Demetrian matrilinear principle and its contesting patriarchal principle, and she finally comes to personify the final triumph of the Apollonian age when the divinity of the mother gives way to that of the father and the presiding goddess becomes Athena.[21] The specter of patriarchal backlash and female complicity with it is thus underscored through this metonymic allusion to woman's historical evolution. In this way, the mother's contradictory nature not only establishes with excruciating clarity the estrangement between a particular mother and daughter that will inform the entire course of this protagonist's quest; it also shapes an archetypal figure that may claim broader cultural significance outside textual particularity.

At the beginning of the initiatory phase of her quest, this female hero finds herself between links in an illusive matrilineal chain: her relationship with her spiritual daughter, Clara, commences; her grandmother dies. She reaches out to play the role of the kind of mother she never was, to become better acquainted with the hidden dimensions of the mother she never really knew. And in this embracing of past, present, and future, she comes face to face with the goddess that was not (her mother), the mythical matriarch whose power was more apparent than real (her grandmother), and the "ox" who sealed her grandmother's fate (her grandfather). This encounter with Magna Mater is not merely blissful or even fearful as it would likely be for the archetypal male hero; instead it constitutes an agonizing confrontation with false goddesses perpetuated and sustained by false gods, with matriarchs deprived too long of their freedom by "los machos castradores e importunos [que] se sobreviv[e]n siempre demasiado" (the castrating and importunate males that always survive too long) (147). The mother as goddess exists as a function of the patriarch, and this constitutes a crucial revelation for the female hero. (Given his privileged position within the patriarchy, such a disclosure would be largely irrelevant to her male counterpart.)

In one particularly shocking recollection-confrontation with her parents, the narrator discovers a key that unlocks the truth about certain subtle intricacies of paternal cruelty and control. One evening, in an oblique and enigmatic manner, the secret attraction between the narrator's father and Sofía, the governess, is exposed. The mother, understandably stunned by the revelation, transforms from her usual Athencan demeanor into the figure of a harpy. But the family has its social obligations to fulfill. The father deems that such ugly outbursts of jealousy cannot be permitted, and disposes of the situation according to his needs. He is "padre-autor" (father-author) (173), and though a cowardly Theseus, a weary Zeus—in short, an antihero—he is still a patriarch, and as such he still possesses the privilege of ascribing and inscribing roles, disguises, and masks to cover up the unpleasantness that has temporarily marred his evening plans—the family's attendance at a ball. Ordering the mother, daughter, and governess to dress up and make themselves lovely and gracious as if nothing has happened, he even goes so far as to make an offering of roses to the abandoned Sofía in a final, grand theatrical gesture, as the guests of the ball—and his betrayed wife—look on.

Through this ritual of patriarchal authorial privilege, the father hides his own weakness, indecisiveness, and inertia. As though they were players on a stage of his making, he distributes the parts of his play and forces the women to act them out. His wife—goddess or harpy—is whatever she may be because he has assigned her a particular role, and he is able to change that role at will: "la diosa convertida unos instantes en arpía, la que él había forzado a comportarse así, la que él había querido así, una diosa a la que sobre todo debía poner él en su sitio exacto" (the goddess transformed for a few moments into a harpy, she whom he had forced to behave this way, she whom he had wanted this way, a goddess whom above all he was supposed to put in her proper place) (179).

The female hero's encounter with her matrilineal antecedents must, then, be colored from this recollection forward by a sharp consciousness of female identity and behavior as a function of patriarchal or paternal authority. But as long as the mother figure complies with such manipulation, the unspoken rage in the daughter continues to seethe. Only if the mother could free herself from the dispositions of such patriarchal authority, could the daughter achieve atonement with her parent of the same sex. The women would have to choose their own roles, do their own naming; they would have to shape the myths that make up the texts of their lives. Sadly, this never becomes possible between the narrator and her mother. Eventually reclaimed by the patriarch—her husband, Julio—the narrator never achieves atonement with her Athenean mother. Unwilling or unable to assume the role of Demeter, the mother fails to save her daughter from abduction. In fact, she remains inalterably compliant with the "patriarchal backlash" and cooperates in ending her daughter's brief flight to matrilinear freedom: "mi madre y Julio se reunirán felices y cómplices a mis espaldas" (my mother and Julio will reunite happy and accomplices behind my back) (228).

The narrator-protagonist not only collides with barriers to her recuperation of matrilinear identity in the person of her mother—that is, on the individual or familial level—but in a wider collective or cultural context as well. This female hero becomes immersed in her culture during that phase of her quest most comparable with the male hero's being swallowed into the "belly of the whale." Her ritual participation in parties, outings, and cultural events constitutes a preparatory phase, a growth of consciousness before initiation, but again her experience is notably distinct from that of the archetypal male hero. In the male "monomyth" (Campbell) the hero plunges into a dark world beyond consciousness, beyond memory; absorbed into this unknown, he prepares to be reborn. For the female hero, being swallowed into the "belly of the whale" may be something other than a gratifying—or even frightening—symbolic return to the darkness of prenatal unconsciousness. Here she is confronted instead with dark images of matrilinear myth parodied and perverted, tantalized by premature images of an androgynous union of opposites. In short, she submerges simultaneously into a grotesque caricature of her collective loss and the elusive phantasm of her desired boon.

In a symbolic trunk of disguises, at a bourgeois masquerade party, among all the farces making up the life and times of her social milieu, the narrator clashes with distortions of matrilinear ritual, ridiculous imitations of female apotheosis, and evidence of "patriarchal backlash." "Una Apoteosis de las Tetas" (an apotheosis of the tits), a sexy panoply of female party guests, recalls through parody the possibility of ancestral matrilinear ritual. An attempted seduction of the narrator by the lady of the house painfully reminds the former of the omnipresence of patriarchal backlash, the impossibility of genuine female union for women like the hostess whose "dueño y señor la trajo de muy lejos para exótico ornato de sus salones y para placer de su cama" (owner and lord brought her from very far to be an exotic ornament in his salons and for pleasure in his bed) (103). These bourgeois ladies—objects of pleasure, virtual prisoners of luxury—are allowed to indulge in false and decadent semblances of matriarchal games, responding all the while to the whims of their likewise decadent patriarchal masters, "los falsos emperadores" (the false emperors).

During a boat excursion with the same vacuous women, the participants play similar games of false witches desperate for release from restrictive social guises. The disrobing of the rich woman and a cover girl acquires an air of decadent fantasy; and just as at the masquerade party, the union of the women is compensatory not heroic, decadent not regenerative, desperate not transformative. As a consequence of entrapment in a glittering world of repressed desires, the women merge on a level of surface titilation and tactile sensations. These games, too, reiterate but a distorted semblance of matrilinear erotic freedom, offering but temporary evasions from patriarchal designs.

Finally, an evening at the theater similarly becomes a veritable descent into Hell, as the protagonist and Clara descend into an inferno of cultural mediocrity and boorishness. The crass materialism and false sensibility of the bourgeois Catalan audience constitutes a netherworld, another dark space from which the two women will emerge attempting to forge another reality. Yet though the imagery for the women's descent into Hell is clearly feminine, it is tinged at the outset with tragic forboding: "esto es una bajada a los infiernos—, el descenso por el estrecho túnel sangriento y aterciopelado, mientras Eurídice sigue dócil tras de mí" (this is a descent into Hell—, the descent through the narrow, bloody and velvety tunnel, while Eurydice follows docily behind me) (132). The narrator's identification with Orpheus of course portends that the coming boon cannot last.

The protagonist seems to long instinctively for matrilinear myths and patterns of behavior, yet she never loses sight of the potential threat of backlash, the image of rape and patriarchal control that affects even the destinies of the most privileged women of her social milieu. Thus Pratt's theory of archetypal matrilinear patterns or aspects and patriarchal responses or counteraspects again enables us to identify and read this dialectic as a consistent thread underlying both the individual and collective dimensions of this female hero's quest. Her presentiment of patriarchal conclusions to the matrilinear adventure is summated poignantly in her mythopoeic characterization of Clara as a new Ariadne: "pienso que desde hace mucho la nueva Ariadna estaba buscando ella también sin saberlo mis mismos laberintos, y que es como yo subterránea, oscura, vegetal, propensa a extraños cultos selénicos y prohibidos [matrilinear], predestinada a debatirse torpemente, lánguida y adormecida, entre las pezuñas agrestes del Minotauro y el aliento denso y ardoroso, el sexo bífido, de Dionisos" [potential for future patriarchal backlash] (I think that for a long time the new Ariadne was unknowingly also searching my very labyrinths, and that she, like I, is subterranean, dark, vegetal, inclined to strange and prohibited selenic cults, predestined to struggle awkwardly, languidly, and numbly, between the wild hoofs of the Minotaur and the dense, ardorous breath, the bifid sex, of Dionysus) (88).[22]

Yet, if anyone in *El mismo mar* seems to possess the potential for enduring, or at least continuing matrilinear mythopoesis, that character is Clara. While the narrator obsessively extracts remnants from her past and reads them according to traditional interpretations of classical myth (she is Ariadne abandoned by Jorge-Theseus, a reluctant Penelope reclaimed by a decadent Julio-Odysseus), Clara promises to be capable of reading into traditional myth and tale messages propitious for her growth as a self-defining woman. First of all, Clara defies the ghosts of patriarchy, inventing a new kind of love, a matrilinear Green World of abundance and polymorphous sensuality. She seeks to eliminate hierarchies and chronological phases—the before and after, the foreplay and orgasmic goal of conventional heterosexual eroticism. Her expansiveness breaks through the barriers of old restrictions and old roles encoded in traditional texts. Both women become likewise Beauty and the Beast ("las dos somos la Bella y las dos somos igualmente la Bestia" [the two of us are Beauty and the two of us are equally the Beast]) (183), thus eliminating the neat division of female, passive sexuality (Beauty) in confrontation with active, male sexuality (the Beast). Through Clara, the two women briefly achieve the ultimate boon of synthesis, a union of opposites, and are thus able to glimpse what Pratt has dubbed the androgynous elixir, aptly symbolized in this novel by the fruit juices and milk with honey that become the mainstay of the lovers' diet.

There is even a glimpse of mother-daughter reconciliation in the union of the protagonist and Clara, for through this relationship between older and younger woman, the former celebrates her rebirth into a realm of maternal and female instinct, and its analogously renewed and previously repressed discourse: "estoy aquí, desnuda, fluyendo entera de mí misma en un torrente de palabras, palabras que tal vez intuí yo hace tanto tanto tiempo

. . . palabras que estuve a punto de iniciar algunas veces cuando la pequeña se dormía . . . pero que no le dije . . . este lenguaje no nace en el pensamiento . . . nace hecho ya voz de las entrañas" (I am here, stripped bare, my entire self flowing in a torrent of words, words that perhaps I intuited a long long time ago . . . words that I was about to begin at times when the little one slept . . . but that I never uttered . . . this language that is not born from thinking . . . it is born fully voiced from the core of one's being) (158). Now the narrator experiences an overlapping of the maternal and lesbian bond, and with it a discourse grounded in the depths of her body and soul. She thus discovers—at least momentarily—the dissolution of polarities between flesh and spirit, sensibility and abstraction, instinct and reason, mother and daughter, an experience precisely and rapturously described by Rachel Blau Du Plessis as a "healing unification of body and mind based on . . . a biological power speaking through us."[23] Discourse, at this juncture, thus ceases to be alienating and defined by the phallogocentric Other; the protagonist instead commences to shape her own text through the enunciation of her maternal corporeal desire.

Yet, though Clara weaves a silken pupa around the protagonist promising chrysalis and the emergence of a truly different future, the paths of the two women ultimately bifurcate: the quest of the older woman becomes truncated by her accommodation to the patriarchal backlash (her abrupt return to Julio, a deadening marriage, bourgeois enclosure). Significantly, she comes to view herself as a manipulated mannequin and a butterfly immobilized and crucified by sexual brutality (thus violently ending her brief flight out from the pupa). The future of the younger woman, however, becomes pregnant with possibility, in spite of her maternal lover's abandonment. The younger companion becomes her own hero as the mature female becomes antihero.

Clara promises to emerge from her end of the adventure prepared for change, equipped with the "freedom to live," as Campbell has named this transcendent ending of the monomyth.[24] If she is called—as are all heroes—to reintegrate herself into the larger context of existence, she will return capacitated for heroic action, her integrity, autonomy, and spiritual purity intact: "ella no regresa arrastrándose ni regresa vencida, . . . intacta o casi intacta su capacidad de andar sobre las aguas" (she does not return dragging herself or conquered, . . . intact or almost intact her capacity to walk upon the waters) (226). Heroic, even Christ-like, Clara cuts the figure of one who has prevailed and will continue to

do so. Her desire to go unaccompanied to the airport is a sign of
her independence; her voice as she announces her decision to the
narrator is firm and possessed of assurance. Now off to another
world, a new and Green World on the other side of the sea, she
just may achieve a synthesis of revolutionary change, love, and art
("la guerrilla y el amor y la literatura con otros en sus selvas
colombianas" [guerrilla warfare and love and literature with
others in her Colombian jungle]) (228). She may become "master
of the two worlds" (to borrow once again from Campbell's terminology)—the old and the new.[25]

Most importantly, as the final words of the novel—those whispered by Clara into the narrator's ear—indicate ("Y Wendy creció"
[And Wendy grew up]) (229), Clara possesses the potential to
reread and consequently rewrite childhood texts and traditionally
perceived myth. For her there is still time to reread the auxiliary
roles of these texts in such ways that may allow her to move
beyond their prophecies of closure and doom (as the narrator was
not wont to do). If Orlando is mad, Theseus degraded and cruel,
Peter Pan incapacitated for growth, Clara's final focus on the
coming of age of Wendy is suggestive. Her break from the old
world of male-centered readings suggests that future mythopoesis
for woman may lie in a transformation from object to subject of
the decentered females in our mythical and literary culture. From
this shifted position, Angelica is ultimately free to choose her own
consort; Ariadne's abandonment by Theseus theoretically leaves
her unattached, able to discover new worlds, begin her own adventure.[26] And Wendy's coming of age allows her to cease playing
mother to little boys and pirates reluctant to occupy their
culturally designated niches in adult patriarchal society.

Clara (as her name, of course, implies) is still clear, unspoiled,
untainted. Her initiation confers upon her a potential for collective as well as personal transformation. In contrast, the narrator—
aging, cynical, held back by habit and inertia—withdraws from
and returns to her familiar world having only briefly tasted what
the elixir of female metamorphosis might be. The bourgeois-
patriarchal backlash is finally too compelling, her integrity as a
woman still too underdeveloped for her to drain the cup to its
dregs. The novel's open-ended synthesis of New World and Green
World myths suggests that matrilinear mythopoesis may ultimately
belong to a less fearful, more daring younger generation, the
uncorrupted daughters of a truly "brave new world."

Meanwhile, Clara stands as one more metonymic trope signifying the particular convergence of discourses that *Os habla* and *El*

mismo mar incorporate. Hers is the juncture between the old and the new; she signifies the younger generation, poised to move beyond the death of the "Great [Political] Father" and Spanish woman's first contacts with international feminism. Her unvanquished departure points to a continuation of poststructuralism's interrogation of patriarchal myth and archetype. Even more, as the victorious student of an aging literature professor, Clara may well signify a new generation of women writers who will inquire more irreverently into the intersection of cultural ideology and text, and who are yet to negotiate even more boldly with the ideological oppositions, disruptions, and transitions of the decade still to come. After the distresses of maternal loss and suppression, a "what if" of recuperation will be entertained and expanded.

Part Three
Gathering Chorus

5
Writing "Her/story"
Reinscriptions of Tradition in Texts by Riera, Gomez Ojea, and Ortiz

Woman must write herself: must bring women to their senses
and to their meaning in history.
—Hélène Cixous, "The Laugh of the Medusa"

When in 1977, at the beginning of the post-Franco era, I went to
Spain in search of the "full flower of feminist fiction" (which at
that time I considered the creation of imaginative alternatives in
fiction to undesirable social realities), I met, quite expectedly, with
disappointment. Cultural history necessarily affects the creative
process, and at that historical moment, so soon after the demise of
social and political closure, women writers were simply not ready
to altogether abandon their ruminations on the chilling effects
that previous history had wrought. It was a time for searching, not
necessarily for finding. Consoling me in my feelings of dis-
juncture from this cultural reality, a feminist friend in Madrid
remarked: "Come back in five years, maybe less, and look for the
same thing. I think you'll find what you're looking for now."

I did come back and I did find, in almost exactly five years, a
new generation that for lack of a more precise (or perhaps more
limiting) label can best be referred to as that of the eighties. As
democratic and progressive ideals began to take root, a more
receptive cultural climate allowed room for ideas that only a few
years before had been little known or simply premature. Into this
more expansive cultural climate flowed more feminist literature
and theory from abroad, bringing with its presence a tendency
among young women writers to often identify more with foreign
models than with their own Spanish literary foremothers.[1] Evi-
dently ideological and cultural changes enabled by the shift in
political regime began to emerge definitively by the early eighties.

127

Crosscurrents of Spanish and trans-Pyrenean thought came to stimulate a continuation and further elaboration of the discursive practices that we have charted thus far in women's narrative from the seventies. The earlier desire to break out of restrictions, both cultural and textual, in writers like Martín Gaite, Alós, and Tusquets is expanded and emboldened in the eighties. While one of the most forceful gestures of writers in the seventies was to attempt recuperation of the often elusive bonds between mother and daughter—often through a refocusing of mythical narratives that shaped these bonds—the historical and cultural constraints of their protagonists ultimately denied lasting atonement with mothers and deferred possession of an(other) discourse for their texts. If this other discourse were ever to become more in the eighties than the elusive fruit of the woman writer as Tantalus, then the discourses of history would have to change along with those of myth. This happened, of course, through changes in external circumstances during the early eighties, but it also took place—and was especially reinforced—by analogous changes in the very historical discourses underwriting narrative itself.

Quite propitiously for the development of further narrative strategies by women, at this time the writing of history was being redefined as a process not unlike the creation of literature, one subject to the imposition of narrative forms and cultural coding.[2] Like fictional narrative, historical narrative appeared to be contained within familiar forms and widely recognized structures, codes perpetuated by the notion that history will say some things and leave others unsaid. Apparently, as Yurij Lotman and B. A. Uspensky have observed, history has left things out because it has responded to culture's "demand to forget certain aspects of historical experience."[3] So history, emerging as a genre not unrelated to fiction, presented itself as a text that could be rewritten; its familiar forms could be interrogated, perhaps even dismantled with materials that a culturally endorsed historical amnesia may have previously suppressed.

As history thus reveals itself as writing, this theoretical insight becomes pivotal for situating (and even producing) the kind of narrative that receives our attention in this chapter. The erasure in this body of narrative of clear lines demarcating boundaries between history and fiction render its production in many ways analogous in strategy and function to the production of historical narrative itself. As woman inserts herself into the aforementioned process of historical revision, she, too, is able to bring back to memory those aspects of historical experience—*her* historical experience—that culture has asked her to forget. Becoming her own historian, she performs these acts of retrieval by dismantling the narrative of forgetfulness with that of remembering—and within the gaps of her own ineluctable forgetfulness, she locates a new narrative of transgressive reinvention. This certainly appears to be the theoretical framework within which are produced *Una primavera para Domenico Guarini (A Springtime for Domenico Guarini)* by Carme Riera, *Otras mujeres y Fabia (Other Women and Fabia)* by Carmen Gómez Ojea, and *Urraca* by Lourdes Ortiz. All published in the early eighties, they remember and/or reinvent forgotten or repressed history, and they incorporate this process into narratives that bridge boundaries between history and fiction. These narratives employ, in even more direct ways than during the previous decade, poststructuralist inspired strategies of displacement and reinscription, bold moves such as the articulation of an(other) discourse grounded in the female body. All share a common resolve to rewrite history (or "her/story," as our gender-inflected neologism makes pointedly specific) from woman's own perspective. Most importantly, each of the aforementioned narratives blends a consciousness of the constrictive nature of traditional historical and mythical accounts of women with a rewriting or reinscription of those discourses in which woman has been inevitably, though often erroneously, implicated.

Riera's *Una primavera* is filled with problems plaguing contemporary Western culture: terrorism, homosexuality, drug addiction, the clash between traditional and newly emergent values. Most pivotal in this novel is the anguished searching of a young woman, Clara, who must decide whether or not to abort. Unfortunately, wherever she looks, she is surrounded by the counsel of inadequate discourses: Marxism, with its exploitation of woman as helpmeet, still "reposo" (resting place) as under Falangist ideology; immature or misunderstood feminism, with its tendency to slip into self-righteous rhetoric and slogans; conservative traditionalism with its acceptance of female repression and suffering as the norm. In addition, Clara's work as a journalist investigating the defacement of a Botticelli masterpiece brings her face to face with the lingering authority of Renaissance patriarchal mythology. Before such unsavory or anachronistic discursive alternatives, Clara, as a sensitive and independent contemporary woman, finds herself obliged to seek more historically appropriate responses to the challenges of her existence and her text.

As Clara follows and records the case of Dominico Guarini's act of vandalism against the "Primavera" for her Barcelona news-paper, she often finds its details contained within a labyrinthine variety of textual models: a lawyer calls the case a horror story fit for the nineteenth century "folletín" or the neorrealist cinema; leftists criticize it as a "western"; the Italian public is fascinated by its melodramatic and sensationalistic aspects. Immersed in this web of textual possibilities, Clara decides to experiment with form and literally write Guarini's text for him. She forges a well-wrought counterpoint of first and third person narration, reveal-ing Guarini's obsessive attraction to Laura, his decision to "love" according to Neoplatonic, Petrarchan concepts, the futility of such an anachronistic posture, and Guarini's growing desire to destroy the Laura who resists insertion into the hyperbolic phallocentric codes of his fantasy. This interpolated text in many ways echoes the psychotic intensity of Sábato's *El túnel* or even the obsessive violence of the film, *Taxi Driver*. However, its primary interest is situated not so much in its portrayal of yet another solitary man driven by angst and the mimetic grandeur of his anachronistic obsessions, as in the issues suggested by its reception.

Alberto, Clara's friend and former lover, reads the Guarini text with a critical eye. His precise analysis of the protagonist-narrator's degraded Neoplatonic "love" introduces to Clara the problem of her apparent identification as writer with the phallocentric imag-ination or that which seeks to make of woman its object. While Clara defends Guarini—the male projection of her imagina-tion—as strong, good, and self-sacrificing, Alberto interprets Guarini as shrouded in myth, incapable of loving, dominating, posessive, paternalistic. Ironically influenced by Clara's third-per-son narrator who has described Laura as changing codes to arrive at a more direct form of communication, Alberto defends Laura with an intensity absent in Clara, Laura's implied author. He thus responds negatively, as reader, to the conservative, traditional codes governing Guarini's behavior, even blasting, iconoclastically, Dante and Petrarch as men, too, who "buscaban el poder a través de su amada" (sought power through their beloved).[4] Alberto's reading, engaging as it does in dialogue with both the text and its implied author, achieves a goal envisaged by Bakhtin: "one would enter into dialogue with texts, open oneself to anachronisms and contemporary issues, and make the entire process an occasion for discovering ourselves and our world."[5] Alberto thus provides the historical dialogical dimension between reader and text necessary for the destabilization of Clara's subjugation to traditional and even phallocentric discursive practices.

If Clara has identified too closely with the traditional discourse of her text, Alberto's more objective, more contemporary feminist, reading seeks to reveal to Clara how her preferred literary creation is mystified, caught within patterns of an anachronistic discourse that today seeks to achieve with "palabras más inteligibles" (more intelligible words) (86) what Dante sought in his own vernacular: "at one stroke, Love and women are both brought under control."[6] Clara's version of Guarini in fact pursues such complete control over Laura that when the latter defies his imaginary codes (quite innocently, quite spontaneously), he pierces the center of her being with the symbolic equivalent of his thwarted phallic authority: "el estilete penetró justo en el centro del pecho" (the stiletto penetrated the exact center of her chest) (103). So Alberto teases Clara's idealizing assimilation of the traditional phallic principle in her text, her admiration of and identification with Guarini's obsessive behavior, as he echoes and adapts Flaubert's famous dictum: "Domenico Guarini c'est moi . . ." (Domenico Guarini is me) (108). Through his spirited criticism and mocking responses, this reader within the text suggests the need for a displacement of myths of domination if Clara is to achieve her own textual/sexual identity as a contemporary woman.

Ironically, events in the actual criminal investigation do subsequently ally themselves with Laura's (or woman's) cause. Laura's mortal remains are not found on the site where Guarini affirmed he had buried them. Instead police find a package of papers and other artifacts, including Petrarch's *Cancionero*. Thus what Clara was remiss to destroy in her textualization of Guarini, Guarini, the suspect, buries (and thus destroys) for her. At the foot of a laurel tree (the tree into which the nymph, Daphne, was transformed to elude Apollo), Guarini's own textual obsession is interred, and his imitation of Petrarch assumes its proper proportions as "un simulacro anacrónico y grotesco" (an anachronistic and grotesque semblance) (118) of life. Not insignificantly, Daphne, in her human counterpart, Laura, survives unravished, once again, as her pursuer comes to acknowledge his folly. Laura's implicit association with the myth of Daphne thus provides an ironically provocative sign at a significant juncture in the text: the resurfacing of the mythical archetype of female survival in this contemporary setting contrasts with Clara's assimilation of myths of female subjection and objectification.[7] The "true-story" of the contemporary crime provides a starkly contrastive object lession to Clara's own unexamined traditional literary imagination.

Later in the novel, the interplay between a professorial exegesis of "Primavera" and memories of Clara's past further serves to underscore the vexing and confining aspects for today's woman of both Renaissance mythology and traditional Spanish ideology.[8] Layers of myth and experience superimpose themselves as the professor explains the mythological pursuit by Zephyr of Cloris, which recalls that of Daphne by Apollo, which recalls that of Laura by Guarini, which recalls that of Clara as a child by a pervert in a movie theater and demonic incubi in her dreams. Contemporary experience seems eminently more sordid than its mythological antecedents, yet Zephyr's pursuit is not without a certain aggressive hostility. The once baleful wind god seeks to possess the nymph so that he may be reborn. In return he bestows upon her the gift of converting whatever she touches into flowers. Then disregarding the nymph's likely frustration from her having too much of a good thing, Zephyr transforms his beloved into Flora, causing her mouth to spew forth roses. Flowers, not words, are Flora's gift from her lover. She is conceded the power to transform him through her beautiful silence. Much like Beatrice in Dante's *La Vita Nuova*, "the woman's desire is nowhere in question, she remains mute, acts against her will."[9] The apparently exquisite metamorphosis of the nymph is thus entirely a process of objectification and silencing by an active male subject. Her will, her desire, her voice (as Spivak theorizes within another context) remain absent and unarticulated.

The reader can juxtapose this theoretical perspective of Renaissance myth with Clara's subsequent recollection of the horrors of contemporary experience, thus linking the two in a striking analogy. A youthful confession in which Clara was rendered mute (the confession is recounted through a priestly monologue), places the discourse of Renaissance myth and that of postwar religious practice under implied indictment for their analogous positioning of the female in the role of silent object. Even at home the words of others threatened the girl with ferocity, that if she were to masturbate she would be condemned to Hell where her mouth would spew forth toads and serpents and the only sound she would emit would be the bestialized language of brays. Autoeroticism (or the language of the girl's own body) would then be punishable by eternal verbal noncommunication, a terrifying and distorted extension of the fate of girls on earth. Schooled in silence ("nosotras hemos venido al mundo para sufrir y aguantar" [we have come into the world to suffer and endure] 139), words for females were appropriate only for prayer or to pardon masculine libertines like Clara's father. This juxtaposition of mythical and contemporary impositions of female silence thus allows a shocking insight into Clara's earlier choice of a male voice for her text. It appears she has never had another.

The professor's traditional exegesis of Venus is hardly more gratifying for the woman in quest of her own voice. Though in "Primavera" Venus may represent Venus Generatrix, goddess of fecundity—some viewers have detected a subtle abdominal protuberance in the painting's central figure—the professorial explicator points out the higher status of Venus Humanitas and Venus Caelestis respectively.[10] Each manifestation of Venus ascends in superiority over the other as she transcends her corporeality, becomes increasingly spiritualized. The celestial Venus, born from the mutilated genitals of her father, Uranus, thus incorporates only the phallic principle; she has no mother. Or as the professor etymologically explains: "rechaza la materia, precisamente por el hecho de no tener madre. Pensad que las dos palabras 'mater' y 'materia' tienen la misma raíz" (she rejects matter, precisely because of the fact she had no mother. Remember that the two words 'mater' and 'matter' have the same root) (144–45). This symbolic affirmation of nonmaternal nonmateriality may provide an apt sign for a young man's spiritual development, his flight from the demands of the mother and what he may perceive as the threatening aspects of the female flesh. Indeed, for the abstract male or patriarchal spirit, Venus Caelestis may be preferable to Venus Generatrix; it effectively cancels out the maternal economy. But for a female, especially a pregnant one, such a rarefied, ethereal figure may provide little more than a cold and alienating indifference to her condition. Clara's memory proves that this is so, for cut off from communication with her mother, she longed as a child for the maternal intimacy of a teacher. The latter rejected the girl's attempts at confidence, advising her to confide her plight to the Virgin (Christianity's version of the celestial Venus). The girl did direct her pleas heavenward. She spoke in prayer, but her tearful monologue was met with silence.

How to make the mother speak seems to be, then, a central historical challenge confronting Clara, or any woman writer for that matter. (We certainly encountered the most direct disclosure of this desire in Alós and Tusquets, its more oblique articulation in Laforet, Matute, and Martín Gaite.) To co-opt the phallic Mother, to make her a "dissident," a renegade of the phallic order, would allow Clara/woman-writer to shape a discourse more resistant to the mystification of paternal discourse and phallicization.[11] Clara does accomplish this *coup de grâce* through an imaginative recollection (a remembering which culture has counseled be forgotten) in which her masochistic mother momentarily claims a single defiant utterance.

Clara's mother, long-suffering the humiliation of an unfaithful husband, was said to have challenged his faithlessness one evening. She was reported to have descended quite regally to where her guests were awaiting her. Accepting their flattery with dignity, she remained composed in the presence of her husband's latest lover, but before she excused herself to give orders to the servants, she made the following announcements and accompanying performance:

> "—Atención, amigos míos, escuchadme un minuto. Todos sabéis con quien me engaña Perico, ahora os enseñaré con quien le engaño yo.
> Con un gesto rapidísimo te arremangaste la falda, deslizaste hacia abajo las bragas de encaje y empezaste a acariciarte el sexo."

> (Attention, my friends, listen to me for a moment. You all know with whom Perico is deceiving me, now I'll show you with whom I'm deceiving him.
> With a rapid gesture you rolled up your skirt, slipped down your lacy panties and began to caress your sex (144).

Such a grandiose and subversive gesture seems incredible to Clara and yet as she recounts it, she affirms precisely its daring brilliance . . . and, expectedly, its consequences: imprisonment of the mother ("te dejaron encerrada" [they locked you up] 144) by the fathers (husband and brother-in-law). The mother is relegated to the object status of an hysteric and yet in spite of her locked-up body, she has spoken and the silence that follows reverberates with echoes of her words. The affirmation of her briefly defiant posture subverts, at least momentarily, the authority of the libertine father, for as the mother ascends the "pequeño estrado" (small stage) (143) during her brief but shocking performance, the figure of the father is at that moment simultaneously dethroned. The mother, fleetingly transformed into a provocative rebel against the phallic order, literally unveils a sign ("el sexo" or autoeroticism) indicating woman's rewriting of herself through her body.

This recollection is fittingly framed by references to Venus Generatrix, whose presence also elicits Clara's defense of her pregnancy. Both women, mother and daughter, are thus implicitly linked by the goddess of fecundity, and as the professor might say, remember that "generatrix" and "genitals" share the same root. For both women, the genitals serve as metaphorical openings to their own discourse, or as Jane Gallop succinctly discloses: "feminine discourse reveals the sex organ."[12] Furthermore, as Clara affirms the maternal—even matrilineal—identity of her future child ("quiero que lleve mis apellidos, no los de él" [I want it to carry my surnames, not his] 142), she begins to name her own text.

Before Clara can arrive at textual/sexual self-definition, she must reject the traditional role of playing mother to her lover, Enrique, and writing his texts for him ("escribía . . . unas crónicas . . . que todo el mundo atribuía a Enrique" [I wrote . . . some chronicles . . . that everyone attributed to Enrique] 171). She must come to terms with her own Three Graces, metonymic representations of other women and their diverse values: the missionary nun, the feminist, and the rebellious young freeloader. And she must accept the loss of her Mercury (Jaime), the only male, besides Alberto, who was capable of inhabiting a nonpatriarchal, paradisiacal space where an untainted language could invent the world anew. As Clara reencounters or remembers these sources of pleasure, pain, and language in her past, much like contemporaneous French feminists, she becomes more acutely aware of "una vida nueva [que] se está abriendo camino en mi vientre" (a new life [that] is opening its way in my womb) (178).[13] Clara learns to reread and implicitly rewrite the mythological codes of "Primavera" for her own benefit, discovering the hermeneutics of chrysalis, the signs of transformation. As she accepts her impending maternity she knows she will become "transformada" (transformed) (196), for now she accepts being alone, implicitly freer of the constraints of repressive myths, prepared to forge her own meanings in the manner of Kristeva's marginal "enceinte": "an 'enceinte' woman loses communital meaning, which suddenly appears to her as worthless."[14] Thus as Clara's homebound train emerges from the darkness of a tunnel, Clara's simultaneous acceptance of pregnancy as a source of transformation, and her solitude as a source of independent meaning beyond traditional cultural coding, confer upon her the potential to fulfill one of Riera's own fondest proposals for women: to cease being spoken and begin to speak.[15]

Also a solitary woman in an urban context, Fabia of Gómez Ojea's *Otras mujeres y Fabia* looks toward that environment as the source of her myths and history. While perceptive of the ugliness and disquieting aspects of her neighborhood, she remains expectant, ready to discover the unforeseen: "sin embargo, a pesar de los ruidos, de las escenas costumbristas y de los tufos grasientos a bárbaros guisos, quizás aquella calle guardara algún encanto que ella no había sabido todavía descubrir" (nevertheless, in spite of the noises, the local color, and the greasy odors of barbarous concoctions, perhaps that street held some charm that she had not yet been able to discover).[16] As Milagros Sánchez Arnosi has pointed out, in Fabia's "barrio," noises and smells even perform an evocative function.[17] And the "sin embargo" (nevertheless) along with repetitive uses of "pero" (but) are locutions that recurrently mark the tone of the text as compensatory: there is always another, and often more hopeful, side of female experience that can be imagined and written.

As a seeker of the hidden bounties of her environment, Fabia belongs to that class of single women in literature through whom authors, according to Annis Pratt, "seem to be clearing out a new space . . . a place that, essentially apatriarchal, contains once-forgotten possibilities of personal development."[18] Of even wider consequence, as a self-appointed historian, Fabia also participates in the rewriting of women's history that might "make the invisible visible, make the silent speak":[19] "a través de esas voces acalladas de mujer—madres, abuelas—como la voz de una juglaresa anónima, no bajó a la tumba la historia no escrita. . . . Gracias a esas madres y abuelas, a través del cordón umbilical de sus palabras, los niños pueden hacer suyo el pasado" (through those silenced voices of women—mothers, grandmothers—like the voice of an anonymous minstrel, unwritten history did not descend to the tomb. . . Thanks to those mothers and grandmothers, through the umbilical cord of their words, the children can appropriate their past) (80). As Fabia implicitly becomes one of those children who recuperates an otherwise buried past, she records for posterity these unspoken, unwritten voices of the mothers, filling in the blanks of forgetfulness left by official historical discourse.

Otras mujeres also bears out Virginia Woolf's maxim that "a woman writing thinks back through her mothers," and again reconfirms my own observations in previous chapters of this book that the female hero's quest for matrilinear identity constitutes a recurrent, archetypal theme in contemporary Spanish narrative by women.[20] One of the first moves in this direction in *Otras mujeres* is Fabia's discovery of a matrilineal chain reaching back historically to the Mother of mothers, passing backward in time through the Carlist Wars, the Enlightenment, the Conquest, the Inquisition, and the Jewish ghetto. The scope of such an undertaking is imposing: "si todas las mujeres de la línea materna se cogieran de la mano hasta llegar a esa Gran Madre común, ella sería la última de la fila y ni poniéndose de puntillas alcanzaría a verla bien" (if all the women of the maternal line were to join hands until they arrived at that Great Mother of them all, she [Fabia] would be the last of the line and not even on tiptoe would she manage to see her [the Great Mother] well) (17). The most recent in the line, Fabia is at once overwhelmed and awed by the grand historical scale of the matrilineal connection.

Now conjured forth, these foremothers animate Fabia's room with their presence, their advice, even their reproaches for Fabia's childless state. As a result, Fabia is brought face to face with the issue of childbearing and her own position regarding this cultural imperative. When she contemplates the advantages and disadvantages of having children, she irreverently undermines a patriarchal myth about procreation (Lao-Tze's birth from a virgin at the age of seventy-two) with her own demythifying candor: "que horror tener en la barriga, años y años, un viejo filósofo malhumorado" (how horrible to have in one's belly, for years and years, a bad-tempered, old philosopher) (20). Rejecting guilt for her nongenerative body, she humorously turns to other voices, those of her Enlightenment foremothers who would likely have said: "es el colmo de los colmos que los ciclos periódicos de tu ovario te produzcan este tipo de desarreglos mentales (it's absolutely absurd that the periodical cycles of your ovary should produce this type of mental disorder) (21). The broad historical scope of this matrilineal vision is capacious enough to contain heterogeneous female voices on the subject of motherhood, thus rendering differences among women not only permissible but a source of irreverent joy.

Still, history is even more imaginatively conjoined with myth to rewrite matrilinear endings for stories told quite differently (moralistically, punitively) by patriarchal myth and history. One hypothetical imagining casts Cleopatra in another, more matrilinear, light: "lo grandioso hubiera sido que, por ejemplo, a Cleopatra la hubiese mordido la mismísima Isis, disfrazada de aspid, para llevársela a las moradas de la luz" (the most magnificent thing would have been, for example, that Isis herself, disguised as an asp, would have bitten Cleopatra, in order to carry her off to the dwellings of light) (29). In another reconsideration of the history of Western culture, the church father, Saint Paul, is conjectured to have required women to cover their heads in church because he sought to veil the terrible wisdom of the prepatriarchal goddess:

"había visto los ojos claros de la diosa de la Acrópolis y se había estremecido, sin comprender la vieja sabiduría de su mirada" (he had seen the clear eyes of the goddess of the Acropolis and he had trembled, not comprehending the ancient wisdom of her gaze) (44). Thus as myth and history are subtly synthesized, traditional interpretations undergo revision and the unspoken desires of women and fears of men are enunciated with a bold new clarity.

Modern and contemporary figures also shift their interpretive implications by being reinserted into revised versions of history. Fabia's grandmother leaps out from her portrait to speak with a tongue of fire and the spirit of a warrior (49).[21] By breaking out from the frame into which time and the course of her personal history have inserted her, this matrilineal image metaphorically escapes being "framed" by the confining restrictions of her culture. Her unbounded pugnacious utterances signify emergence from the frame of historically bounded patriarchal discourse. Another character, Señora Efe, would be a hero if she could become her own revised version of Queen Urraca, daring to speak against her father, renting patriarchal political discourse with her protest: "a mí porque soy mugier, dejaisme desheredada" (me, because I am a woman, you leave disinherited) (78). But Señora Efe cannot find the denouement to her own plot ("faltaba el desenlace" [the ending was missing]) (79); she cannot name her emptiness, in spite of her degree in literature. Señora Efe can only blame men for her malaise and engage in a certain irascible and disruptive iconoclasm. It is Fabia who must sift through the implications of these and other attempts to reinscribe woman's personal cum collective histories. As a result, her grandmother implicitly breaks from the past into the future; Señora Efe warns of spineless desire. Fabia's ultimate model would seem to lie, then, in the unself-conscious vocalizations of "las pechugonas [que] tienen que comunicarse como sea" (the big-bosomed women [who] have to communicate no matter what) (75).

The word "pechugona" as sign expands and reverberates with meanings and connotations: big-bosomed, shameless, brazen, insolent, bold, single-minded women. If Señora Efe is brazen, she is not sufficiently single-minded and bold. It remains up to Fabia to be the woman who makes the bold and single-minded step toward linking up with the myths and texts of her historical foremothers and her contemporaries. The word that signals her technique is metonymy (99). Each woman fans out, as it were, into a multitude. Through metonymy Fabia discovers how she can draw her inspiration from the world and words of women, the voices of present and past.

So Fabia becomes, as Sánchez Arnosi has indicated, "una especie de juglar, o mejor dicho de cronista objetivo de una historia anudada a su propia historieta individual" (a kind of minstrel, or better said objective chronicler of a larger history tied in with her own personal tale).[22] Fabia searches not only through the intertext of Spanish foremothers but in the example of their lives for codes that may prove useful for her, her text, and others of her generation. The secret of Pardo Bazán, for example, was her practicality, a quality lacking in the scandalous Señora Efe, whose complicity with what she considered her unfortunate fate was at least partly to blame for her limitations, real or imagined. Instead of only disparaging the codes of courtly love and quoting from the classics, Señora Efe might have done well to look also toward the tradition of popular literature for women (like "la novela rosa") for a fuller understanding of herself and other women.

As we have seen Martín Gaite affirm in *El cuarto*, Gómez Ojea seems to imply that popular fiction by and for women may not only be an unjustly denigrated window to the female imagination; it may also provide a source of textual coding rich in pleasure and surprising sources of wisdom. Fabia is able to pierce beyond the popularized image of *Gone with the Wind*'s Scarlett O'Hara and regard her a strong woman, a survivor;[23] and she can glean wisdom despite this American best-seller's tearful sentimentality: that though love may be fleeting and illusive, there is hope in change. Probably of key significance for Fabia, and the maturing writer she represents, however, is *Gone with the Wind*'s evocative mythic ending: its "subdued autumnal promise" of transformation and rebirth.[24]

In the late summer of her life, Fabia seeks to discover forms of discourse more appropriate for her development as a mature woman and implied writer. Like Clara of *Una primavera*, she finds that Botticelli's image of woman in "Primavera" is less valid for her now than it might have been in the past. Though once likened by a lover to Simonetta, Fabia can but vaguely recall traces of that youthful love and the idealized image she represented to that shadowy lover in the springtime of her life. This particular rendering of Neoplatonic Renaissance mythology can no longer encode the feelings and desires of her maturing generation, women and men who, like Tinkerbell, have lost their magical wings and from now on "sólo se arrugarían" (would only grow wrinkled)

(100). That Botticelli's pictorial language has fascinated and left its imprint on both Riera's Clara and Gómez Ojea's Fabia is certainly noteworthy. Yet, even more remarkably, there emerges in both texts an uneasiness with this mythological inheritance; admiration turns to struggle as these contemporary writers and their protagonists similarly move beyond traditional and largely fixed metaphorical significations toward a more disruptive, expansive, and metonymic discourse of their own.

Finally beyond economic bondage (she has won the lottery), a more mature Fabia can afford to enjoy the luxury of reading, studying, and observing her neighborhood with its often hidden and unexpected qualities. And as she confronts the counterpoint of female figures that pass through her imagination and speak to her in a variety of voices, Fabia's capacity for a broader spectrum of human relationships seems to grow. The wisdom of her grandmother's maternal discourse ("lo que me pasma de tus tiempos es ese remachar, dale y dale, sobre asuntos del sexo") (what astonishes me about your time is that stress, over and over again, on sexual matters) (53)—strikingly similar to American writer May Sarton's critique of the same subject ("what is becoming tiresome now in the American ethos is the emphasis on sex")[25]—foretells Fabia's own movement, as a mature, single woman, toward widening fields of human interaction and discourse. As her street appears longer and longer ("larga, larga") (109), a seemingly endless road toward possibility, her relationships and her text analogously promise to extend beyond the solely erotic ("no tenía amante") (she had no lover) (100). As Fabia uncovers cultural meanings that lie submerged in her "barrio," and as she begins to recuperate and reinscribe her collective history and mythology, she engages in subtle moves to write herself—and other women of her generation—anew.

Very little is known about the personal life of the twelfth-century monarch, Queen Urraca. As Bernard F. Reilly has affirmed after minute and painstaking archival research, "the study of the reign of Urraca, for all her prominence, remains a study of her public acts and the public institutions of the realm itself. There is as yet no feasible method of penetrating her thoughts or her councils."[26] Unlike Reilly's meticulously documented approach, the accounts of earlier historians tend to demonstrate recognizable narrative structures rather than a strict fidelity to observable fact. For example, nineteenth-century Juan de Dios de la Rada y Delgado portrays the woman as victim, defending the queen as weak, the object of manipulation, detractors, and false stories imputing her morality.[27] E. L. Miron, writing during the early years of this century, offers another narrative apologia for a victimized woman: although acknowledging the queen's strength as head of her troops, he also portrays her as the victim of a brutish husband, and his Victorian discourse insists that Urraca and Count Pedro Gonzalez de Lara were lawfully wed.[28] Though these historians were no doubt sincere, the historicity of their own discourses is clear: the paucity of concrete evidence concerning the personal details of Queen Urraca's life has resulted more often than not in conjectural conclusions based upon prevailing narrative structures or modes of discourse employed by each historian in question.

Before such speculative views of this fascinating Castilian monarch, how does one create a narrative capable of compensating for partiality and omission? One makes the most of the least, as *Urraca's* author, Lourdes Ortiz, explains: "precisamente la escasez de referencias históricas verdaderamente documentadas era alicente para la invención" (precisely the scarcity of truly documented historical references was an incentive for invention).[29] By taking advantage of the gaps in recorded history, Ortiz could invent a narrative text free to recreate those psychological processes that are often veiled by the thin or insufficient structures of traditional historical discourse. And since, as Jane Tibbets Schulenburg has pointed out, official chronicles of the twelfth century were extremely biased and narrow, and woman's spheres of influence began to shrink, what better vehicle could today's woman writer choose for rewriting such exclusion and loss than a new chronicle, one written by woman herself.[30]

Queen Urraca narrates this new chronicle, one that clearly seeks to displace previously deficient historical narratives with her own voice: "ellos escribirán la historia a su modo; Urraca tiene ahora la palabra" (they may write history in their way; Urraca now has the floor).[31] Authored and narrated with the corrective passion of a contemporary female perspective, *Urraca* is thus a compensatory text including elements often omitted from more traditional chronicles. This novel does not shrink from employing a sordid naturalism to demythologize official accounts of male heroism or patriarchal myths about womanhood; neither does it demur before the affirmation of female eroticism and intimate considerations of the female body. The tone of Urraca's new chronicle is thus personal, sensual, yet subtly chronological, without losing its air of spontaneity, its approximation to the flow of consciousness and natural, spoken discourse. Above all, Urraca's new chronicle is a daring attempt to reinvent and reconstruct a particular woman's history, while at the same time its implications reach beyond the confines of the individual.

In captivity as a result of the order of her son, Urraca's sole interlocutor is a monk, Roberto. The context of the queen's narration is already a sign for her existence in a broader sense: she must struggle to make her own word credible, a mark of authority in an environment largely shaped by a masculine drive for power and cultural-spiritual hegemony. Urraca's characteristically medieval world of Reconquest Spain is a vast field of shifting alliances, a world in which lovers kill each other with more than tender kindness. The characters of this world, as seen through the recollections of the queen, are driven by intense passions: erotic, bellicose, religious. These three passions often overlap as the bed is recalled a battleground of aphrodisiac sin, a den of conspiracy; the battleground is remembered as the dust and sweat perfumed boudoir of the queen's love of empire; the church is evoked as the bishop's bedroom and the planning chamber for intrigue and the satisfaction of his lust for power. In this context, Urraca reveals herself as no ordinary woman. Albeit a victim of her times, she also emerges a hero, fighting indefatigably for her idea of empire, premature by some four-and-a-half centuries.

Urraca challenges official accounts of history by forcing us to view persons and events in a manner to which we have not been accustomed by standard or traditional historiography. For example, she flies in the face of a sacred cow like El Cid, calling him "un mercenario sin escrúpulos" (an unscrupulous mercenary) (135). Though Urraca's view of Rodrigo Diaz is no doubt conditioned, in part, by her family ties—that is, even if her perspective reflects her bias as her father's daughter—she ends up disclosing an important and recurrent historical truth: "un guerrero metido a justiciero tiene siempre algo de buitre" (a warrior who takes up righteousness is always something of a vulture) (136). As the national hero is displaced, the baser actions of heroism are unveiled.

In another retelling of historical events, as Urraca recounts the uprising of the burghers of Sahagún, her fantasy carries her from official versions of the royal-clerical alliance against the citizens to a vision of rebellion which we might name, borrowing from Roland Barthes, "doubly perverse."[32] Couching her narrative in the subjunctive, hypothetical mode, Urraca imagines herself as a townswoman dancing frenetically "la danza loca de la libertad" (the mad dance of freedom) (186). Recreating herself as rebel, she creates a subversive text which, in a Barthean manner, "simultaneously and contradictorily participates in the profound hedonism of all culture . . . and in the destruction of that culture."[33] As a monarch reinscribed by historical fantasy, in her role as dancing townswoman, she simultaneously occupies the position of participant in the hedonism of culture and subverter or destroyer of that same culture. Envisioning herself thus as celebrant in a mad rite to undo her own officialdom, Urraca's text appropriates and voices a spectrum of contradictory desires that might otherwise remain silenced by authorized univocal historical discourse.

If we juxtapose Urraca's new text to a traditional historical account of the queen's alliance with the abbot (such as the one we find in Reilly), we are amply persuaded that the chronicle rewritten by Urraca dares to provoke, undermine, even overturn that alliance.[34] In her own text, the queen imagines herself participating in "la danza obscena de las mozas desnudas en la plaza . . . los sueños de ser libres" (the obscene dance of naked maidens in the square . . . dreams of freedom) (186). She transposes herself into an agent of transformation, endowing herself with dreams that transcend her own personal, and even national, history. In this way she transforms into a sign for the new woman writer, who, writing through her body, articulates an(other) discourse for women. Urraca's new chronicle thus marks difference in a way noted by Mary Jacobus; that is, it challenges official historiography—and even more broadly, official cultural discourse—through multiplicity, joyousness, and an even contradictory heterogeneity.[35] While Urraca's interlocutor prefers accounts that speak only of heroism and honor, she often insists on her own—more naturalistic—versions of events: "mi crónica es más sórdida" (my chronicle is more sordid) (107). Part of her text's heterogeneity is even the queen's willingness to expose her own cruelty and treachery, the dark side of her own character. Not only the Cid, then, but also his female antagonist elude the chronicles of sanctioned historical discourse. With joyful perversity Urraca now exposes the corporeal, contemptible, and similarly less-than-heroic aspects of royal and other personages of renown.

Urraca's rewritten chronicle also transforms negative medieval beliefs about woman into images and accounts affirming a more positive view of female power. Of a statue portraying an adulteress with a close resemblance to the queen, Urraca fashions a compensatory deity affirming love and life. Throwing down her gauntlet before the bishop, she affirms her own triumph in a blasphemous celebration of vitality: "la mujer adúltera reina en tu catedral; tú me has igualado al Altísimo, sin proponértelo" (the adulterous woman reigns in your cathedral; you have made me an equal of the Almighty without intending to do so) (130–31). Subsequently challenging Roberto's impossible desire for the solely symbolic woman—his Marianism—Urraca ironically proves his likewise irresistible need for "la madre, el cuerpo femenino. Yo, Urraca" (the mother, the female body. Me, Urraca) (153). Through her seductive discourse, Urraca bares the other side, the repressed body of womanhood in medieval religious iconology and clerical doctrine. In these ways Urraca diplaces the tendency of medieval phallogocentric ideology (and, implicitly, its more contemporary manifestations) to polarize woman into separate categories of good and evil, spiritual and corporeal.[36] The queen further questions prevailing phallocentric notions of the tainted nature of female corporeality by juxtaposing them to evidence of Alfonso's bloody cruelty to his subjects. Here the resultant irony is that the king's political cruelty was, of course, far filthier than any of the natural processes of the queen's female body.

Urraca's sexual desires are potently exposed in her chronicle: first teasingly and temptingly ("no voy a hablarte de ellos todavía . . . no son temas para una crónica" [I won't talk to you about them yet . . . they're not themes for a chronicle]) (47); then in a more direct and uncensored manner ("Pedro de Lara . . . necesito esa borrachera del juego y del abrazo, cuando todo era posible. Mi garañón, es tu cuerpo lo que quisiera ahora, tu cuerpo y tus palabras obscenas" [Pedro de Lara . . . I need that drunken play-fulness and embrace, when everything was possible. My stud, it's your body that I desire now, your body and your obscene words]) (176–77). This recollection of the play of erotic discourse privileges an enjoyment "which exceeds exchange"[37] (another coun-terdiscourse) in a field dominated almost exclusively by sex as strategic political weapon.

Yet alongside the private and the sexual, Urraca continuously juxtaposes the more Amazonian matters of political deeds, in-trigue, and the machinations of war: "estas manos han sostenido la espada y han lanzado el dardo con precisión" (these hands have borne the sword and have hurled the dart with precision) (146). Urraca's chronicle thus speaks against any unidimensional, par-tial, or gender stereotypical accounts of either her desires or her deeds. She discards, equally, popular, mournful balladic versions of her marriage to Alfonso ("la desdicha de su reina, a quien llaman la malquerida" [the wretchedness of his queen, whom they call the despised one]) (80), or fairy-tale versions ("Erase una reina que quiso casar con el monarca de un país vecino" [There once was a queen who wished to marry the king of a neighboring country]) (69), or traditional historical accounts ("un rey déspota, un rey maricón que maltrató a su mujer" [a despotic king, a pansy king who mistreated his wife]) (80). Writing out from such an intertext, Urraca opts instead for her own self-created version of her past marriage and stormy relations with Alfonso. By sifting through the varieties of textualization that have heretofore characterized and defined her and her intimates, Urraca again suggests the theoretical and practical need for compensatory voices and texts by women. To texts articulated by others, she proposes to attach her newly authorized supplement.

Even though textual tradition would advise Urraca to be sensible and recognize that "una crónica debe ser elegía, canto, glosa triunfal" (a chronicle should be elegy, song, triumphant gloss) (99), she insists on expressing other tones and contributing further to an alternative theory of the historical chronicle and its uses for women. Of her husband Alfonso's character, she chooses to highlight his erotic eccentricities, especially his irresistible taste for menstrual blood: "Alfonso acudía especialmente a mí en esos días para bañarse en la impureza, para extraer vigor de lo que más le repelía: la mancha" (Alfonso approached me especially on those days to bathe in impurity, to extract vigor from that which repelled him most: the stain) (112).[38] Given medieval superstitions about menstruating women, Urraca had to pay for her husband's desire with imprisonment. But to "la crónica, la que escriban los demás" (the chronicle, that which others may write) (110), Urraca adds, in her account of her confinement, her own version of the magnitude of her powers and her status as a source of fearful magical potency. Perhaps her point of view rests upon her intuitive knowledge (as Jane Gallop has remarked) that "menstrual blood . . . marks woman as woman with no need of man's tools."[39] So, though imprisoned as the seemingly hapless victim of her husband's fear and desire, the queen's subsequent counterchronicling of his desperate moves to protect male power serves to expose them and displace them in a subtle manuever against phallocentric sexual/textual authority.

The queen's resistant or independent voice can be traced to two mentors whose initiation of the adolescent princess conferred upon her the signs and letters of an alternate maternal, androgynous, and self-affirming text. Poncia, a wise old woman and mother figure, initiates the pubescent Urraca as "única sucesora en la tierra de la gran reina madre" (sole successor on earth of the great queen mother) (60). Cidellus, the Jewish physician of Urraca's father, introduces the young future monarch to the concept of androgyny, a force that will empower the queen to become soldier, lover, mover of men, moved by men: "Yo seré ese Andrógino, ya que no de cuerpo, sí en espíritu y voluntad" (I shall be that androgyne, if not in body, then in spirit and will) (171). Not unlike the philosopher's stone of the alchemist, the "elixir" of androgyny empowers the young monarch with the strengths of both genders, "la unión de los contrarios, mujer y hombre" (the union of opposites, man and woman) (171).

Most importantly, the magical lessons of the two wise mentors have direct bearing upon the generation of the queen's alternative text. From Poncia, Urraca acquires maternal or matrilinear discourse: a language derived from the sea and the moon, a knowledge of herbal healing. Cidellus teaches the young princess alchemy, through which she discovers a link between the body and the text and the importance of recombining letters. Via his presentation of alchemy, Cidellus functions as a sort of medieval writing coach, his instructions to his young student incorporating a theory of writing as rewriting or reinscription: "delante del papel vacío juega con las letras, mézclalas, permútalas, trastócalas, hasta que tu corazón se exalte y, cuando te des cuenta de que de esa combinación surgen cosas nunca antes dichas ni sabidas, cosas que jamás hubieras podido conocer gracias a la tradición, concentra tu mente y permite que fluya la imaginación" (before the blank page play with the letters, mix them up, interchange them, reverse them, until your heart leaps up and, when you realize that from that combination things never before said nor known emerge, things that you never would have been able to know thanks to tradition, concentrate your mind and let your imagination flow) (162–63). So, though in confinement as a consequence of her son's edict against her, Urraca compensates for her physical imprisonment with flights of memory and imagination. Recalling her usually silent mother Constanza's songs and tenderness, Poncia's matriarchal ritual, and Cidellus's alchemical (textual) initiation, Urraca forges a text that at once strains for androgyny and the energizing mythos of her matrilinear connections.

Through the linking of her text with the desires of her female body, Urraca, as narrator, succeeds in creating the kind of text envisioned by recent French feminist theory, or as Hélène Cixous has proclaimed: "women must write through their bodies, they must invent the impregnable language that will wreck partitions, classes, and rhetorics, regulations and codes."[40] The very words Urraca employs to describe her sexual games with don Pedro are analogous to the theory and practice of this kind of text: "el deseo . . . requiere la construcción, el invento . . . sólo se desea aquello que sorprende, lo que se arranca al tiempo, lo que provoca" (desire . . . requires construction, invention . . . one only desires that which surprises, that which is wrenched out of time, that which provokes) (122–23). Through these moves, this inventive game of words and bodies, "la historia se recompone" (history is recreated) (176). Thus by combining documented history with novelistic fabulation, Ortiz, through her royal narrator, succeeds in fashioning a text that blends together what Hayden White would call a "discourse of the real" (history) with a "discourse of desire" (fiction).[41] This alchemical melding of genres—which enhances both the authority and desirability of woman's discourse—emerges as final testimony that the queen and her writer descendant have successfully incorporated into their text both the elusive union of opposites and the boldness of their self-articulated female desire.

Any consideration of narrative texts from the early eighties would hardly be complete without a few more remarks on the relationship between textual and cultural history. Because literature rarely exists in a vacuum, the textual transformations we have been charting in this chapter also point to the revised roadmap of cultural terrain we noted earlier. The quest for a self-defined sexual/textual voice may be seen to also correspond to woman's struggle during the early eighties for more resonance in the political arena. The two go hand in hand, for as Cixous maintains: "a woman without a body, dumb, blind, can't possibly be a good fighter."[42] Urraca applauds her own deeds as a warrior; the words of Fabia's grandmother are impelled by her warrior spirit; Señora Efe would go to the ends of the earth with an Urraca "sin pelos en la lengua para decir lo que pensaba del injusto trato" (outspoken enough to say what she thought about unjust treatment) (78); Clara decides, on her own, to forego abortion for the transformative powers of childbirth. Perhaps these characters—straight talkers, fighters, women in full possession of their bodies—are fictional analogues of extratextual women, enmeshed in the discursive negotiations of dynamic cultural (ex)change. Perhaps these fictional protagonists encode the projects of their counterparts in contemporaneous Spanish society, engaged in an ongoing struggle for complete and legal control over their bodies, for a voice in a government, which, though democratic, was still largely dominated by men. If one speaks only of the politics of high culture, then these narrative voices can be heard to cry out, too, for recognition in a literary marketplace, which, though officially uncensored and open by the early eighties, still bestowed more generously of its support and promotion upon "los consagrados" (the "hallowed" ones). Though the threads binding text to the whole of culture are often implied and subtle, the quest for voice, autonomy, and self-definition is seldom confined solely to the inscription of black marks upon a white page. The "other voices" in narrative by women at the beginning of the eighties may have sought to recuperate and articulate nothing less than those aspects of "her/story," which, as Evelyne García has noted, "el poder en todo tiempo y lugar ha usurpado o coartado" (those in power at all times and in all places have usurped or restricted).[43]

6

Parody and Defiance
Subversive Challenges in the Texts of Díaz-Mas and Gómez Ojea

> The laughter that takes hold of me when I observe him in those very areas where he wishes to be distinguished . . . that is my best weapon.
> —Annie Leclerc, "Parole de femme" (Woman's Word)

> The transformation of literature and criticism as cultural institutions demands a language of defiance rather than the silent or unquestioning mimetic complicity expected of us in order to sustain phallocentrism.
> —Elizabeth A. Meese, *Crossing the Double-Cross*

By the mid-eighties self-reflexive or self-conscious writing by women takes yet another turn: now the voice is that of reveler, joker, irreverent deconstructor of revered traditions and respected texts. The young woman writer continues to undermine the paternal symbolic contract as a site of sacrifice, but now her intolerance wields a new weapon—laughter. Joyful affirmation reconfirms and expands earlier quests for a female or maternal source of woman's own voice. Paternal plots are turned on their heads, expected texts are inverted, subverted, and ultimately displaced with an(other) discourse, a multiplicity of women's voices that refuses to be easily pinned down. Of special interest for their engagement in these ludic tendencies are two narratives of the mid-eighties: *El rapto del Santo Grial* by Paloma Díaz-Mas and *Los perros de Hécate* by Carmen Gómez Ojea. The two are in the foregoing tonal and functional ways plainly and closely interrelated.

Díaz-Mas, as a medieval scholar, chooses for her site of contest the revered legend of the Holy Grail. Within the context of her medieval sources, the author's strategy seems to emanate from the very parodic tradition of the Middle Ages—those dialogized jousts between the sacred and profane—that Bakhtin has identified and defined.[1] In *El rapto,* though, the dialogized dispute is between a now desacralized tradition and its destabilizing alternatives. When chivalric values are exposed as martial ones through the imminent presence (or threat) of harmony, parody dialogues with its sources, reveals the latter's hidden attributes, and sets up discursive oppositions that it offers as superior to convention.[2] *El rapto*'s parodic destabilization of a mystified tradition subverts its supposed sources through a mix of external or intertextual and internal or structural irony. Its strategy of recurrent inversions, reversals, and ambiguous confusion thus serves to oppose its origins and suggest the desirability of an(other) less deceptively dangerous text. Most importantly, *El rapto*'s playfulness insists upon a supplemental, indeed, amusing voice in active opposition to the sobriety of canonical tradition, as Díaz-Mas indirectly confirms: "la verdad es que yo la literatura la veo como una cosa bastante humorística y bastante . . . lúdica" (the truth is that I view literature as considerably humorous and considerably . . . ludic).[3]

Gómez Ojea's *Los perros* takes up where her *Otras mujeres y Fabia* and Díaz Mas's *El rapto* leave off. It continues, with spirited good humor, to undo and disrupt textual expectations that have been internalized by such master narratives as the biblical, epic, Gothic, social realist, poetic, and best-seller. Under the aegis of Hecate— ancient goddess of maternal discourse—[4] this playful narrative defies textual conventions and unquestioned complicity with them. Through the disruptive power of parody and perversion, *Los perros* refuses to designate any discourse sacred or exempt from its all-encompassing game. Like *El rapto, Los perros* thus humorously undermines and defies tradition and consecrated texts; by subverting a given textual legacy, it replaces it with shocking to amusing alternatives of its own. The result of such irreverence is to blithely traverse the limitations erected by phallocentric discourse by raising up (in the spirit of Annie Leclerc) the most irresistible arm of trangression: laughter.

First let us imagine King Arthur surrounded, as one might expect, by his knights of the Round Table. His eyes are filled with tears, but no one notices for he is old, and besides, tradition has repeatedly portrayed him as an effusive weeper upon the departure of his beloved entourage. But at this supper his crying is of a different sort. Tradition seems to swerve; the familiar is dislocated. The king's source of woe now turns out to be an entirely unexpected inversion of Arthurian tradition: he announces the facile availability of the Holy Grail, now guarded by a bevy of maidens who will gladly relinquish their charge just as soon as any of the knights arrives to pick it up. After all these years, the elusive booty can be theirs for the taking, so the knights of the Round Table are packed off by their king to fetch the Grail. At a fixed hour they head for an exact destination, all according to a specific itinerary. No longer will they leave their horses to chance upon the way through thick and misty forests. But why are the king and his men so sad? After all, the Grail promises to usher in a new age of peace, justice, and goodness, an end to fratricidal conflict, hunger, disease, and injustice. The knights, grown old and grey, have spent their entire lives fighting for this anxiously awaited moment, but now that their once yearned-for hypothetical kingdom of peace becomes visible and attainable, they fear the purpose of their lives will be effaced. Their traditional text is threatened; their customary plot is coming to an end. In the gaze of Gawain, Lancelot reads as in an open book: "y ahora, qué?" (and now, what?).[5] Dispossessed of textual convention, they are also divested of meaning. They are characters about to embark on a journey beyond the pages of their familiar book.

Consonant with Díaz-Mas's scholarly background in medieval studies, *El rapto*'s rewriting of the Grail legend participates in historical attempts to reevaluate the Grail tradition. *El rapto* thus forms part of a critical-historical intertext that punctures the mythical portrayal of Grail knights as ideal and lofty beings.[6] Removing the veil of mystification and baring the dark side of chivalric concepts such as heroism and honor, *El rapto* exposes, for example, Arthur's ironically perverse awe before violence and bloodshed: "es la costumbre de matar a sus semejantes el más noble hábito del hombre" (the custom of killing one's peers is the most noble habit of man) (21–22). Echoing Gawain's uncertainty, the king is unable to envision a world in which men no longer have war as the central motivating force of their existence: "mis caballeros, que toda su vida se dedicaron a la lucha y a la guerra, ¿qué harán? ¿Cómo vivirán en adelante?" (my knights, who have dedicated their lives to fighting and war, what will they do? How will they live from now on?) (22). War, says *El rapto*'s Arthur, is what makes the world go round. His assessment suggests not only the glory and heroism of war but its baser, more material spoils such as jobs, wealth, and power. If this characterizaton breaks with traditional Arthurian idealization, it nevertheless delineates a scenario familiar to the reader. The narrative's medieval setting soon claims the qualities of a metaphor for modernity; the rewriting of Arthur becomes hauntingly contemporary.

The story here is, in fact, so familiar that a specific textual reversal like this one calls attention not only to the violence inherent in the chivalric intertext or in the lessons of recent history, it also interrogates through irony the more generalized patriarchal discourse of blood and violence that has, for centuries, underwritten textual and cultural legitimacy in the West. If we chuckle at Arthur's distorted values and bewilderment, we find ourselves laughing subversively at the perversity of our own culture's dominant values. Ultimately textual strategies such as this enjoin us to laugh these discursive notions of power and violence out of their privileged position. That same subtle wit then invites us to imagine a playful alternative, that which might emerge from what Annis Pratt has called the "disruptively feminist element" underlying masculine violence in Grail material.[7] These strategies of reinscribed reader-text complicity introduce, at *El rapto*'s outset, its challenge to a major patriarchal discursive system and to the texts that system has traditionally produced.

The older, well-known knights, Lancelot and Perceval, refuse to accept the possibility of a world without masculine conflict and unfulfilled desire, so they soon hatch counterplots to Arthur's unwelcome and unexpected plot. Perceval, here consistent with his traditional forebears, surrenders to a despair so extravagant that his tears create a river upon whose banks a luxuriant flora begins to grow. But though his sorrow engenders a fecund nature, he is not content to be on the verge of quelling desire. Echoing Machado and Becquer, he prefers to cling to "aquella espina dorada" (that golden thorn) (28), and turns to a traditionally staunch friend, Gawain, for aid. Gawain, proposing that Perceval carry through with his unpleasant assignment, offers to do his best to prevent the attainment of Perceval's objective. By appealing to a traditional and well-known intertext, Gawain justifies his ironically inverted act of friendship: "En todas las bellas historias de nobles barones valerosos ha habido siempre una traición y no pocas veces un héroe ha alcanzado la gloria gracias a un traidor . . . yo te traicionaré para que nunca llegues a tu destino" (In all the beautiful stories of noble, valerous men there has always been a betrayal and more than occasionally the hero has achieved glory thanks to a traitor . . . I will betray you so that you will never arrive at your destination) (29).

Gawain thus self-consciously scripts a plot retaining roots in textual antecedents familiar to him and to Perceval; his alternate plot is designed to preserve a known and privileged text in the face of threatened change. Though a plain-talking, textually self-conscious parody of his antecedents, Gawain still seeks to conserve the salient properties of his late "Vulgate" namesake; that is, his counterplot is to be the "carrier of deadly 'values.'"[8] Yet, though we may find Gawain's insistence on betrayal shocking, we smile wryly at the textual resonances in his speech and at the clever way in which *El rapto* at once grounds them in tradition and humorously inverts them. We thus respond amply to this narrative's skillful parody: here there is more at stake than the ridiculing of style; beliefs, too, are clearly made the object of ridicule.[9] Underlying the noble ring of the knightly promise lies a mocking note of absurdity, a ripple of laughter that playfully destabilizes the apparent nobility of Gawain's pledge.

Lancelot, along his route through the woods, meets up with a roughhewn woodsman. Thereupon ensues a humorous clash of discourses, as Lancelot queries the rustic about his activities and is repeatedly met with blunt replies at the margins of knightly discourse. For example, when Lancelot explains the belligerent function of a lance, the woodsman replies subversively: "Sin duda eres un poco tonto para ir por el mundo con semejante cachivache" (Undoubtedly you're a little daft to go around with such a piece of junk) (33). Yet in spite of the humorous distance that separates their experience, Lancelot enlists the woodsman in his counterplot. After explaining that his insignia is for his greater glory—not to indicate the direction of the wind (as the rustic believes)—and after hearing another literal but cleverly well-founded response ("tan inútil me parece gloriarse de un trapo" [it seems so useless to me to be proud of a rag]) (33), Lancelot enjoins the rustic to be his enemy. The woodsman, attracted by the more concrete promise of sudden wealth, willingly accepts his new role and dubs himself Caballero de la Verde Oliva (Knight of the Green Olive Tree) after the tree he was chopping when the plot of his life suddenly changed.

But, as the text's mixture of external and internal irony would have it, neither Perceval nor Lancelot become unambiguous victims of their own, self-inscribed plots. Perceval gets caught up in a rewriting of the ballad of "El conde Arnaldos" (Count Arnaldos), boarding a ship with "velas de seda" (sails of silk) whose singing captain insists: "yo no digo mi canción sino al que conmigo va" (I don't sing my song to anyone except he who goes with me) (52). Still, much like his antecedents, Perceval takes his king's orders so literally and so naively, that when the ship reaches land, he commands the captain to keep sailing. After all, his route to the castle was to be by sea. His ironically strict attention to the literal level of the word forces the ship to navigate on land, and consequently become "landwrecked." The siren call of the ballad's captain then inverts to become the voice of a doomed servant, fatally victimized by the stubborn insistence of his noble lord. While the revised legendary captain reluctantly expires in a sea of humus, Perceval dies serenely in knightly honor.

This exaggerated series of ironic reversals and inversions renders Perceval's death sublimely ridiculous. Later, in an instance of internal irony, when Gawain wonders how he will carry out his act of treachery against Perceval, he discovers the corpse of Lancelot, while the cause of the latter's death remains ambiguous. Whichever way these heroes eventually die, whichever ironic twist finally ensnares them, Díaz-Mas seems to make a point analogous to the theories of French feminist, Annie Leclerc. Describing male heroism as "played out in the face of death," Leclerc questions if greatness is meant to lie in death and laments the "carrion-eating values that have polluted the whole world."[10] Similarly, as the parodic perspective of *El rapto* undermines and subverts those very "values" the heroes try so resolutely to sustain, the quote from Leclerc with which this chapter begins again becomes ever more suggestive. Here lamentation is conjoined with the weapon of laughter in a kind of extended oxymoron, the effect of this device being to simultaneously undermine and displace both a specific intertext and the cultural ideology upon which it historically has been grounded.

One knight does genuinely desire the Grail and does not engender a counterplot to thwart possessing it. Instead, *she* begins to suggest a different text. El Caballero de Morado (the Purple Knight), daughter of an old knight with seven daughters and no son, effectively argues to secure a place for herself in Arthur's small band of reluctant Grail seekers. The king's first reaction to her offer of joining the quest is negative and based on a lack of textual precedents: "Nunca se oyó en mi reino ni en ningún otro que doncella alguna vistiese armas y entrase en combate singular" (It has never been heard in my kingdom nor in any other that any maiden bore arms or entered into a single combat) (14). The maiden knight's gesture thus constitutes an entirely unfamiliar plot device in the king's text (his kingdom) and in the chivalric intertext (in any other kingdom), so she appeals to another textual tradition to justify her claim: "habrías de considerar necios y locos a Aristóteles, a Ovidio, a Plinio y a otros muchos autores de la Antiguedad que en sus historias narran lo que aconteció en el país de las Amazonas. ¡En verdad que en aquel reino no había varón que ciñese espada!" (you might consider Aristotle, Ovid, Pliny, and many other authors of antiquity silly and crazy because in their stories they narrated what happened in the land of the Amazons. In truth in that kingdom there was no man that bore a sword!) (14). Against this appeal to another intertext, the king resorts to the handy argument that "anatomy is destiny," citing the girl's rounded breasts as a liability for sword bearing. But, undaunted, she effectively rejects that argument, too, logically describing how such anatomical difference is rendered invisible beneath a coat of armor.

Proving that she is not to be taken for a madwoman for daring to utter a different discourse, the king finally accedes—on the condition that the Purple Knight prove her prowess with a sword. But the test for female martial skills is inverted and sounds curiously like a trial for virginity: "júrame que es la primera espada que tocas y que jamás antes envainaste ninguna otra. He de ver si te heriste o no con ella y si brotó sangre cuando la metiste en tu vaina" (swear that this is the first sword you have touched and that you have never sheathed another. I must see if you have injured yourself with it and if blood flowed when you placed it in your sheath) (16). Her answer is also inverted and sounds more appropriate as a proof of chastity than of military prowess: "hay una mancha de sangre. ¡Sólo a quien es muy inexperto en el manejo de la espada puede ocurrirle esto!" (there is a spot of blood. Only someone who is very inexperienced in the wielding of a sword can experience this!) (16). More than likely the king, fearing he cannot control this maiden knight as well as his men—given her position on the margins of his shared patriarchal text—seeks to assure himself of her lack of skill at handling a sword, and thus of her potential for failing to secure the unwanted Grail. More generally, this ironic reversal from the chivalric intertext underscores the persistence of other (sexual) values for women—purity rather than prowess as the requirement for female honor.

Still, this female knight passes her absurd test and proceeds to choose her colors and her arms: purple for her clothing, a mirror of Venus for her shield. In these choices of the signs of chivalry, she allows the reader further glimpses of an alternate text. Purple, for the ancients (to whom the female knight has already appealed for authority), was not purple but burgundy, the color of blood, especially menstrual blood that often signified matrilineal kinship in a sacred clan.[11] In the same context, Venus was the Roman name for the Great Goddess; yet even in her modern version as goddess of love, the choice of this female deity rather than the Virgin Mary reverses the symbolism of traditional Grail iconology and restores to it its pre-Christian origins.[12] So the sally of the maiden knight in *El rapto* subverts key aspects of the traditional chivalric intertext by: 1) reversing the gender of one of its key participants; and 2) pointing to further rewritings of the chivalric genre by allowing a shift in referents for two key symbols from their customarily paternal to revised maternal associations. Perhaps these elements of the text restore resonances of archaic Celtic symbolism, which earlier readers of the Grail tradition, like Weston and Loomis, have identified.[13] Certainly, the posture and choices of the maiden knight begin to disrupt the male characters' insistence on patriarchal plotting and symbolism.

The Purple Knight fails, however, to reckon with the fact that she must function, as Hélène Cixous would say, "within the discourse of man," one which diminishes, stifles, indeed annihilates life.[14] Along her journey, she meets up with Pelinor, a youth who was her beloved and who was sent by Arthur to prevent the acquisition of the Grail. In a broad stroke of internal irony, the Purple Knight and Pelinor come to confront each other, each ignorant of the other's identity. Pelinor even thrusts his lance in honor of his beloved, unaware that she stands before him. Still, the Purple Knight, faithful to codes of chivalry if not to its traditional plot, insists on keeping her identity secret. Attempting desperately, however, to stave off Pelinor's sword from her throat, she narrates her version of the ballad, "La Doncella Guerrera" (the warrior maiden). In this retelling, analogies to the Purple Knight's own narrative are absolutely clear to the reader, and we expect that Pelinor will likewise recognize the story's analogues and similarly decode the tale of his beloved. The maiden's narrative is designed to appeal to the noblest sentiments of the listener ("que perdonéis a quien es capaz de narrar tan linda historia" [may you pardon the one who is capable of narrating such a comely story]) (60), and leaves such bold hermeneutic stones along its path that decoding should be obvious and facile indeed. Yet Pelinor blindly, or deafly, ignores its implications. To Pelinor, the narrative is nothing more than an inconsequential old wives' tale, unfit for male articulation and, even more, undeserving of male interpretation. Lying outside his textual tastes and training, he disparages it and ultimately rejects it. Thus two codes or discourses clash unremediably.[15]

Increasingly desperate, the Purple Knight requests that Pelinor remove her headgear so that he may see her identity, but he wants only to hear the knight's name and nothing more. Each insists upon a different mode of identification, making communication between them impossible. Pelinor's insistence on his abstract principle stops at nothing short of death, so the Purple Knight becomes yet another casuality of extreme masculine violence: "Pelinor hizo entrar su espada en la herida no una, sino varias veces, y cuando hubo terminado, se alzó, se reafirmó las ropas y degolló al caballero con la misma espada" (Pelinor thrust his sword into the wound not once, but several times, and, when he had finished, he stood straight, readjusted his clothes and beheaded the knight with the same sword) (63). Pelinor never removes his victim's headgear to verify her identity. Instead, boldly and coldly he proceeds according to an authorized masculine plot.

Yet Pelinor's stubborn fury does not go unnoticed; the narrator's final moral commentary strips away all possibility of chivalric idealization with the irony of understatement: "en verdad obró muy mal en esto" (in truth he acted very badly in this situation) (63). Having unquestioningly internalized the discourse of martial values, Pelinor could not pardon anyone—even, ironically, his beloved—from its harsh demands. Gawain's lament when he discovers the corpse of the felled Purple Knight is telling: "¡Ah, dulcísima doncella, que en todo quisiste emular a los varones! No está el mundo hecho para estas cosas" (Ah, sweet maiden, who in everything wanted to emulate men! The world is not made for such things) (81). The mistake of this woman was to have sought participation in a plot inscribed by men desirous of acquiring or maintaining power, men deaf to conciliatory voices and narratives, men blindly destructive of values different from their own.

Pelinor, however, is not spared the fate of the other three Grail knights. In accordance with the ridiculously unrelenting predominance of death and violence, he, too, must die.[16] And he meets his doom with his namesake, the rustic Caballero de la Verde Oliva in service to Lancelot.[17] When the two Knights of the Green Olive Tree encounter each other, Pelinor is never named; the identity of both men remains ambiguous and oblique. Meeting in a narrow passageway called Garganta de los Ecos (the Throat of Echoes), the encounter of these two identical figures seems like a confrontation with their own mirrored images. As we are unsure of who is who, they are uncertain if their opponent is outside or inside themselves. It is as if each man were confronting

himself or the fantasm of himself in search of absolute self-
mastery and control.[18] The voices of the two knights utter the
same injunction against continuing to the castle of the Grail. Each
challenges the other in the same manner and echoes of thousands
of voices, all exactly alike, respond. Their blows are magnified
into thousands, their swords are multiplied into thousands of
reflections. The two knights are thus transformed by the irony of
hyperbole into a vast array of physical violence so exaggerated
that the reader is overwhelmed with the absurdity of its dimensions. Finally one Caballero de la Verde Oliva kills the other.
Ambiguity prevails and the reader is not certain which of the two
knights has been slain. Not until later, when Gawain discovers the
corpses of three Grail knights—Lancelot, the Purple Knight, and
Pelinor—do we learn that the victim of the battle of the Throat
was King Arthur's youngest knight.

Once we establish the identity of the slain Knight of the Green
Olive Tree we are able to reread and savor the irony of the rustic's
success in penetrating the Grail Castle and its occupants. The two
chapters in which this episode occurs form a narrative parenthesis
in the text of otherwise exaggerated masculine violence, and *El
rapto*'s parody of chivalry shifts from its undermining of deadly
forces to its playful proposal of compensatory, life-enhancing
values. Unlike the surrounding text, which mocks a relentless
ideology of male mastery and annihilation, this hiatus relocates
the narrative perspective in an(other) more female-centered discourse. Here the reader may rediscover, as an alternative to the
pervasive cult of death, the underlying female or feminist element
already present in the traditional Grail legend.

The surviving Knight of the Green Olive Tree comes to rest in a
paradisiacal space outside the portals of the castle of Acabarás
wherein is located the Grail. In a scene containing topics from the
restorative imagery of romance—softly warm air, green and florid
landscape, the song of a goldfinch—the knight sits to regenerate
his powers. While he rests, the castle's inhabitants espy his
"poderosa lanza" (powerful lance) (71). Some on the sly, others
more boldly, admire and ask about "aquella reluciente y enorme
verga que llevaba el caballero desconocido, pues nunca habían
visto otra igual ni sabían cual era su utilidad" (that brilliant and
huge rod that the unknown knight bore, for they had never seen
its equal nor did they know its purpose) (72). The reader immediately chuckles at this lexical ambiguity that begins to transform
courtly service from its more lofty notions to pure animal delight.
For the first time in this text, the arms of a knight are named with

a term possessing the double meaning of rod and phallus, and it remains possible to read this double meaning throughout the chapter. In one such instance, the leader of the Grail maidens, Blancaniña, gazes admiringly at the arm's potency: "me llena de alegría la visión de una lanza tan inhiesta como la tuya, que me parece de las mejores y más robustas que he visto" (the sight of such an erect lance as yours fills me with joy, for it seems to me one of the best and most robust that I have seen) (72). She suggests directly that the knight's lance "ha de cumplir bien su cometido y que ninguna dama a cuyo servicio la pusieres quedaría enojada o poco satisfecha" (is bound to successfully carry out its task and that no lady in whose service you might put it would be left angry or dissatisfied) (72). When the knight agrees to put his lance in the service of all the maidens of the castle and prove "como no desmayaba" (how it would not wither away) (73), the distance between chivalric metaphor and the claims of the body continues to close; the concept of service slips further into the realm of corporeality.

The doors of the castle open, and the hundred maidens take turns touching the captivating "weapon" of their benefactor: "una a una fueron tomando la lanza con sus manos blancas y pulidas y comprobaron cómo era de robusta; y, tras lavársela con agua de azahar y pesársela, le pidieron todas a una voz que les enseñase a embrazarla" (one by one they took the lance into their white and polished hands and verified how robust it was; and, after washing it with orange blossom water and appraising it, they all asked him in unison to instruct them how to grasp it) (73). The knight tirelessly pleases all of them, including the castle's mistress, and as a reward for his service, he is offered the Grail. The final reward rounds out this delightful inversion of chivalric values from their traditional intertext: no longer does the lady reward the knight with her sexual favors for his chivalric exploits or service, but for his sexual service he is rewarded the ultimate spoil of chivalry— the Grail. The dominant chivalric ethos is thus effectively reversed and shifted back to woman's physical perspective; the word merges with the flesh, the symbol is reabsorbed by the body. After all the maiming and killing is done, the episode at the Grail castle deliciously restores what French feminist Chantal Chawaf has called the "verbal paganism of the Middle Ages" through which the book is reconnected with the body and with pleasure.[19]

This recent textual move to displace male violence with female desire and pleasure seems to draw upon inherently feminist elements in the Grail tradition. Jessie Weston, in her now classic study of folkloric and pre-Christian elements in the Grail legend, has indicated that ancient oriental religion provides a remote source of Grail material, and that within that source the phallus was a dominant symbol of its fertility cults. Complementarily, in specific cults associated with ritual death and rebirth, "the most noticeable feature . . . was the prominence assigned to women."[20] Weston also cites the possible presence in the Grail legend of the Wild Huntsman figure and other phallic demons of fertility who kept company with fair women. These and numerous other observations by Weston are illuminating not only as an explanation for the sources of original Grail material, but for the mythical power that these sources still may have for women writers, like Díaz-Mas, who seek to recuperate the traditional intertext for its rewriting from a contemporary female perspective.

Preserving the now widely accepted interpretation that the Castle of the Grail is, as Joseph Campbell has maintained, "a sanctuary in which sexual symbolism is both appropriate and inevitable," the contemporary woman writer turns that symbolism to her own ends.[21] She reassigns the phallus its place as the source of female satisfaction, not domination, retrieving from archaic archaeology the playful function of the phallus as "made for her pleasure and fulfillment."[22] Today's writer, like Díaz-Mas, discovers the secret Tantric self-discipline practiced by some courtly lovers whose "aim was not selfish pleasure but only gratification of the lady," and endows her own hero with such stamina and selflessness.[23] And today's writer is able to select from the Celtic substratum of the Grail material its matrilocal or matrilineal symbols, recreating "the lady of the castle who chose whomever she pleased" and then bathed her guest, "artistically massaging him."[24] Finally, she blends romance with fabliau in order to stress the humorously immediate gratification of female desire. In short, the kind of writer exemplified by Díaz-Mas culls from history, legendary lore, and literature for women who woo and choose and enjoy their sensuality, assigning them prominence and displacing with them a patriarchal mythology in which noble men shun such pleasures, seeking theirs in violence and death.

In the passages cited from the episode of the Grail castle, Díaz-Mas inscribes these shifts and more. *El rapto*'s maidens become enchanted after their dalliance with the Knight of the Green Olive Tree in an amusing reversal of the Grail topic of enchanted maidens. Traditionally, maidens being held under a spell are released by the noble services of a knight; they do not become enchanted after having been served (or, in this case, serviced) or by feeling their skirts grow too tight and too narrow. After *El rapto*'s maidens communicate their predicament to the beautiful green knight, he earnestly explains:

> "a decir verdad nunca puse mi lanza al servicio de una dama, que no le pasase esto al poco de yo servirla: perder la [sic] color de la cara y estrechársele el brial día por día. Pero vosotras me pedisteis que pusiese mi lanza a vuestro servicio y yo no pude resistirme, pues al fin soy caballero y hubiera hecho muy mal si me negase

> (to tell the truth I never employed my lance in the service of a lady when this did not happen to her shortly after my having served her: she lost her blush and her skirt grew tighter and tighter every day. But you asked me to put my lance at your service and I could not resist, for after all I am a knight and I would have acted badly had I refused) (76).

With these words we chuckle once again at the genial manner in which *El rapto* retrieves ancient Celtic motifs symbolizing fertility and life and enfolds them into this playful reversal of chivalric service.

If Pelinor recalls his traditional namesake, a "maimed" king discovered by Weston in a certain manuscript of the Arthurian cycle, and if he symbolizes death, then his double, or the knighted rustic, would suggest the opposite: an amalgam of Wild Huntsman, fertility demon, and rebirth.[25] The purpose and signification of the two green knights now becomes clear: the one associated with the plot of violence and death is subverted by irony; the one who survives becomes the bearer of ancient matriarchal symbols unheeded by his double. The rustic's lance would then be linked symbolically to the Grail of the maidens, for as Weston discovered the lance represents male, the cup female reproductive energy.[26] The humorous reversals of the episode in the Grail castle underscore, then, the desirability of recuperating this life-enhancing and resurrecting symbolism, creating a marked contrast to the fatal martial values parodied in the preceding chapters.

One more key resonance in these alternative chapters should be acknowledged for it results in a definitive overturning of the honor code, which the Purple Knight was unable to accomplish. The Grail maiden's name, Blancaniña, recalls the epithet naming the protagonist of "Romance de una fatal ocasión" (Ballad of a Fatal Occasion). As the reader will recall, in that ballad a maiden, addressed as "blanca niña," protects her honor by stabbing a

knight who wished to dally with her at the foot of a "verde oliva."
Adroitly weaving these references into the Grail episode, *El rapto*
reverses events by having Blancaniña and her companions welcome their knight of the "verde oliva." After having taken their
pleasure, their "briales" grow too tight, unlike the closely guarded
"brial" of the ballad's heroine as she tucks it up to avoid soiling it
with dew. These reversals from their ballad source effectively
cancel out the ballad's patriarchal moral lesson and free the Grail
maidens for their playfully subversive project.

But unfortunately there is no place for these females, with their
life-enhancing games, in the deadly lands of Arthur. Because they
are all pregnant and polygamy is prohibited by Christian doctrine,
the group unanimously decides to take off for the land of the
Moors. Ironically, they absentmindedly pack the Grail amid sacks
of flour and forget about it as they depart for Turkey. In another
twist of irony, the Grail and its guardians leave for the land of the
infidels—not to fight for or defend Christian values but, presumably, to settle into the sensual pleasures of the East. Left behind is
a landscape dotted with fallen chivalric heroes.

Pelinor is buried with all due ceremony near an altar, and a few
steps behind him is laid the tomb of the warrior maiden he had
loved and ironically killed. In a final and definitive reversal from
the traditional Grail plot, the dead young knight is declared king;
the beginning of the Wasteland is proclaimed. From that day
forward the land would be covered with ash, women would be
sterile, orchards would transform into rock and stone, cities
would be hushed into cemeteries, music would be silenced, all
books would lie covered with dust in the libraries, and mothers
would cease to tell their children ancient tales in archaic languages. In this land of infertility, existent texts would henceforth
go unread and future matrilineal discourse would be silenced.
The reign of death and infertility signifies, then, the demise of all
texts—chivalric and matrilinear. Only a portrait of the dead king
reading remains above Pelinor's tomb; his text, archaic and spent,
is rendered frozen forever in his hands. The regime of death has
answered Gawain's initial question with "ahora, nada" (now,
nothing). A society deaf and blind to woman's voice and vision is
ironically left with no voice at all. "What do men's eyes see?" asks
French feminist Viviane Forrester. "A crippled world, mutilated,
deprived of women's vision."[27] Yet at least the wasteland of *El
rapto* is localized; the damage is confined to a specific patriarchal
space. In the Orient, the woodsman's numerous progeny may
resume using the banners of knighthood for weathervanes, and

on those erased chivalric surfaces, their multiple mothers may inscribe the differences of their playfully subversive maternal texts.

If the Grail Maidens were to write, their text might resemble that of Tarsiana, the principal narrator of Gómez Ojea's *Los perros,* and those of her accomplices. Tarsiana as a libertine and former prostitute—not a conventionally "nice" person at all— also stands outside the margins of the sacrificial paternal text. Her likes and dislikes are never veiled by what might be right and proper for women to say, and what she does voice is often outrageously intolerant. If this outsider detests motherhood, and is terrified by housewifery, she minces no words; her preferences are rather voiced through wild flights of the imagination (such as her "sucios deleites" [dirty delights] from a nightmare in which an anthropophagous seamstress devours her newborn.[28] This fantasy, the first shock or perversion in this novel, provokes the reader into reassessing textual expectations, especially those inherited from the patterns of social realism and even the first wave of sociopolitical feminism. Tarsiana, unlike those more grave and practical predecessors who chose the subordination of imagination to mimesis and social reform, prefers to jolt her readers through the kind of defiance counseled by Meese in this chapter's opening quote.[29] Tarsiana's (and by extension, Gómez Ojea's) strategy is to function outside dominant culture rather than attempt to reform it from within. Like the transplanted Grail Maidens, she prefers to occupy an(other) space.

By casting herself as a "cínica libertina" (cynical libertine) (31) who consciously selected the occupation of prostitute (127), Tarsiana encodes within herself the disruptive, subversive potential that such a figure is capable of projecting. The libertine or the pervert, Foucault reminds us, "deliberately breaks the law," most especially the law of marriage and the order of desires.[30] And as Jane Gallop similarly suggests, the prostitute who engages in her trade not only for money but also for pleasure is a subversive force.[31] Thus, in a world "regido por la sombra dominadora de Abraham" (ruled by the dominating shadow of Abraham) (126)— a world in which, like Sarah, women are the objects of exchange— Tarsiana's lucid position ("tengo plena conciencia de lo que quiero," [I am fully conscious of what I want]) (127) disrupts woman's mindless subjugation to the patriarch's desire or the rule of paternal law. Instead, Tarsiana wishes to be Circe, a goddess, and learn the sorcery of this and other goddesses (23). Positioning herself on the margins of patriarchal discourse rather than engaging in direct confrontation with it, she invents and rewrites (9) and imagines the "central patriarchal text" (as Edward Said has called the Bible)[32] going up in flames: "el libro del Génesis arderá entonces en todos los hogares" (the book of Genesis will then burn in all the hearths) (38). Tarsiana's is the imagination of modernity that decenters and deconstructs the very foundation of Western beliefs.

From the self-cloistered location of her room, Tarsiana organizes multiple narratives about herself and numerous persons of her acquaintance. Unlike other more conventional enclosed females of literature, such as young girls forced into nunneries by cruel elders or Gothic victims imprisoned by demonic villains, Tarsiana chooses her own space—a den of inactivity and focused attention— since this seclusion is deemed essential for the spinning and sharing of yarns. Tarsiana takes her cue for this decision from Teodora, an old friend of her mother, who was bedridden by a lingering illness. Teodora's chamber, into which passes numerous interlocutors, thus serves as a prototype for Tarsiana's later narrative enterprise. Its recollection suggests the site and plants the seed for Tarsiana's own narrative experiment, her collection and creation of disruptive, shocking narrations: "Escuchaba el murmullo de las conversaciones, las voces femeninas que llegaban hasta mí, llevando a mis oídos retazos de historias terribles y sangrientas" (I used to listen to the murmur of the conversations, the feminine voices that reached me, carrying to my ears remnants of terrible and bloody stories) (53).

The motif of blood (which we have seen reconsidered in *El rapto* through parodic hyperbole) has often been silenced in women's literature. Considered more appropriate for the masculine genres of war and crime, it is, however, in *El rapto* and in *Los perros* reinstated as a recurring obsessive and disruptive sign. This lust for blood may signify the surfacing of previously suppressed attributes of female sexuality (as Hélène Cixous desires for women's literature in "The Laugh of the Medusa" or as we have seen in Ortiz's *Urraca*), or it may express an impulse to reinscribe the original violation or reviolate masculine turf (as Nancy K. Miller has described in another context).[33] While the undermining of violent masculine turf dominates in *El rapto*, examples of both these tendencies of the blood motif abound in *Los perros*.

Regalina, Tarsiana's regal servant and narrative accomplice, alternately shocks and awes with the bloody monstrosity of her life and fantastic stories: the veteran of numerous abortions, she conceives miraculously during her menstrual period, yet decides to keep the child she knows is sacred, a girl, and doomed to die at eight months. Later she devours huge amounts of raw meat as her pregnancy advances. By exaggerating the bloody dimensions of life and death, and by possessing an uncanny knowledge of these forces, Regalina disrupts traditional images of servility and assumes a sexual power that overturns traditional textual patterns of female weakness during pregnancy. Bruna Fel, a friend of the narrator, bewitches Tarsiana with her bloody, viscous words, her exaggerated and unwelcome fertility, and her pathological attraction to her husband's perversions. Bruna's language of blood is transformative, for it gives voice to contradictory aspects of female sexuality often suppressed and silenced by more mimetic narratives.

Tarsiana's godmother committed suicide through self-mutilation under the aegis of St. Walpurga (the Christianized version of the pagan goddess of witches). While paternal voices judge the godmother insane, nothing but a sexually frustrated hysteric, her act and legacy (her eternal presence in the margins of Tarsiana's books) signify an implicit disruption of the paternal, Symbolic Order and its inadequate explanations of women's mysteries of body and blood. Moraima, Mo Lue, Melisa a Xaneiriña, and Tarsiana's grandmother, Isolda, are all portrayed as ogresses (48), caught by the narrator in the act of drinking blood, and thus metaphorically linked with the power to reinscribe the original violation in which the female victim is made to bleed. Finally, the stories that Tarsiana heard from her paternal grandmother disrupt expectations about demure grandmothers by revioling masculine turf: "solían ser crudas y terribles, referidas casi siempre a acciones bélicas sangrientas y perversamente heroicas" (they were usually crude and terrible, referring almost always to bloody military and perversely heroic actions) (66). This text's insistence on the hyperbolic dimensions of blood displaces our moorings of comfort and complacency; its ludic vengeance hurls itself repeatedly against our unexamined taboos.

Just as varied and insistent as the bloody stories are the traces of perversion that lace Tarsiana's defiant narrative web. They are bold, fanciful, funny, disturbing; their disruptive playfulness underscores, once again, Los perros' function as a ludic text. In one instance, Tarsiana recalls being awakened as a girl by the insidious whispers of hydrangeas in her eccentric godmother's garden. The talebearing flowers were telling a little frog about the perversions of their mistress (182). Such vegetal assessments of human eccentricities adds another dimension of whimsical play not only to the portrayal of one odd character but to the entire tone of Tarsiana's text. Talking plants are then joined to talking pots, which a grandmother of three of Tarsiana's storytellers received as a wedding gift. The lady's cooks were shocked by the obscenities of the cookware and the lechery with which the medium-sized saucepan tried to seduce the little baking pan. This animated universe—with its talk of perversions and its perverted talk—tweaks the nose of domestic order, tranquility, and more mimetic texts grounded on such disputed certainties.

The humor of perversion also bares the dark side of bourgeois respectability, as in the case of Valeria. "La violenta Valeria" (violent Valeria) dedicates herself to terrorizing "administrativos adiposos, caballeros maduros" (adipose administrators, mature gentlemen) (83) by humiliating them with forced fellatio and the subsequent required drinking of its product from a feeding bottle. Valeria "goza intensamente con su perversión" (intensely enjoys her perversion) (83), the narrator informs us, thus defiantly inverting dominant male fantasies about such activities. Valeria's crude language also subverts traditional expectations about propriety and woman's speech.

Yet not all in *Los perros* signifies disruptive rejection. This narrative also celebrates the pure sensuality of literature and language at the same time that it engages in its enchanting retellings of tradition. Tarsiana's delectation of a text she is reading doubles as a description of the one she is generating and we are reading:

Es una historia hecha con retazos de sueños prodigiosos, visiones, conversaciones con los gnomos y los elfos que pueblan el pomo cristalino de mi narguile. Es simple escribir palabras, bellas y suaves palabras, cuya tibieza, cuya forma cálidamente redondeada puede obnubilar de placer y solazar los raciocinios más obtusos. Ojeo y toco con avidez y lujuria esos folios.

(It is a story made from remnants of prodigious dreams, visions, conversations with the gnomes and the elfs that populate the crystalline bowl of my narghile. It is simple to write words, beautiful and soft words whose mildness, whose warmly rounded form can enthrall with pleasure and relax the most obtuse of minds. Avidly and sensually, I thumb through and touch these pages) (42).

Above all, the criterion for Tarsiana's narrative enterprise has to be pleasure, for herself and for her readers:

A veces pienso que debería escribir con orden y rigor. . . . Pero . . . no sería un trabajo divertido. No me haría sonreír más que un par de veces a lo sumo; y, por otro lado, no creo que su lectura reportase ninguna clase de gozo a nadie.

(Sometimes I think that I ought to write with order and rigor. . . . But . . . it wouldn't be an enjoyable enterprise. I wouldn't make myself smile more than a couple of times at most; and, on the other hand, I don't think that its reading would provide any sort of pleasure to anyone) (79).

As reader and implied writer, Tarsiana knows what does not give her pleasure, and the textual peccadillos of others serve as foils for her own preferences. Hipólito, an aging intellectual of the sixties, loves words but uses them with dogged indiscretion. Still caught up in the hackneyed lexicon of existentialism and Marxism, he drives Tarsiana to desperation: "Hipólito, Hipólito, sigues siendo el joven infatuado y petulante, un ser inmaduro, incapaz de romper los cacharros litúrgicos del antiguo culto, las burdas imágenes de la vieja idolatría" (Hipolitus, Hipolitus, you continue to be the same infatuated and petulant youth, an immature being, incapable of breaking the liturgical vessels of the archaic cult, the clumsy images of the old idolatry) (93). She has little patience with those, like him, who keep telling the same story over and over again through the paradigms of an outdated discourse. Neither can she bear the writings of Vasthí, a successful woman writer who produces "lo que al fin y al cabo se espera que escriba una mujer" (that which after all is expected that a woman write) (144), in the narrator's words: "relatos pringosos de trampas y traiciones . . . una aburrida historia doméstica" (greasy stories of traps and betrayals . . . a boring domestic story) (144–45). The most objectionable aspect of Vasthí's commercially successful writing for women is its lack of humor and its writer's inability to poke fun at herself. Tarsiana, as the irreverent deconstructer of convention that she is, needs to impertinently elude the traps of complicity; she would rather challenge tediousness with imagination and maintain her marginal position vis-à-vis predictable domestic plots.

Though Tarsiana may seem insensitive to women's issues, it is really only whining and complaining that leave her unmoved. She, in fact, derives her discursive preferences from women, but from the proud and even impudent daughters of Eve who dare to answer the paternal interdiction with a resounding "no." Plainly conscious of her "pecado contra el dios de mis padres" (sin against the god of my fathers) (34), Tarsiana declares herself one of the rebels against patriarchal religious authority. Replacing Christian orthodoxy with pagan defiance, she proclaims, "me santiguaba y rezaba, pequeña idólatra, pérfida politeísta, adoradora de Hécate y de sus hermanas. La enigmática diosa tricéfala me asistía" (I blessed myself and prayed, little idol, perfidious polytheist, adorer of Hecate and her sisters. The enigmatic three-headed goddess assisted me) (34). References to Hecate surface and resurface repeatedly throughout the text, as this Greek trinitarian goddess displaces the Trinity of patriarchal dogma, and the goddess's "mother's Words of Power" become the focal point of Tarsiana's narrative.[34] She even leaves room for such evasions of patriarchal law among followers of the Christian godhead for one of Tarsiana's memories concerns a young novice "que buscaba su camino lejos de las leyes patriarcales del otro lado de la tapia del convento" (who searched for her path far from the patriarchal laws of inside the convent wall) (129–30). Tarsiana herself maintains an eclectic position regarding the texts of her repudiated faith. Missals and other religious books for devotions and rituals of the church fascinate her, and the beads of her rosary serve as a kind of magic carpet to places of her imagination. A source of sensual and visual pleasure, the rosary becomes a vehicle capable of linking Christian with pagan and of effecting a return to pre-patriarchal, maternal realms—in short, to the garden before the fall ("misteriosos jardines de gozos verdes" [mysterious gardens of green pleasures]) (169).

With a great and persistent desire to return to the past ("Ah, cómo me gustaría aspirar el aire perfumado de una noche de primavera del siglo quince" [Ah, how I should like to breathe the perfumed air of a springtime night in the fifteenth century]) (61), Tarsiana devises narrative schemes whereby this desire is transformed into textual reinscription. Once she inserts herself into the poem of the Cid in order to imagine a ritualized destruction of the bellicose epic and its simultaneous rewriting from the perspective of nonviolent female power:

> Era la niña de nueve años, asomándose con timidez por entre dos versos de arte mayor, como dos hojas de roble, porque un guerrero castellano llamaba a mi puerta. Mientras me acercaba al cerrojo para abrirle, crecía y crecía mi pelo; las trenzas me llegaban hasta los pies. Mio Cid, no vayas a guerrear. Siéntate ahí y bebamos. Quemaremos un cantar de gesta, haremos esta noche una refulgente hoguera con los versos de tus amadores, con todas las voces que van a pronunciar tu nombre; fuego con las palabras del juglar que tan bien te sirvió.

> (I was the nine-year old girl, appearing with timidity from between two twelve syllable lines, as if from between two oak leaves, because a

Castilian warrior was calling at my door. While I approached the lock to open it, my hair grew and grew; the braids reached my feet. My Lord, don't go to battle. Sit here and we'll drink. We'll burn the epic poem, we'll make a roaring fire tonight with the verses of your admirers, with all the voices that will pronounce your name; a fire with the words of the troubadour that served you so well) (37).

On another occasion, Tarsiana revisits the sixteenth century, specifically Counter Reformation Trent. With her contemporary Italian clerical lover, she collaborates in the reinvention of her sixteenth-century self as lover of cardinals and sinners. The fabrication of stories repeats itself in temporal and spatial layers as Tarsiana playfully glides across the borders of history from one dimension to another. And at still another moment, as she remembers one more lover—this time an Israeli who sang Sephardic songs he learned from his former wife, who in turn learned them through a female line from laundresses on the Tagus—Tarsiana playfully transforms a well-known and well-loved poem by Machado: "Israel, siempre estarás en mi corazón. Sión, mística e inalcanzable, vas conmigo, mi corazón te lleva" (Israel, you will always be in my heart. Zion, mystical and unreachable, you go with me, my heart carries you) (74). Diverse textual sources are thus juxtaposed and metamorphosed in dynamic heterogeneity. The display sparkles with invention. Still, aware that the reader may question such unabashed, thinly veiled borrowings as the Machado source, the narrator absolves herself from possible censure: "Muy poco original, la verdad, pero es que la recreación literaria me vuelve loca de placer" (Not very original, this is true, but it's just that literary recreation drives me crazy with pleasure) (74). In her poetic game and gloss she thus sums up her entire textual enterprise as literary recreation.

Though Tarsiana as narrator rejects the self-pitying complicity of "women's literature"—the overtold stories of the "mater dolorosa" and the self-flagellating masochism of the "malmaridada"—and though she is utterly annoyed with the overworked, exhausted strategies of social realism, Tarsiana does not repudiate all commercial writing. In fact, she writes and sells trashy fiction to one Sam of Bif, a millionaire writer of humble origins. Writing for Sam allows her to indulge baser pleasures as she perverts the self-righteousness of legitimate aesthetic sensibility: "me deja sumida en una especie de pútrida cloaca, en la que chapoteo como una lechona voluptuosa experimentando deleitosas sensaciones groseras" (it leaves me submerged in a kind of putrid sewer, in which I splash around like a voluptuous pig feeling delightfully gross sensations) (148). Crossing the thin line from kitsch to parody, she explores the ludic potential of "trashy" sentimental writing. As a result, we chuckle at titles such as *Te estaba esperando, Siempre te seguiré, Ya sabes que he de volver, Aunque me desprecies, Canto mientras cuece mi fabada* (*I Was Waiting for You, I Shall Always Follow You, You Already Know That I Shall Return, Although You Despise Me, I Sing While My Stew Is Cooking*). Tarsiana is not the only "guilty" one; a professor who surreptitiously indulges in the transgression of writing popular fiction receives his absolution by yielding to Tarsiana's seduction. And she poses, finally, that respectable, conservative writers such as the Valdés brothers and Menéndez Pelayo read licentious pulp literature. By subverting proper lettered types, she defies textual propriety, turns it on its head, and affirms the dark pleasures of literature's more seamy side.

Tarsiana has other accomplices in defiance and disruption. Her cousin, Blandina, also turns literary expectations on their head, for she lives what used to be relegated to the imaginary and imagines the sordidness of the so-called real. She experiences an idealized Petrarchan fantasy (a chaste adventure with "un desconocido moreno de ojos febriles" [a dark stranger with febrile eyes]) (80), while she writes "novelas descarnadas de un neorrealismo sorprendente . . . fábulas tremendistas" (bare novels of a surprising neorealism . . . crudely realistic fables) (81). For Blandina, idealized life "deconstructs" demystified realist texts in an ironic reversal of conventional hierarchical notions of imagined and real. Solange, who married her first suitor because she feared being designated "soltera, soltera, soltera" (spinster, spinster, spinster) (101), attempts to compensate for her conventional bourgeois marriage with pastoral desires that "un poeta y peregrino [la] besara y amara en un ameno y umbrío prado verde" (a poet and a pilgrim kiss her and love her in a pleasant and shady green meadow) (100). Ceaselessly, she also creates oral literature, but Solange is not as fortunate as others who share their tales with Tarsiana. Solange, like so many female voices throughout history, is a "juglaresa sin público" (troubadour without an audience) (102). Her family is deaf to her continuous fabulations, but at least her insistence on speaking gives voice, in a Lacanian sense, to the imaginary. As Solange speaks of her desire, she textualizes it and thus articulates something that might otherwise have remained a blank and vacant silence.

Regalina, Tarsiana's maid, exceeds all the other narrators in her capacity for textual disruption and reinscription. An "excelente fabuladora" (excellent storyteller) according to Tarsiana, her talent expresses itself through oral and epistolary vehicles. Thus positioned on the margins of print, Regalina is redolent of a more ancient past; she proudly assumes the identity of "la última narradora de las tierras astures, la última barda de este viejo reino" (the last female narrator of the Asturian lands, the last female bard of this old kingdom) (107). As might be expected, she hates Gutenberg, and asserts that "las historias deben ser contadas en alta voz por el que las inventa" (stories should be told out loud by the one who invents them) (107). As a result, all books are suspect, even the Bible. Regalina's retellings of Holy Scripture as matrilineal lore are nothing less than delightful: "Según Regalina, que lo sabe por su abuela y ésta por la suya y así sucesivamente desde los días anteriores a la llegada de los moros, Jesucristo era un hijo de Salomón, un brujo, y su madre, Miriam, inventó la olla a presión y la cocción al baño María" (According to Regalina, who knows it from her grandmother who knew it through hers and so successively since the days before the arrival of the Moors, Jesus Christ was the son of Solomon, a sorcerer, and his mother, Miriam, invented the pressure cooker and the double boiler) (108). With a narrative power lying in exaggeration and untrammeled fantasy, Regalina can bewitch her mistress with delirious epopees, like that of her fantastic mother who could eat like Gargantua, sever her fingers, have them grow back, and make her husband mute. Finally, Regalina's epistolary creations supply Tarsiana with precious additions to her growing collection of 1,305 "real or fictional" letters. Regarding a supposed missive from her family in which the birth of a monstrous child is described, Regalina comments on the phenomenon, dismissing it as a common occurrence and lamenting that women are fools to cede the power they could enjoy through their agency in such anomalous events. Ironically, both letter and gloss turn out to be Regalina's own inventions, as the maid proves herself a fair match for the textual power and irreverence of her mistress.

It might be useful at this juncture to explore the possible causes of Tarsiana's narrative defiance. At the novel's close, Tarsiana recalls a childhood haunted by the ghosts of sacred texts and that of her dead twin brother. The death of her male twin permanently embittered the mother and turned her against Tarsiana. The mother had wanted "un varón para adorarlo—pequeño ídolo" (a male to adore—small idol) (193), and deprived of such a privileged male subject, she turned, forever, against her daughter. Abandoned also by her father and her husband, Tarsiana's mother resorts to always reading the same book—presumably that of a woman rendered incomplete and rigid by recurrent male escapes from her hold. Tarsiana (like Alós's Electra before her) is therefore consigned to living as an outsider, a woman marginal to the paternal economy.

But unlike her deficient mother, endlessly reading the text of her unrequited desire (and unlike Electra, who can never definitively elude the patriarchal economy), Tarsiana turns to alternate, woman-defined strategies of inscribing her life. The end of her narrative augurs her approaching union with Hecate—presumably her death. Yet her death is not ending but beginning. From the burning of the patriarchal Genesis early in the novel, another "génesis se inicia" (genesis begins) (196). Now aiding Tarsiana in her transition and rebirth are Circe—Homeric witch and shaper of creation—and Medea—wise one, Mother goddess, and (in Sanskrit) bearer of "female wisdom."[35] Like Circe, Tarsiana's hair grows to endow her with new powers. In her bag she holds an apple, the sign of her status as new Eve, undoer of paternal sacred textuality, shaper of revised texts, both sacred and profane.

Tarsiana's posture vis-à-vis her textual heritage and the writing process links up with and expands other narrative strategies we have observed thus far. The defiance of Tarsiana and her accomplices seeks to displace frozen idols and replace them with transformational, dynamic signs of a new female-defined textuality. These moves continue to affirm, by analogy, how the woman writer and *her* accomplices can perform the multiple disruptions of first "refusing the authority of the already signified," and then changing the rules of the game to break previously forged narrative chains.[36] As we have seen, Gómez Ojea is a veteran of these strategies, having already engaged in them in her previous narrative, *Otras mujeres y Fabia,* wherein matrilineal narrative links are created among women across broad expanses of time. We also discovered how Carme Riera's *Una primavera para Domenico Guarini* agonizes and provokes woman into seizing her own word, and how Lourdes Ortiz's *Urraca* retells history through the displacement of partial or inaccurate accounts with revised perspectives. Undoubtedly all writers seek to write the previously unwritten, yet today's women writers often add other, more specific concerns of their own. Their position as generic other, consigned to the margins of paternal or patriarchal discourse, often pushes them to deconstruct the barriers that have historically excluded them. But what is so delightfully different about the parody and defiance in Díaz-Mas's *El rapto del santo grial* and Gómez Ojea's *Los perros de Hécate* is that their particular forms of subversion have added yet another dimension to an already dynamic process of articulation in Spanish women's narrative. While these texts (as the narratives of the preceding chapter) effect a replacement of inherited limitations with something more capable of speaking directly—and often unabashedly—of the potential of woman's own desire, they do so with a wit and humor that render anything other than irreverence potentially suspect. Amid the sounds of their salutory mockery, the gloom of tradition appears henceforth, and in no small measure, silly.

7

Beyond the Father
Desire, Ambiguity, and Transgression in the Narrative of Adelaida García Morales

> Era un lugar fantástico. . . . (It was a fantastic place. . . .)
> —Adelaida García Morales, *El sur*

Lest we naively believe that the strategies of rewriting and subversion discussed in the previous chapters have erased all traces of paternal discourse, and that now the woman writer can be free from all restrictions to articulate as she will, we need only read the narratives of Adelaida García Morales to rediscover the lingering ghosts of patriarchy or the insinuating presence of the paternal sacrificial contract. But still, though situated in the delicate position of writing in spite of and around the intimidating ghosts of the symbolic, this woman writer seeks out the interstitial spaces where other ghosts might be enlisted for her own project. In this way the woman writer fights ghost with ghost, employing strategies of the fantastic to engage the phantoms in their own language. The subversive gesture of this kind of text acquires the uncanny capacity to slip and slide among layers of culture and the imagination. The ambiguity of the phantasmal becomes woman's very strategy for textual and cultural transgression.

García Morales has created fictional worlds in *El Sur*, *Bene* and *El silencio de las sirenas* that are both of and beyond what is most familiar to their readers. *El Sur* and *Bene*'s domestic confines are situated on a lonely stretch of road, cut off from village or town. The village of *El silencio* is similarly secluded, perched among the surrounding peaks of Las Alpujarras. Silence reigns over these isolated spaces, and into the gaps left by the absence of speech, the whispers of ghosts and the spirits of the past insinuate themselves. The listeners of these voices of silence are three young women whose characters closely resemble one another, especially in their almost absolute physical and ontological solitude. Theirs is an introverted, internalized world—even a confining and restricted one—and whatever they tell us about the world beyond them becomes colored and shaped by their solitary imaginations. In the narrative space of *El Sur, Bene,* and *El silencio* there hovers a lurking presence of unspecified evil and intimations of prohibited desire. Allusions to incestuous desire link Adriana of *Sur* and Angela and Bene of *Bene,* and strange psychic powers and evil spells surround the obsessive passion of Elsa of *El silencio.* Into this rarefied atmosphere, ghosts of fathers, lovers, and father/lovers seem to emerge uncannily; they float in rhetorical ambiguity, evading attempts to grasp at them and confine them as the either/ or of reality or fantasy. Even the young narrators or protagonists (Adriana, Angela, Bene, and Elsa) are at times seen as monsters, to be pitied, yet to have no lasting place in a world only reluctantly tolerant of the elusive, the unmanageable, the unclassifiable, and most disconcertingly, the inexplicable.

If anything is clear, the narrative worlds of Adelaida García Morales exhibit the now familiar characteristics of the unfamiliar worlds of fantastic literature. Many of the recurrent features of the fantastic that Tzvetan Todorov has classified and analyzed are present in the narratives that receive our attention in this chapter. The events of all three texts take place in what Todorov has called the "duration of uncertainty," the temporal-spatial realm in which the need to choose between the natural and the supernatural is often held in abeyance.[1] The reader is thus obliged to hesitate between opposing explanations of occurrences, the rhetorical ambiguity of the fantastic text rendering such options untenable. On this ambiguous middleground, then, the narratives of García Morales as fantastic texts examine "desire in its excessive forms," and "preoccupations concerning death [and] life after death are linked to the theme of love."[2] These themes of the fantastic identified by Todorov are also those that link *El sur, Bene,* and *El silencio de las sirenas* into a series of interconnected narratives that defy the logical structuring of desire.

The narrative strategies of García Morales might be sufficiently served if we were to analyze them solely in terms of Todorov's catalog of structural and thematic attributes characterizing the fantastic. However, without reference to cultural implications of the fantastic, this reading could only partially address how the strategies of fantastic discourse serve also as a means whereby today's woman writer challenges her readers to reassess their cultural positioning. The fantastic has long been repressed and marginalized and for good reason:[3] it characteristically operates outside dominant value systems, subverting laws and beliefs that seek to insure cultural order and established ideological hegemony.[4] If the fantastic is a literature of desire—which Todorov establishes and Rosemary Jackson reaffirms—it is so primarily because it dares to articulate the unsaid or give voice to that which is customarily prohibited by culture.[5] The fantastic therefore violates "normal" or common sense perspectives as it insists on its discourse of transgressive desire. To achieve this disconcerting mode of articulation, practices such as sadism, incest, necrophilia, murder, and eroticism recur as themes structuring interrelationships and ultimately the text itself. Recurrent motifs like ghosts, shadows, vampires, werewolves, partial selves, reflections, enclosures, monsters, beasts, cannibals all serve to erase rigid markers of dream and reality, gender and genre.[6] The presence of cultural prohibitions thus assails the reader into perceiving reality as shifting—perhaps even shifty—and by no means predictable and stable.

As indicated by Jackson, one of the ways in which women writers have employed the fantastic is "to subvert patriarchal society— the symbolic order of modern culture."[7] The female narrators of García Morales must, of course, also grapple with this symbolic order, for that cultural given presents itself over and over again as the unavoidable hurdle for all writing. Yet as woman seeks to convert the content of her imagination into the symbolic order of culture, her desire collides repeatedly with the contradictory tensions of the text. Her gender inflected voicing may elicit costly negotiations. One way out of entirely sacrificing her imaginary realm for the strictures of the symbolic is to opt for a rhetoric of ambiguity. Though such a posture is by no means gender specific, it is one effective way woman can elude the often rigid demands of the symbolic order. With this in mind, along with Andrés Amorós's conclusion that "lo fantástico supone, desde luego, el deseo de profundizar en la realidad para captar sus estratos más íntimos" (the fantastic assumes, after all, the desire to delve into reality to capture its most intimate levels),[8] I should like to read, by means of the narratives of García Morales, how the cultural dis-ease often felt by contemporary woman may inscribe itself into the ambiguous and transgressive fantastic text.

I shall approach García Morales's texts as a continuum, guided by the central concerns of each: my reading of *El Sur* will trace the seductive power of the paternal enigma and the Father's Law, discourses that initially hold the daughter's desire in their sway; reading *Bene* will reveal another insistence on the ambiguity of desire as, this time, the enigma of the mysterious housemaid is left elliptically incomplete; and finally, *El silencio de las sirenas* will be read as a meditation on the sources, processes, and pitfalls of love story writing, as woman attempts to negotiate the treacherous terrain between the Symbolic Order and her imagination. In all three texts the power of the paternal (symbolic/sacrificial) contract is finally elided/eluded and left stealthily on the margins of the narratives' discourse.

> It is his desire which prescribes the force, the shape, the modes, etc. of the law he lays down or passes on, a law that reduces to the state of "fantasy" the little girl's seduced and rejected desire—a desire still faltering, barely articulate, silent perhaps, or expressed in signs, a desire that must be seduced to the discourse and law of the father.
> —Luce Irigaray, *Speculum of the Other Woman*

Every daughter is "daddy's girl." Sooner or later every female becomes enfolded into the embrace of her father's discourse. She absorbs its terms perhaps unconsciously, and so her utterances may seem entirely her own. Yet at some time her search for self-articulation must at least attempt to come to terms with this invasion, or perhaps less sensationally, this permeation. *El Sur* (South) is the story of just such a reckoning.

Narrated by the daughter, Adriana, and addressed to the deceased father, *El Sur* recounts the narrator's formative years under the authority of her father, his suicide, and her later investigation into the nature of his secret past life. Through the course of the daughter's maturation and investigation the father loses his apparently magical powers and takes on more human proportions. He acquires poignancy as one who has made mistakes and paid dearly for them, but if he begins as an enigma for his daughter ("para mí eras un enigma" [you were an enigma to me]),[9] he is never fully clarified. As García Morales herself has observed, the figure of the father remains "de una manera ambigua, conflictiva" (in a certain way ambiguous, conflictive).[10] In his ambiguity, he reflects the daughter's own ambivalent attitude toward him, for though she comes to understand her father better, understanding is somehow not sufficient ("comprender no era suficiente") (51). Like the masked image in an old photo, the father can never be fully revealed; something deeper remains hidden and continues to insinuate itself uncannily into the deeper levels of the daughter's consciousness. Desire for (and through) the father, in spite of his betrayal, leaves its mark upon the daughter and her text.]

During her early childhood, the daughter was at odds with others in her perception of the father. She endowed him with magical powers ("pensaba entonces que tú eras un mago" [I thought then that you were a magician]) (5), but between the father and the women of his household, there was great enmity. The mother complained of isolation and imprisonment, while the daughter was oblivious to the suffering of other females under the aegis of paternal rule. For her, the father signified nothing less than a tender and luminous presence. Mesmerized by the pendulum that functioned as the external signifier of the father's power and authority, Adriana believed she shared his magical powers. She was even seduced or reduced into accepting her own virtual imprisonment—her father prohibited her from attending school—perhaps as an oblique sign of her privileged status within the hierarchical disposition of paternal law.

The narration by Adriana of her childhood feelings toward her father are revealing to the reader, even if they remain for her the blind spot of her captivity and her text. We see how she placed the father-daughter bond beyond the familiar and normal, or into what seemed the space of the fantastic: their special union was "familiar y mágica a un tiempo" (at once familiar and magical) (16). She was seduced by their eerie sharing of prohibition: "me sentía hermanada contigo en aquello que teníamos en común: el mal" (I felt joined to you in that which we shared in common: evil) (16). She felt the frightening thrill of her transgressive posture reconfirmed by those outside the magical circle: her mother's gaze was like a mirror that reflected "aquel monstruo que ya veía yo aparecer en mi interior" (that monster which I already saw appear inside me) (15). At that time the daughter perceived her father as the transgressor of traditional gender identity—in the traditionally maternal role of comforter offering unconditional love— while others—females—ironically appeared censorious. She could not see that she was being set up for an eventual fall, that the father was hiding behind his enigma and would be unable to tolerate such challenges to traditional paternal law.

Things inevitably change, then, as Adriana's narrative follows the master plot for female development. The father-daughter bond has to be broken, at least from the father's side. Prohibition has to be invoked. The father's imposition of silence on the household becomes all enveloping, finally not even exempting or privileging the daughter. A family secret that definitively separates the spouses (something to do with a woman from the past) also severs the secret bond between father and daughter. Still, while rhetorical ambiguity veils the ghosts of desire past ("silencios tensos, palabras con segundas intenciones" [tense silences, words with double meanings]) (25), it fails to erase the daughter's desire for her father: "me sabía tu cómplice y eso me acercaba de nuevo a ti" (I was convinced I was your accomplice and that drew me closer to you) (26). To borrow from the words of Jane Gallop: "the daughter's desire for her father is desperate".[11] She is reluctant to give up his discourse, whatever form it may take.

More than ever Adriana wants to fill herself with the father's texts and find words to bridge the gap that divides them: "libros, cuadernos, carpetas. Deseaba tanto leerlas" (books, notebooks, folders. I wanted so much to read them) (26). His texts—his discourse—seduce her in his absence, for physically he has already abandoned her: "sentí que me habías abandonado" (I felt you had abandoned me) (27). Sometimes he returns, but he imposes severe prohibitions: "imponiéndome brutalmente unas normas rígidas" (brutally imposing rigid rules) (31). As a result, she hates him and desires him at once: "surgió en mí un amago de odio hacia ti. Entonces tuve un deseo: casarme contigo" (signs of hatred loomed up in me. At that time I had one desire: to marry you) (31, 34). Hatred and incestuous longings well up simultaneously for ambivalence becomes the only possible response to paternal evasion, but finally the possibility of dialogue or closeness between father and daughter is ruptured definitively. The father commits suicide.

Unable to bear her loss, the daughter again invokes the fantastic and erases the distinction between this world and the next: "en un acto supremo de voluntad decidí no creer en la muerte. Tú existirías siempre (in an act of supreme will power I decided to not believe in death. You would exist always) (38). Though she newly desires closeness with her widowed and unloved mother, some obscure force still divides them: "deseé acercarme a ella, pero me sentí paralizada" (I wished to approach her, but I felt paralyzed) (39). The unnamed ghost of the father separates mother and daughter (at least for the moment) and impels the daughter to reject all signs of division between life and death. Here the fantastic seems to underwrite the persistence of the daughter's unholy desire. As a result, she is driven to seek the father still further among traces he left behind in the city of his past, Sevilla.

But Sevilla provides other texts from other perspectives, texts that begin to rupture the obsessive desire of the daughter, texts of Gloria Valle (the other woman), Emilia (a "medium"), and Miguel (Gloria's son and Adriana's half-brother). These other voices serve to weaken and destabilize the absolute hold of paternal discourse on the daughter. By chance, Adriana discovers the letters of Gloria Valle, writings that hold answers to the secret of the father's other life. From Gloria's differing point of view, they tell a story of abandonment, of the father's cynical insensitivity to Gloria's plight, of Gloria's strength and bravery. They imply to the daughter the abandonment of both families, a kind of infinitely reversible "Catch 22" in which two women, son, and daughter were all the objects of the father's brooding manipulations. Adriana discovers a situation, then, which the silent enigmatic father never fully disclosed and one which the daughter ironically never suspected: "Yo sabía tan poco de tí" (I knew so little about you) (42).

In the role of medium, the old housemaid, Emilia, conjures up another aspect of the past. Telling of the father's childhood and youth, she evokes for the daughter the "living ghost" (45) of the father. And Miguel, the father's abandoned son, writes a diary on the margins of paternal discourse: "la imagen de un padre era algo extraño e innecesario para él" (the image of a father was something strange and unnecessary for him) (47). The father is thus never fully unveiled by these "Sevillan texts," but their pieces of ambiguity assemble a puzzle that begins to reshape the dead father's image. The daughter discovers the cynic, the coward, the man forever hidden by a carnival mask. This is enough to restore the threshold dividing the living from the dead. The revelations of those from the past sufficiently alter the paternal enigma to drive a wedge between father and the daughter's desire: "Y en este escenario fantasmal de nuestra vida en común, ha sobrevivido tu silencio y también, para mi desgracia, aquella separación última entre tú y yo que, con tu muerte, se ha hecho insalvable y eterna" (And in the phantasmal scene of our shared life, your silence has survived, and to my dismay, [so has] that ultimate separation between you and me, which with your death, has become insurmountable and eternal) (52). Thus read the final words of the daughter's narrative and the end of her epistle to a father who finally is allowed to grow silent and die.

The ending of *El Sur* is painful; its sense of total loss is profound. Yet this dismal conclusion nevertheless seems hopeful; this pain seems to promise birth and rebirth. Why? How? Let us consider this: besides its links with the fantastic, *El Sur* has much that recalls the Gothic novel. The enclosure of female figures in a gloomy space controlled by masculine authority and desire; the existence of a mysterious family secret; the daughter's ambivalent fear and desire of a paternal figure who confines her along with a maternal figure who shifts between nurturance and indifference: these are familiar themes of the Gothic that reappear in *El Sur*.[12] Like the traditional Gothic, *El Sur* moves toward the release of its captive females, the explication of the family secret, and the freeing of the daughter from danger and unholy desire. As the following analysis of Rafael Llopis coincidentally reconfirms, the novel ends in a way characteristic of the Gothic: "el mundo del padre, deseado en la infancia y rechazado definitivamente en la juventud, se convierte en un mundo arcaico y corrompido pero amenazador . . . la mujer se erija en figura racional, como portadora de luz contra las sombras de un pasado exclusivamente varonil (the world of the father, desired in childhood and definitively rejected in youth, transforms into an archaic, corrupt, and menacing world . . . woman rises as a rational figure, as the bearer of light against the shadows of an exclusively masculine past).[13] When Adriana raises the "círculo luminoso de mi linterna" (the luminous circle of my lantern) (52) to light the abandoned objects of her dead father, she performs the same ritual of separation and renewal. This rebirth implicitly frees her to establish future bonds and articulate other discourses outside the restrictive boundaries of the Father's Law.

After the father's death, when Adriana's mother is released to visit Santander and the daughter decides to make her pilgrimage to Sevilla, there is some promise of rapprochement between mother and daughter. The gap left by the father's absence opens the possibility that in the future it may be filled with a newly forged bond between mother and daughter. And in Sevilla, the daughter's incestuous longing for the father is displaced by Miguel's attraction to Adriana. Though she escapes from her half-brother's physical presence, she leaves a note that she loves him, confusedly beginning to shift the locus of her desire away from the father. Though the half-brother might seem another forbidden object, its importance as a sign for change nevertheless derives from its position outside the ambit of the Father's Law. Miguel is the product of an exclusively maternal world ("aquel mundo que Gloria Valle había tejido para vuestro hijo" [that world that Gloria Valle had woven for your son]) (51). If Adriana tries to insure the permanence of her half-brother's desire, she is, in this sense, creating the inverse of the prohibition that tormented her. By setting up an(other) transgression—the image of a union defying the paternal prohibition—she creates a signifier perhaps more friendly to the expression of female or feminine desire.[14] As Jane Gallop has concluded: when woman's complicity with father-love is curtailed, then she may "rediscover some feminine desire, some desire for a masculine body that does not respect the Father's law."[15] The desire to insure her continued presence—spiritually if not physically—within the aura of the brother's maternal "atmósfera de encantamiento" (magical atmosphere) (52) is thus born of a separation from the father's house of the dead. In the luminous circle of her lantern's light, Adriana bids farewell to the abandoned objects (the signs of death) of her father and places herself metonymically into the realm of the maternal fantastic. The paternal affair has ended.

> Transgression belongs neither to day nor to night. . . . No before, no during, no afterwards. It is as if it were another region, a place different from all places.
> —Maurice Blanchot, *Le pas au-delà*

Opening *Bene* is a dream sequence in which the first person narrator, Angela, addresses her brother, Santiago. She dreams of him walking at her side through a eucalyptus grove, having returned to stay with her. They see Bene, their housemaid, holding a missal with the burnt imprint of a human hand on its cover. The brother then disappears, leaving the narrator alone with Bene. Bene's eyes blaze intensely and the narrator attempts to flee. Instead, as a result of her exertion, the dreamer awakens without having solved the mystery of Bene's sudden departure. Outlined thus is the enigmatic axis of this novella. In keeping with the volume's title, *El Sur seguido de Bene (South Followed by Bene),* an enigma continues to structure this narrative, though now its locus shifts from the paternal figure to that of a woman named Bene. The narrator's desire continues to fix itself implicitly upon a fraternal object, Santiago. This highly charged first passage thus "dreams" its reader into a strange and uncanny realm of prohibitions and concealed desires. Bene somehow threatens disruption of the established order. Here, at least, her association with the burnt holy book casts her as a fearful accomplice in some unholy desecration of consecrated textuality. Yet, as will the entire text, the oneiric passage refuses to solve its enigma. A microstructure of what follows, the opening dream inscribes a rhetoric and structure unceasingly protective of its ambiguous undecidability.[16]

Much like Adriana of *El Sur, Bene*'s Angela is an isolated young adolescent. During the time of the narrated events, age and education began to separate the girl and her older brother whose intimacy she desperately desired. Angela was rarely able to experience life except as it passed by on the lonely road beyond her iron gate enclosure. Bulls frequently passed, flaunting their powerful masculine gait. Caravans of silent gypsies passed, wordlessly signifying ethnic and class differences, unspoken dimensions beyond the girl's economically privileged yet highly restricted world. The spatial disposition of the girl's sphere vis-à-vis the outside world thus establishes at the outset of the novella a world of gender and class divisions, a world that exerts great power over the narrator's imagination and an uneasiness that can only intimate the unsaid regions of culture.

The culture underlying the girl's observations is thus understated, implied, and part of the perplexing nature of her perspective. She can only describe what she sees, and that from the point of view of one for whom reality has been consistently censored and repressed. As a result, the narrator's observations of Bene reflect that same hesitancy or incertitude: Bene's expression has something "indefinible, inaprehensible" (indefinable, inapprehensible) to it,[17] and the death-like mask that suddenly clouds Bene's visage lies beyond the narrator's powers of description; it is "inexplicable" (61). Similarly, Bene's widely dissimilar reactions to the conditions of her servitude (from authoritative self-possession to complete helplessness before her employer) may say as much about the narrator and her text as about the character. Unnameable fears and unspoken impotence link the child narrator and her family's new servant: both are marginal, both "déclassé" because of gender, age, and in Bene's case, class. Either or both lie outside the boundaries of cultural certainties; the narrator, as a female child without authority, is denied the position of unequivocal purveyor of truth.

Others in the household suspect Bene of some heinous past, and their rhetoric, in contrast to Angela's, is more like that of the governess in *Turn of the Screw*. Aunt Elisa and Doña Rosaura, each in her way, would impose what Shoshana Felman has called "the vulgar, literal and unambiguous" on their textualizations of the enigmatic Bene.[18] When Angela reflects upon Aunt Elisa's suspicions of Bene, her words seek to reflect the degree to which Elisa reduces the ambiguity of her subject: "tía Elisa dudaba de la bondad de Bene o, más bien, estaba convencida de su maldad" (aunt Elisa doubted the goodness of Bene or, rather, she was convinced of her evil) (63). While Angela produces a text that privileges ambiguity and "won't tell" (in the manner of Felman's James), Elisa reduces rhetoric and seeks to repress the chances of uncertainty. Her moral vision is largely restricted to concerns about her widowed brother's amorous exploits, but professorial doña Rosaura warns Elisa about less visible sources of Bene's putative evil. Doña Rosaura's reality lies on the other side of Todorov's schema; she is convinced that Bene's dead lover/father was a demon and that he still holds Bene in his power. She cannot accept the "duration of uncertainty" of the fantastic, but seeks to convince Elisa of the certainty of supernatural presence. As Angela explains, the language of doña Rosaura "parecía destinado sólo a nombrar lo obvio" (seemed destined only to name the obvious) (68), and though Angela finds doña Rosaura's bold assertions compelling, her own observations of Bene cause her to hesitate before the others' rhetorical certainty: "no podía concebir que anidara en ella algo tan terrible como insinuaban las palabras y las voces temerosas de aquellas mujeres" (I couldn't conceive that she harbored something so terrible as the words and fearful voices of those women insinuated) (68). Something beyond articulation links Angela with Bene in a realm similarly outside the "literal and unambiguous."

Bene and the children have a custom of picnicking in some nearby eucalyptus groves. These excursions give rise to more contradictory feelings, for while Bene brings along delicious desserts and serves them attractively, some incomprehensible tension (at least for Angela) grips the threesome. Santiago, as he becomes more estranged from his sister, seems to share in some uncanny conspiracy with Bene. And when Bene suddenly dons her death-like expression, Angela is further repelled and frightened. Something here lies beyond the girl's capacity to understand and articulate. That inexplicable and unnameable something that drains Bene's countenance and leaves upon her a look of death-like suspension in "un extraño sueño de encantamiento" (a strange dream of enchantment) (87), recalls the mysterious, inexplicable force that overcomes the schoolgirls in Peter Weir's 1975 film *Picnic at Hanging Rock*. Does a spirit similar to the one that haunts and bewitches the girls of that film exercise a similar force here on Bene and Angela? Does that unnamed and elusive disrupter of an arid Australian Victorian order similarly insinuate itself into the patriarchal bourgeoisie of Spain's similarly arid Extremadura in the guise of Bene and her phantom lover? Bene's haunting by the doomed ghost of her gypsy lover also recalls the irresistible pull of the ghostly lover in de Falla's *El amor brujo*

(*Bewitched Love*). Do both ghosts say something about man's possessive hold on woman, even after death? The questions suggested by these intertextual echoes all point to cultural and sexual forces that evade the mastery of direct and unequivocal replies.

More and more Bene comes to occupy the region of these and other unanswered questions. When she is missing from her bedroom, she may or may not be with the children's father. Her absence is never balanced by an alternate presence, and intimations of adult sexuality remain for the narrator "algo misterioso y casi diabólico" (something mysterious and almost diabolical) (73). Expectedly, Angela's conjecture about the compelling enigma of her father's pleasures is followed by the apparition outside her window. As in *The Turn of the Screw,* unnamed sexual desire apparently transforms into fantasmal signs visible only to those for whom sexuality is still repressed in ignorance or irresolution (Angela, the governess).

The sign of sexuality, the least verbal in *Bene,* is nevertheless the most pervasive as it is the most elusive. After the father leaves the household on one of his customary "pleasure" trips, he leaves a vacuum into which Santiago is drawn. Angela has already observed Bene's signs of seduction on the picnics ("los detalles de seducción que ella dirigía a mi hermano" [the details of seduction that she directed at my brother]) (83). But as the separation between brother and sister becomes definitive in the father's absence, it seems to Angela that her brother has fallen completely under Bene's spell. She sees him as a body without a soul, one whose love was like "una posesión sobrehumana" (a superhuman possession) (99). In a kind of oedipal displacement for both children, Bene comes to occupy the place of rival, the mature woman whose powers appear as superhuman or even supernatural to the young girl. Angela is no match for adult sexuality, and the brother slips entirely out of her range: "tu olvido de mí era irremediable" (your obliviousness to me was irremediable) (98). The thwarting of Angela's incestuous desires is somehow transferred and translated into Santiago's uncanny necrophilia, an amorous desire on his part that seems to come from "la misma muerte" (death itself) (99). One transgression is thus subsumed into another while sexuality continues to function as a negation of rhetorical and implicitly cultural restraints.

Something unspeakable lies always beyond the boundaries of the household gates. Try as she might, when Angela attempts to pry information from her poor friend and Bene's sister, Juana, she is thwarted. The barriers of class and privilege separating them perforce separate their very use of language, so Angela can never solve the enigma of the "other side." Juana only reinforces the enigma of Bene, reaffirms her sister's difference ("no es como los demás" (she is not like others) (81); and Juana's later insinuations about Bene's work (she supported the family) and love life (it was said Bene had many sweethearts) only play against the reader's most conventional expectations and prejudices. Sexual innuendos and rumors, things that people say, might simply be based on cultural divisions and bias: "la gente es muy mala y odia a los gitanos" (people are evil and hate the gypsies) (94). Bene's putative evil may be entirely "positional," coinciding, as Jameson has observed, "with categories of Otherness."[19] As Juana refuses to surrender all the secrets of her class to Angela— virtually her only possessions—she insists upon her right to conceal ("se negaba a revelarme algo . . . era como si se le hubiera impuesto la sagrada obligación de ocultarme algo" [she refused to reveal something to me . . . it was as if someone had imposed on her a sacred obligation to conceal something from me]) (92). That obligation to conceal is Juana's right to self-protection. The narrator's inability to ascertain secrets and share her own uncertainties reaffirms once again the text's refusal to bow before the interrogations of cultural dominance and reduce its rhetoric to simple or comfortable answers.

In spite of prohibitions by those who would seek to master meaning by keeping the inexplicably demonic at bay—doña Rosaura with her "no te asomes a la cancela, ni hables con desconocidos . . . no escuches ni mires a nadie" (don't appear at the gate, don't talk to strangers . . . don't listen to nor gaze at anyone) (99)—the signs of the Other or the gypsy apparition multiply. Even closed doors become ineffective barriers against the forbidden; having lost their capacity to cordon off the culturally undesirable, they have become permeable. As meaning thus splits and divides and the sole source of it resides in the narrator's and reader's reception of the phenomena, the only precise, unquestionable thing is the narrator's panic: "sus señales eran inaprehensibles. Sólo mi pánico era preciso, incuestionable" (his signs were inapprehensible. Only my panic was precise, unquestionable) (101). Even the narrator herself is decentered, deprived of ontological certainty: "ya no sabía quién era él ni tampoco quién era yo" (by now I didn't know who he was nor even who I was) (101–2). Uncertainty and ambiguity intensify.

The horrified household finally expels Bene, and Santiago joins her. However, two weeks later he is returned forcibly by civil guards, and Angela is delighted to have him to herself again. Soon the veil protecting Santiago's secret return and Angela's pleasure is removed by Aunt Elisa, who demands a full accounting of Santiago's activities: "que me vas a contar todo lo que ha pasado con esa fulana" (you're going to tell me everything that went on with that hussy) (107). Occupying a position similar to that of the governess in *The Turn of the Screw*, Aunt Elisa attempts to grasp at meaning; her suspicions demand interpretation, a posture that can result only in suffocating, stifling, and killing the ambivalence before her. Her insistence on resolving the enigma of Santiago's flight has as its sole consequence a reactive stance by Santiago: his total self-enclosure into a realm of silence and, finally, death. Like the text itself, Santiago refuses to surrender to easy explanations. Santiago's need for "silencio total" (total silence) (110) mirrors what Felman has called the "reserve of silence" or that which literature is incapable of speaking (or refuses to disclose).[20] The narrator, too, surrenders to a kind of death, a perfect blackness, in her ostensible desire to join the brother, and in so doing she recapitulates his challenge to a unified, unequivocal reality. By embracing death, or a kind of ghostly semblance of death, the fraternal pair underscore the text's insistence on its culturally transgressive role.

As the ghost, that indeterminate specter of meaning hovers in our minds, we realize that what we have just "witnessed" (read) is the unnameable, elusive slippery stuff that is the "bogeyman" of all writing, most especially that of women. The "ghost" is that which defies articulation, try as the narrator might to join the ranks of the sensible majority. But the marginal element—the female, the child, the underclass—is never guaranteed such a comfortable cultural position. The job of the ghost story writer is, then—as Jackson suggests—to "make visible that which is culturally invisible and which is written out as negation and as death."[21] (In *Bene* those areas of invisibility are disclosed by the ghostly apparitions, the brother's death, and Angela's figurative death.) Most importantly, as Jackson continues, "the cultural, or countercultural, implications of this assertion of nonsignification are far-reaching, for it represents a dissolution of a culture's signifying practice, the very means by which it establishes meaning."[22] To voice such a horror as a woman is to transgress to "another region," by fleeing the circle of determinate meaning that culture underwrites by force of its (patriarchal or paternal) Law.

They no longer had any desire to allure; all that they wanted
was to hold as long as they could the radiance that fell from
Ulysses' great eyes.
                           —Franz Kafka, "The Silence of the Sirens"

The mountainous world of *El silencio de las sirenas (The Silence of the Sirens)* is another solitary and isolated place in the words of the novel's narrator: strange, atemporal, silent. Here, in the harshness of village life, hardy widows live stoically beyond desire, and the presence of ghosts is just as natural as the breath of the living. Into this space, far from urban culture and within the shadowy presence of exotic Africa, comes María to serve as teacher. More important than María's ostensible professional function in the village is her role as ad hoc hypnotist of Elsa, another outsider, who is experiencing a deeply passionate love for a man she hardly knows. With María's regular assistance, Elsa tells and increasingly embellishes her account of love, eventually transforming it into a nineteenth-century romantic fiction.

El silencio de las sirenas thus tells an old story from a new angle: this love story is as much a meditation on its generation as on the nature of love itself. Though Peter Brooks reminds us that "texts are always implicitly or even explicitly addressed to someone," *El silencio*'s explicit use of the Lacanian "dimension of dialogue" makes of it a self-reflective text in ways that *Sur* and *Bene* are not.[23] While Adriana's epistle to her deceased father and Angela's recounting of a dream and reflections to her late brother express at least one side of the dialogic transaction, *El silencio* depends for its very existence on multiple dialogues. María draws out the threads of Elsa's tale, playing at analyst and enthralled by her role as interlocutor. She also transmits, comments upon, and rewrites Elsa's notebooks. Multiple as is María's "intervention" in Elsa's narrative (as Brooks might call such a role),[24] it facilitates the text's "transference" and contributes to its interpretation. This collaborative enterprise of two women is consequently rich in implications about the sources, processes, and pitfalls of love story writing (and living) for women.

Prompted by Lacan, Shoshana Felman asks if all stories, all narratives imply a transferential structure, that is a love-relation that both organizes and disguises, deciphers and enciphers them.[25] While Felman's question or hypothesis is more a rhetorical introit to *The Turn of the Screw* than a firmly answerable proposition, it serves us well here as a suggestive entrance to *El silencio*. Elsa is blatant in her affirmation of the "love-relation" structuring her narrative. Even more, in her notebook she interrogates the process whereby imagined love becomes a more potent organizer of her narrative than anything she has actually experienced: "Me pregunto cómo pueden los sueños tejer una historia que me va enredando más que la vida misma" (I ask myself how dreams can weave a story that ensnares me more than life itself).[26] She also ponders the sources of her imagery: "Y me pregunto también de dónde provienen estas imágenes" (And I also ask myself where these images are coming from) (51). One answer to her queries precedes the questions themselves: "he visto y ahora ensueño" (I saw and now I envision) (51). By the end of her notebook entry, she realizes that an initial visual experience has taken on its greatest power within her imagination.[27]

At the same time Elsa is impelled to enunciate the content of that imagination—her desire—and must resort to enciphering its imagery through the mediating function of the Symbolic Order. Elsa's powerlessness to name this ("esto") that is more than love ("no sé qué nombre dar" [I don't know how to name it]) (52), articulates the difficulty of applying the Symbolic Order to the Imaginary. Worse still, as Juliet Flower MacCannell reminds us, crossing over into the symbolic often entails a sacrificial positioning for woman. But has she another option? Perhaps, in her desire to bridge the alienating gap between the two orders, she may attempt to position herself astride them; for woman may imagine herself, as MacCannell through Kristeva has advocated, "at the threshold between the imaginary and the symbolic."[28] Elsa and María's collaboration temporarily achieves this synthesis, but ultimately the project miscarries.

To achieve and maintain this position is demanding since the Symbolic Order traditionally expects to speak for woman (as we have especially witnessed/heard in chapter 2). If she tries to speak for herself, she may find herself subject to dangerous crosscurrents. Elsa is buffeted in just this way. At one moment, a brief communication between Elsa and Agustín results in her elated recollections of the fullness of language: "no recuerdo en toda mi vida que la palabra hubiera sido algo tan pleno para mí (I don't remember any other time in my life when the word was so full for me) (60–61). She seems to participate fully in the Symbolic Order. Later, however, when Elsa's speech is met with Agustín's indifference and even silence, her discomfiture in this role causes her to rail against the symbolic circumscription of her oddity: "¡No soy un monstruo! ¡No soy un monstruo!" (I am not a monster! I am not a monster!) (62).

Elsa's eccentricities frighten Agustín, and he takes refuge in the
posture of Ulysses: he fills his ears with metaphorical wax, deafen-
ing himself to her words. To him, Elsa's expression of desire seems
the traditional siren's call: seductive and treacherous, outside the
security of his symbolic boundaries. The novel's allusion to Kafka
suggests, however, that the sirens are not as menacing as Agustín's
fears might portray them. Admittedly the sirens of Kafka are
silent; initially they seem to wield a power outside language or the
symbolic. Yet, as Ulysses eludes them, they lose their desire to
allure. They instead fall dependent on the hero's radiance (a
metaphorical projection of the symbolic) in the same paradoxical
gesture which is that of the woman who seeks to write. If Kafka's
sirens could speak, their words might lament how woman, desir-
ing to speak (or write), is necessarily and eventually captivated by
the Symbolic Order, but then regarded by it as a monster and
named accordingly. Elsa, as another casualty of the symbolic's fear
and flight from woman's discursive eccentricities, finds her desire
ignored, frustrated and even misread.[29] Her difference is regarded as aberrant.

Still, as in García Morales's other narratives, the monstrosity of
El silencio's encipherment is underwritten by a layering of fantastic
elements in the text, thus rendering it transgressive as well as
sacrificial. The village setting, the presence of magic and ghostly
echoes in Matilde's (an older village woman's) rituals and stories,
and not of least importance the collaboration between María and
Elsa produce levels of strangeness that make the monstrosity of
Elsa's desire more poignant and subversively suggestive than if it
were solely the consequence of Agustín's personal misreading. Its
transgressive attributes resist absolute containment within the
sharply etched contours of the symbolic. Even when Elsa's notebook shifts from the village to Venice, that setting is also phantasmal and ghostly. There, too, the lover emerges as a product of
fantastic space, as an emanation of the imaginary and its unauthorized desire.

Yet, the transgressive seems constantly assailed by the sacrificial, for while Elsa writes in Venice, she feels herself a monstrous
siren again, deciphering her feeling as a sign announcing the
impossibility of physical or concrete union with her lover. Elsa's
problematical dependence on the wary dispositions of her lover—
with the recurrent feelings of monstrosity that such a position of
dependence on his symbolic power implies—may well double as a
subtle sign of the difficulty of woman's writing herself out of her

imaginary and of the chastening consequences that such transgressive moves within the symbolic may summon.

María attempts to act as a kind of midwife for the Symbolic Order, seeking to usher Elsa's imagination into the realm of language. But this ritual or ceremony has its price. Foreshadowings of the sacrifice appear in more and more ornate renderings of the ongoing story. Once Elsa dreams of "Eduardo" (Agustín) receiving a manuscript written by various authors that he will have to rewrite in a different way. Though the dream is set amid the romantic intrigue of late nineteenth-century Germany, Elsa feels "anulada" (annuled) (109) by the mysterious transactions of the dream. Could it be that her collaborative text will eventually be rewritten? Later Elsa records in her notebook that her love cannot be realized in any other way than to be written for Agustín. Somehow as the concrete lover becomes more shadowy, his power over what and how she writes increases. When inquisitorial soldiers pursue her in another dream, she suspends her narration in terrified mystification. Silence is her only escape from these threatening agents of the symbolic. Inexorably, Elsa's estrangement causes her to retreat more and more from word or action: "ella no era capaz de decir, ni de pensar nada" (she was not capable of saying, nor of thinking anything) (132).

María finally urges Elsa to face the prosaic notion that the latter's narrative of love participates in an old literary tradition in which women die or go mad. But Elsa refuses to see her own passion—or the literary models she chooses as vehicles—in such categorical terms. Yet her insistent obsession threatens to obliterate other discursive options. Attempting to wrench Elsa out of her obsession, María reminds her that the tragic love plot "es casi una ley" (is almost a law) (146). Under that portion of the symbolic contract that governs narrative convention in our culture, this "masterplot" has long been customary. There may be no escape once a woman has submitted to it, and Elsa—like Kafka's sirens—has been drawn inexorably into its terms. Eventually, under the provisions of this particular masterplot, Elsa may have to die or go crazy.

And so she does. Elsa becomes but a phantasm occupied by the image of her lover. Having completely internalized him, she herself is nothing. Accordingly, Lacan has voiced such a predicament: as the subject installs his [in this case, her] demand in the Other, "the phantom of the Omnipotence" is introduced.[30] When the concrete "lover" makes his appearance to articulate his stern prohibition of Elsa continuing her communications to him, her sense of selfhood is definitively obliterated. Severing the thin thread of words connecting her to life, Agustín's demand erases Elsa's remaining will to live because she lived to write to, for, and about him. As Elsa's dreams foretold, Agustín effectively ends her text for her and implicitly chooses its inevitable conclusion: insanity *and* death. The plot of *El silencio* is thus signed with a cautionary paradox: to face the inescapable demands of the symbolic may be to eventually cede all, but to shift desire outside the symbolic may be to regress to absolute silence and, in this case, death.

Here the narratives of Adelaida García Morales seem to hang in abeyance, caught in the impasse of this disquieting paradox. The only way out of this impasse would seem to require the non-polarized, unifying richness of the threshold position between the two orders. Though this may prove treacherous and slippery terrain, its successful negotiation may also be the only means to stake a claim on writing and, indeed, on life. Curiously, the chronology of García Morales's writings may offer a clue to this theoretical conundrum and perhaps a model for the woman writer's continued evasion of Ulysses's symbolic scorn. *El silencio* was conceived and its writing was begun in 1979, prior to the beginnings of *El sur* and *Bene* (1981). This chronology of the works' inception, rather than of their publication, might explain why *El silencio* may seem a perplexingly paradoxical regression. It would also allow *El Sur seguido de Bene* the last and more transgressive word in García Morales's defiance of our culture's ordering of the imagination. Through revisions and interrogations of narrative order, and through increasingly fantastic flights of imagination, this writer voices unspoken regions of the culture while she challenges the pitfalls that lie in wait, inevitably, when woman is daring or mad enough to attempt their articulation.

Part Four
Conclusion

8

Rewriting the Future
On the Proliferation and Continuation of Difference

> Insist also and deliberately upon those blanks in discourse
> which recall the places of her exclusion. . . . Reinscribe them
> hither and thither as divergencies.
> —Luce Irigaray, *Speculum of the Other Woman*

Chapter by chapter, the foregoing study discloses intersections as
well as divergencies of discursive concerns and strategies in postwar Spanish narrative by women. The maternal trope that ush-
ered us into these readings may now serve as a summarizing sign
for each text's position in a field of cultural and literary discourses.
Through this sign we are able to review the evolution of our texts
from their anguished absorption of dominant discourses to their
interrogation of them and, finally, to their varied attempts at
evasion.

The double voicing of Laforet's *Nada* invokes a subtle countermove by the mother-daughter dyad against complete absorption
by the dominant paternal or patriarchal discourses of the early
postwar period. From the mother figure, the daughter, as potential writer, receives a legacy of creative language that future
women writers will bring to fuller flower. An absence of the
nonphallocentric maternal trope in Soriano's *La playa de los locos*
and Quiroga's *La enferma* signals an invasive presence of phallocentric and patriarchal discourses and an analogous absence of
an(other) voice, or even, finally, of any voice at all. Later, in
Matute's *La trampa*, a maturing narrator is similarly unable to
assume the powers of Kristeva's nonphallocentric Mother. She, as
other maturing women of the earlier postwar period, occupies a
vexing, shrinking space where the discourses of Others eventually
leave her in multilayered exile and without a voice of her own.

By the seventies, or the period of transition, the maternal is still problematic, but it is interrogated and summoned up as a support for alternative discourses. In Martín Gaite's *Retahílas* motherhood or the maternal is recollected and questioned by the novel's interlocutors through the topics of their oral exchange. Memories of maternal space evoke an alternate textuality, while the role of mother begins to be redefined as new bonds and discourses develop between a mature woman and a young man (in marked contrast to the severed ones in *La trampa*). Through the pair's reassessment of the discourses that have made of them—like their predecessors—a site between contradiction and repression, possibilities for nonpolarized alternatives are suggested in ways that were historically unlikely before. In Martín Gaite's *El cuarto de atrás,* the androgynous nocturnal interlocutor acquires maternal qualities as he provokes and soothes the writer in his role as facilitator of her text. During the same period, Alós's *Os habla Electra* and Tusquets's *El mismo mar de todos los veranos* destabilize archetypes of the patriarchal or phallocentric quest myth with matrilinear or maternal alternatives. These narratives by Martín Gaite, Alós, and Tusquets implicitly counter, then, the ubiquitous discourses of the phallocentric or patriarchal Other that invaded and absorbed the tentative voices of their maturing foremothers in *La playa, La enferma,* and *La trampa.*

Narratives of the post-Franco period are most consistently evasive when challenging the privileges of phallocentric discourse. While *La playa's* protagonist lamented her failure to conform to alien discourses, Riera's *Una primavera para Domenico Guarini* questions the kinds of historical and mythical discourses that caused pain, frustration, and voicelessness in mature foremothers. Allowing for the surfacing and articulation of the nonphallocentric Mother, Riera concedes to the daughter a boldness to assume an(other) discourse. Such links between mother and daughter revisit and widen the open road of *Nada's* ending. Gómez Ojea's *Otras mujeres y Fabia* goes beyond the individual maternal voice to reforge collective matrilinear connections. This novel's single, maturing protagonist is not finished, but instead also embarks upon an open road, reassessing, as did *Una primavera,* the feminine icons of Botticelli. Unlike her narrative foremother in *La playa,* she no longer desires conformity to them. Singleness and maturity in *Una primavera* and *Otras mujeres* thus become newly empowering when connected by the maternal trope to a recuperation of matrilinear history. In Ortiz's *Urraca,* Queen Urraca becomes herself a figure of the Great Mother, recuperating maternal sources of history, language and creative power. Parodic evasion of phallocentric discourses grounded on violence is effected by the maternal trope in Díaz-Mas's *El rapto del Santo Grial*. And the protagonist of Gómez Ojea's *Los perros de Hécate*, another single woman, is empowered with an(other) discourse by means of her connection with Hecate's maternal words of power. Of the most recent narratives, those of García Morales (*El Sur seguido de Bene* and *El silencio de las sirenas*) come closest to being reabsorbed by paternal discourse and the symbolic Order, but they manage, finally, to affirm a transgressive evasiveness through their links with the ambiguity and strangeness of the ghostly fantastic.

A constant disclosed by the maternal trope in these and other texts is woman's desire to rewrite herself out of (discursive) bounds. For obvious cultural and political reasons, this process is articulated during the earlier postwar period with implicit subtlety; more recently, given an opening cultural and political climate, it has acquired a growing urgency and intensity. Also, in this poststructuralist, deconstructionist age, the production of self-conscious writing is almost de rigueur. Still, even in the early postwar years, the novel of adolescence, especially, stands as a metonymic milestone in this process. As *Nada* moved beyond Gothic and Freudian narrative contracts, other novels of female adolescence or development subsequently and similarly charted their transitions from more socially acceptable narrative forms (often the more pleasant, gratifying ones of childhood) to the more disturbing and disruptive ones of the mature woman writer seeking to voice the silenced and unspoken. The remainder of these concluding remarks will briefly survey other texts that also incorporate some of the discursive strategies discovered in these pages, and it will close with an ear poised toward a continuation of such writing in the future.

Other postwar narratives of female adolescence display a self-conscious desire to write and rewrite. Natalia of Martín Gaite's *Entre visillos (Among Window Curtains)* and Marta of Laforet's *La isla de los demonios (The Island of the Demons)* compose diaries. In hers, Natalia attempts to forge an autonomous text as a complement to the prearranged and limited discourses of her provincial patriarchal environment. Marta makes of hers a compendium of demons and legends of the Canary Islands where she has been forced, by historical circumstances and the authority of adults, to take up temporary residence. When Marta becomes conscious of the evil surrounding her, she must relinquish the comforting texts of her childhood and assess her position in a world of conflicting adult (and frequently paternal) discourses. Matia of Ana María Matute's *Primera memoria (First Memory)* also seeks temporary refuge in childhood books and stories until a consciousness of adult cruelty forces her to renounce them: "no existió la Isla de Nunca Jamás y la Joven Sirena no consiguió un alma inmortal" (the Island of Neverever did not exist and the Young Mermaid never got an immortal soul).[1] Matia's diminished childlike qualities and her awakening to the less than magical world of adults make of her "una Alicia un tanto sospechosa" (a somewhat suspicious Alice) (213), thrust out from the security of make-believe and into another field of warring discourses.

The liminality or outsider status of adolescence or youth thus unites many protagonists of the narrative of female adolescence or development in their lone reassessments of hallowed myths, legends, and texts of childhood. Outside the security of the childish imagination, they reluctantly relinquish Anderson, Alice, Peter Pan (Matia), yet they also sense that those adored stories of childhood do not always bode well for young women (Carmen Kurtz's Carla of *Al lado del hombre* [*At Man's Side*] would like to reverse "Beauty and the Beast," and Esther Tusquets does indeed later revise this and other childhood stories in *El mismo mar de todos los veranos*).

Words in themselves, like Lorena's neologisms in Carmen Kurtz's *Cándidas palomas (Innocent Doves)*, encode a growing discursive assertiveness and spiritedness in the narrative of female adolescence during the transition. Though precision in language is sought earlier by Cristina of Concha Alós's *Los cien pájaros (Two in a Bush)*, who searches for "las mejores palabras. Las más claras, las más atractivas" (the best words. The clearest, the most attractive).[2] A desire to voice in the most independent, direct, and exact way is common to these youthful protagonists. *Nada* certainly implies early on that the forcible silencing of women's lips is nothing less than offensive to the young woman. When Andrea goes out with Gerardo, that which characterizes him most is his propensity to speak too much: "Gerardo hablaba tanto . . . hablaba como un libro" (Gerardo spoke so much . . . he spoke like a book) (142). Andrea "iba callada a su lado" (walked silently alongside him) (143). In the oppressive shadow of his "paternales consejos" (paternal advice), Andrea is silenced, dispossessed of her voice. Gerardo imposes his on her. Female lips are silent in the presence of Gerardo; they only serve to be cleaned (when Gerardo cleans the lips of a statue of Venus) or kissed (when Gerardo kisses Andrea for the first time).

The disgust felt by Andrea upon this first kiss implies something beyond the mere physical or psychological revulsion that a young girl may feel upon her first brush with male carnality. It may also serve as a disturbing metaphor for the struggle in which the young woman writer attempts to evade the undesired planting of male lips upon her own; that is, the imposition of men's words (or the paternal symbolic contract) upon her own silent or silenced lips. When Andrea escapes from Gerardo and the imposition of his texts—he spoke citing continuously from books he had read— she escapes metaphorically from the oppression of utterances alien to her own. By reclaiming her right to speak—her own words—she prepares territory for her descendants so that they, too, can revindicate their own autonomous discourse. This is perhaps the least apparent legacy of *Nada*, but it is without doubt the most lasting, the one of most enduring inspiration.

Later mature descendants in narratives about aging are still pulled back by the undertow of alien discourses, but their troubled struggles to articulate persist. Even in recent narratives about aging one can still read the troubling denouement of voicelessness. Elena Quiroga's *Presente profundo (Profound Present)* resonates, in its character Daría, with thematic and theoretical echoes from *La enferma*. This time a mature woman commits suicide in the sea, experiencing her only moment of self-possession as she enters the waves. Before her death she was marginal to events, alienated from her family, and reduced to a silence that is re-emphasized after her death when another village priest attempts to explain how she died. Again, others cannot begin to understand the older woman's untold story of silence and death. Only Soledad, an independent and single woman (perhaps in this way distanced from the power of dominant paternal discourse) attempts to set straight the record about Daría. Martín Gaite's 1976 novel, *Fragmentos de interior (Interior Fragments)*, recalls *Retahílas* in its concern with interlocution. In this later narrative, Agustina— aging and separated from her husband—looks back at letters that have ceased to have meaning. She lives only among old papers that remain frozen in the past without connection to the present. A woman with only one story, she becomes, in maturity, a floating, disembodied voice.

Still, *Nada* and other narratives of female adolescence or development have initiated an unquellable questioning of plots or narrative contracts—juvenile and adult—which may hem-in the spirit, the imagination, indeed, the voice of woman as writer. This quest for other plots is evident in Alós's rejection of a set generic ending for the plot of unwed Cristina's pregnancy in *Los cien pájaros*. Instead of ceding to the traditional narrative contract of sentimental novels ("he llegado incluso a imaginar que me acogería y que, como en las novelas sentimentales, nos casaríamos y llegaríamos a ser felices" [I even began to imagine that he would comfort me and that, as in the sentimental novels, we would be married and find happiness]) (246), Cristina rejects security, the possibility of marriage, and opts to seek the "birds in the bush." Leaving to welcome an uncertain future for herself and her un-born child, Cristina takes a bold step toward an(other) autono-mous maternal discourse, following the legacy of *Nada* and anticipating the decision of *Una primavera*'s Clara.[3]

As women writers struggle to rewrite texts from their own point of view, the quest for maternal relations and matrilineal roots often becomes crucial for setting up an alternative to paternal logic and discourse. *El mismo mar* presented one protagonist's attempt to recuperate her lost matrilineal roots and a potential for female mythopoesis, but this quest ended in failure, given the inexorability of confining patriarchal social arrangements. This protagonist's predecessor, in Alós's *Os habla,* also disturbed us with the tragic implications of her quest to recognize and internalize the strengths and powers of the mother. In the meantime, the same thematic concern has reappeared time and time again in narratives by these and other women writers. Tusquets herself returned to it in the third novel of her trilogy, *Varada tras el último naufragio (Stranded after the Last Shipwreck),* in which her pro-tagonist discovers aspects of her mother she has never seen be-fore, "aspectos insospechados, improbables" (unsuspected and improbable aspects) and eventually discovers that her own mater-nal ties are impelling her by means of rushing, explosive, unre-strained discourse to a newly discovered contentment and high pitched state of creative potential.[4]

Alós has also reiterated woman's desire for maternal relations, her quest for lost matrilinear identity. In a recent novel, *Argeo ha muerto, supongo (Argeo Has Died, I Suppose),* the victimization and subsequent wisdom of Jano tell the story of lost matrilineal strength. Though *Argeo* seems to recapitulate earlier stories of woman's increasing enclosure in the patriarchy, it still leaves visi-ble between-the-lines, or inscribed within the gaps, a potent image of matriarchal power. As the image of the idealized male, Argeo, fades into nothingness, Jano and her mother (the mother who, along with her daughter, used to form a matriarchy) reestablish intimate links of communication. As they share their dreams of adventure, quests for buried treasure and magical lamps, we glimpse a muted story of female power and imagination that, though temporarily displaced by the violence and deceit of Argeo, rises again like a Phoenix. Jano and her mother affirm that the female mind never completely loses its "ancient wisdom" even if the body becomes imprisoned in the house and culture of patriarchy.

The bleakest plot of matriarchal loss, by far, concludes what might be considered Alós's matriarchal trilogy. In *El asesino de los sueños (The Dream Assassin)*, a protagonist and a mother with the attributes of Electra and Jano resurface (in fact, the narrator calls herself the inventor of Electra). The narrator is thus a self-conscious writer who calls our attention to the choices of texts and plots made by the characters. Since both she and her lover, Marcelo, are writers, they attempt to textualize their experience, yet the gap between their romantic imaginations and the sordid reality of their Barcelona environment results in a tragic denouement for their plot. The narrator's mother, like mother Electra, has sold out to the patriarchy, trading her matriarchal power for security. While Marcelo may idealize love in his letters, the plays he writes are inspired by O'Neill whose *Emperor Jones* provides a more potent intertext for the plot of his life. Finally overcome by their phantasms, like O'Neill's protagonists, the lovers are banished from their idealized texts. Their plots close off according to a much more desolate tradition: with Gothic submission to patriarchal propriety and only the faint, lingering echo of matriarchal power.

As compensation for this dark denouement, we might remember Riera's *Una primavera* in which we watched as the protagonist's mother made her single, grandly subversive gesture to displace, temporarily, the "Law of the Father." Or, in Montserrat Roig's *La ópera cotidiana (Daily Opera)*, a mother-daughter link literally shuts out the father (as punishment for his obsessive desire to control), and this maternal connection (incomprehensible to the father) leaves him distraught with envy and thwarted paternal desire. Rosa Montero's *Te trataré como a una reina (I Shall Treat You like a Queen)*, presents a middle-aged single woman who discovers the mother within her through a brief love affair with a younger man; eventually she comes to welcome the potential for new links with her own mother. Thus again and again, from the edges to the centers of these narrative texts, the desire for recuperating and revitalizing relationships between mother and daughter is articulated with increasing frequency and intensity. Though popular belief has often cast the Spanish mother into the role of domesticated matriarch, there is something more powerful and subversive about these female-defined figures. They desire nothing less than to escape being spoken and to become the redefined subjects of a different discourse.

We have explored in detail how Riera works with the challenges of rewriting in *Una primavera*. Nevertheless, Riera's earlier narratives already incorporated her theoretical ideas about the growing autonomy and difference of woman's voice. Her fascinating short story collection, *Palabra de mujer (Woman's Word)*, begins impressively as its first tale plays with many of the reader's conventional expectations. It seems to follow faithfully the familiar pattern of those traditional feminine love stories in which a young girl falls hopelessly in love with an older man. Little by little the narrator reveals the details of this remembered relationship, but the most significant detail is reserved for the final words of the story: the female name of the lover. That revelation causes the reader to reassess and reinvent images s/he has been forging throughout the text; s/he must invert signs and images to recuperate a region of reality often silenced in the past. What emerges is akin to what Geraldine Cleary Nichols has identified in Tusquets's *El mismo mar de todos los veranos:* "the love in this love story is . . . a perversion of the conventional boy-meets-girl plot, and a subversion of the sociosexual system which underwrites that plot."[5]

Ortiz's *Urraca* and Gómez Ojea's *Otras mujeres y Fabia* have also shown us how narratives may successfully effect that synthesis between the appropriation of discourse by woman—her insistence on rewriting from her point of view—and a reconsideration of history that current theories suggest we recognize. As she insists upon her own word, Urraca reinvents her place in history as Cixous has urged women to do. Closely linked with Urraca in discursive function, Fabia, of *Otras mujeres*, voiced for us a kind of minstrel or chronicler, searching through the lives and texts of foremothers for the history of her matrilineal past. We heard her, too, rescue and retell history from woman's point of view, inserting, as Irigaray has insisted, woman's word within the gaps left by "their" written history. Montserrat Roig has also worked with the problem of telling or retelling women's history in *Ramona adiós (Farewell Ramona)*, a narrative in which contrapuntal technique parallels the lives of three very different generations of women. The result is a disclosure that the lives of women from widely varied backgrounds are related by common frustrations of desire, human potential, and imagination. By means of such a "contra-saga" (countersaga), as C. B. Cadenas has called it, women and their personal histories intersect and blend with national history (as Cixous has celebrated). They are no longer accessories of male-inscribed history but rather key players of their own.

Roig has consciously set out to supplement other historical omissions in yet other rewritings. In *La hora violeta (The Violet Hour)*, Natalia affirms: "Me parecía que era necesario salvar con las palabras todo lo que la historia, la Historia grande, es decir, la de los hombres, había hecho impreciso, había condenado o idealizado" (It seemed to me that it was necessary to salvage with words all that history, history with a capital "H," that is, that of men, had made imprecise, had condemned or idealized).[6] The women of that novel reflect upon and tentatively engage in their own "discurso" (discourse), their own "lenguaje común" (common language) (72, 74), doing so with mixed feelings and mixed re-sults, but always with an inevitability integral to their condition. They are young, intellectual professionals, women plagued by all the contradictions inherent in their situation—that paradoxical crossroads somewhere between tradition (the ghosts of romantic passion) and freedom (the cool autonomy of economic indepen-dence). Finally, in Roig's more recent *La ópera*, orality informs and sustains the novel as characters of different ages and genders recount their own personal histories within the backdrop of con-temporary Spanish society. The accounts of a phallocentric nar-rator become increasingly unreliable as he recounts his futile attempt to totally possess and control his wife. An elderly woman reshapes her personal history according to her fantasies and thereby invents the portrait of a headstrong young woman with the qualities of Catherine Earnshaw and Violeta Valery. She also employs a young companion to read and reread to her from a certain sentimental novel, thereby weaving from it the strands of her fictional existence, and eventually entangling the young woman in the same narrative web. Each narrative invention in this novel thus involves a gender and even age-specific blending and rewriting of contemporary history and literary convention. As the characters spin out stories of their lives, ironic implications emerge about power relations surrounding the telling and recep-tion of narratives by interlocutors of different ages and genders.

A primary locus of woman's subversion and escape from the power of phallogocentric discourse has been, most recently, her own body. This sign perhaps more than any other—given the

imposed silences of censorship and traditional morality surrounding it for so long in Spain—has burgeoned as a source of multiple
meanings in new women's narrative. Again, Tusquets has been a
trail blazer, inscribing into her trilogy redefinitions of love and
language vis-à-vis the female body. Geraldine Cleary Nichols has
meticulously shown how the love affair in *El mismo mar* incorporates the "infinitized" and diffuse experience of the female body
called for by French feminism, especially Irigaray.[7] Concurrently,
Catherine Bellver has analyzed how Tusquets's women become
the designers of romance, thus defining female sexuality from a
feminine point of view.[8] Though female sexuality is not always the
"positive, beautiful, and enjoyable force," that Bellver would have
it be, it certainly is powerful and subversive.[9] In Tusquets's *El amor
es un juego solitario (Love Is a Solitary Game)*, sexual pleasure is
inextricably linked to decadence and selfishness, and purity is
inseparable from suffering. Elia, the maturing protagonist, nevertheless becomes the means whereby the pleasures of the female
body are explored with directness and intensity. The writing out
of Elia's boundless sexuality is analogous, throughout the trilogy,
with the text's own infinite syntax, a syntax clearly related to the
female body in ways imagined by French feminism.

When woman's body speaks, given its usual insertion within the
discourse and desires of men, it is not always satisfactorily understood. In *La función delta (The Delta Function)*, Rosa Montero's
novel of 1981, the voice of the female body as it lies dying is
permitted the luxury of reliving the apprenticeship, mastery, and
ripeness of female-defined sexuality. Lucía's lovers, past and present (Hipólito, Miguel, and Ricardo), roughly correspond to these
three states; and as accomplice, fellow adventurer, and loving
companion respectively, each man grapples with the text of
woman's body. Hipólito largely misreads Lucía and her intentions;
Miguel reads Lucía's body and her desires with an open tenderness; Ricardo reads Lucía's text (and her body) with irreverential
yet affectionate honesty. Ricardo, as Lucía's last interlocutor, offers insights into the problems of male lovers/readers confronting
female bodies/texts. He tends to view mood shifts and contradictions as unreliability or lack of verisimilitude. Thus the claims of
Lucía's body and her text may be judged by categorical imper-
atives alien to legibility and comprehension. More disastrously,
still, in Montero's later novel, *Te trataré como a una reina*, the bodies
of women and men merge without communication; metaphorically speaking different languages, there is no alternative but
eventual rupture of all intimacy between them.

Similarly, in Roig's *Opera,* Mari Cruz's speaking body ("las palabras me salieron como si no fuese yo quien las dijese, sino mi cuerpo" [the words emerged from me as if it were not I that uttered them, but my body])[10] goes unheard and misunderstood by her fleeting lover, señor Duc: "los dos estábamos en mundos diferentes, en dos galaxias que no se entendían, irreconciliables, como si hablásemos dos lenguas distintas" (we two were in different worlds, in two galaxies unintelligible to each other, unreconcilable, as if we were speaking two different languages) (122). Though this alienation is disturbing, it is not at all surprising, for Duc was unable to read his wife's boundless ability to love until his blindness became tragic and irreversible. When he finally realized that his wife had eluded her husband's desperate grasp because she was "capaz de sentir, de querer más allá de los placeres de alcoba" (capable of feeling, of loving beyond the pleasures of the bedroom) (188), it was too late. As a schoolgirl, Mari Cruz may have been provided by the "Law of the Father" with surrogate kisses and an adoptive father for paternal naming; but when she grows up, the language of her body is distorted and silenced by that same law. The inscription of a different discourse in this narrative does not eliminate paternal or phallocentric presence; it does, however, reveal its toll.

Marta Portal's *Un espacio erótico (An Erotic Space)* struggles with the ghosts of phallocentric alienation while attempting to effect, through the articulation of female desire, that escape from "male desires for domination" called for by Cixous. Employing the intriguing metanovelistic strategy of a female narrator attempting to convey the most intimate dimensions of her female subject, who is likewise a writer trying to penetrate the hidden dimensions of her own body and soul, *Un espacio* peels away the outer, inherently deceptive layers of discourse to reveal the voluptuous honesty of female corporeal desire. Elvira, the protagonist, returns to Spain after a disastrous marriage in Mexico. With her she brings disturbing memories of sexual domination and degradation at the hands of her Mexican husband, and for a time she suffers the deadening effects of this experience on body and spirit. Eventually, an affair with a younger colleague, Montoro, brings her body back to life, and it is at this juncture that the connection between body and text becomes most apparent: the life and expression of one is intimately linked with the generation of the other. Afterwards, feeling more alive, she associates erotic pleasure with a renewed capacity to write: "¡La sorpresa acezante del placer! ¡La sorpresa anhelante de una nueva página! ¡La posibilidad de lo inédito!" (The breathless surprise of pleasure! The yearned for surprise of a new page! The possibility of something never voiced before!).[11]

It is not only writing that is unleashed but an unpredictability outside the laws of convention, beyond the boundaries of the known. A subsequent erotic relationship with her cousin, Elena, carries Elvira farther along the path toward her own untrammeled discourse. That experience, in which the maternal achieves primacy, promises to open even greater frontiers of expression: "fue dejándose invadir por la capacidad maternal . . . por ese saber sin fronteras que de un cuerpo de mujer tiene otro cuerpo de mujer" (she let herself be overcome by a maternal capaciousness . . . by that borderless wisdom that one female body has of another) (123). It suggests to Elvira a new myth of maternity within the Christian myth of the annunciation: the "prescindibilidad física del Padre" (the physical dispensability of the Father) (125) implied by the conception of Jesus reveals to Elvira a surprising message of erotic self-sufficiency and "la negación del Padre" (the negation of the Father) (126) so often advocated by French feminism.

Implicit in this re-vision is the potential for rewriting within the maternal realm of what Kristeva has named "nonsymbolic, nonpaternal causality."[12] Since this novel is ultimately about the challenge of one female writing about another, about her struggle to capture the other as if she were the same as the writing self, the erotic space referred to by the work's title is just that place where writing seeks to break through the boundaries of the symbolic word to become flesh. The site of utterance ceases to function as symbolic vessel or even metonymic substitute for the concreteness of corporeal discourse. When the narrator enunciates through the body, she leaves the insufficiency of words behind and chooses to end with nothing less than the self-sufficiency of the erotic, corporeal text: "Cómo yo pasaría la punta de mi lengua por tu boca, dibujándola con mi carne, en vez de describirla con mi palabra. Que tú eres carne, Elvira, carne crispada en el orgasmo, estremecida por mi mano, palabra hecha carne, hecha deseo" (As I would pass the tip of my tongue over your mouth, drawing its outlines with my flesh, instead of describing it with my word. For you are flesh, Elvira, flesh contracting in its orgasm, trembling under my touch, word made flesh, made desire) (184). The narrator must close the verbal text at this point, for the word has become flesh; in this revised incarnation, there is nothing left to approximate with mere words.

The narratives that we have read in detail and briefly surveyed all reveal a common impulse toward the difference of reinscription. This impulse voices itself repeatedly and heterogeneously through the rewriting of narrative contracts such as the Gothic, myths, history, Arthurian romance, the fantastic and articulations of female corporeality. As each generation succeeds another, these writers are impelled to create and recreate with increasing boldness and authority. This history of divergent and self-defining discourse may mean seeking renewed bonds with beleaguered maternal figures or affirming maternal power from a female perspective. It may produce the subjection of traditional myths and history to scrutiny, and later it may mean executing their complete inversion. It may involve exposing the female body, shaking off layers of suppression and repression to reveal reverberations of erotic and textual desire. Subversion in today's texts by women may constitute a paean to female desire as Queen Urraca's insistence on the improvisational and inventive aspects of her erotic experiences and text. It may shift the location of joker and butt of joke through irony and parody as in the narratives of Díaz-Mas and Gómez Ojea; it may introduce a slippage and ambiguous elusiveness from the discourses of the Father and the symbolic contract as in the fantastic narratives of García Morales; or it may be combative and even violent, like Bella's physical revenge against male treachery in Montero's *Te trataré como a una reina.*

Whatever posture she chooses, as today's Spanish woman novelist bares aspects of woman and culture that have often been submerged and silenced by the Other, she cannot be expected to submit to the legislation of consecrated codes and discursive laws. Claiming the freedom of heterogeneity and multivocality, she welcomes theories of difference as suggestive sources of influence and stimulating ideas for inventing the future. These theories have not been, nor are they likely to become, prescriptions for univocal predictability. Our pleasure now as readers is to continue hearing these long, lingering, and diversely nuanced sounds.

Notes

Introduction

1. Lawrence Lipking, "Aristotle's Sister: A Poetics of Abandonment," *Critical Inquiry* 10 (1983): 62.

2. Constance A. Sullivan, "Re-reading the Hispanic Literary Canon," *Ideologies and Literature: A Journal of Hispanic and Luso-Brazilian Studies* 4 (1983): 97.

3. Leopoldo Rodriguez Alcalde, "Las novelistas españolas en los últimos veinte años," *La estafeta literaria* 25 (1962):6.

4. Janet Pérez, "Some Desiderata in Studies of Twentieth Century Spanish Fiction," *Siglo XX/20th Century* 1 (1984): 6.

5. Fernando Alvarez Palacios, *Novela y cultura española de postguerra* (Madrid: Edicusa, 1975), 120–21.

6. John Butt, *Writers and Politics in Modern Spain* (New York: Holmes & Meier, 1978).

7. Alvarez Palacios, *Novela y cultura,* 124.

8. Alvarez Palacios includes only one woman, Elena Soriano, among his interviewed novelists, probably because her presence was made manifest as editor of the literary journal, *El Urogallo.* Ironically, among Soriano's comments is her severe reprobation of Spanish criticism's falsification of "nuestra historia literaria actual" (our contemporary literary history) (Ibid., 256). One wonders if she was thinking of the omission of women as well as of writers unacceptable to official culture.

9. Besides Sobejano, Garcia Viñó, and Corrales Egea, other critics of the period have grappled with the problem of including women (for example, Santos Sanz Villanueva, Ignacio Soldevilla, and Robert Spires); have chosen to virtually ignore the presence of women writers within their theoretical boundaries (for example, Pablo Gil Casado in his *La novela social española (1920–1971);* or continue to provide rich source materials or scattered references to the works of women (José Maria Martinez Cachero's critical bibliography in *La novela española entre 1936–1975).* See Gonzalo Sobejano, *Novela española de nuestro tiempo (en busca del pueblo perdido)* (Madrid: Prensa Española, 1975); M. Garcia Viño, *Novela española actual* (Madrid: Prensa Española, 1975); José Corrales Egea, *La novela española actual: Ensayo de ordenación* (Madrid: Edicusa, 1971); Santos Sanz Villanueva, *Historia de la novela social española (1942–1975)* (Madrid: Alhambra, 1980), and———, *Tendencias de la novela española actual* (Madrid: Editorial Cuadernos para el diálogo, 1972); Ignacio Soldevilla, *La novela desde 1936* (Madrid: Alhambra, 1980); Robert Spires, *La novela española de posguerra,* (Madrid: Cupsa Editorial, 1978); Pablo Gil Casado, *La novela social española (1920–1971)* (Barcelona: Seix Barral, 1973); José María Martínez Cachero, *La novela española entre 1936–1975* (Madrid: Castalia, 1979).

10. Juan Goytisolo, *El furgón de cola* (Paris: Ruedo Ibérico, 1970), 11.

11. Alvarez Palacios, *Novela y cultura,* 256.

12. Olga Prjevalinsky Ferrer, "Las novelistas españolas de hoy," *Cuadernos Americanos*, Año 20, Tomo 118 (1961): 212. Translation is my own.

13. Ibid., 222.

14. Ibid., 218.

15. Two recent publications that confirm how feminist theory has revitalized the reading of contemporary Spanish narrative by women are Mirella D'Ambrosio Servodidio and Marcia L. Welles, eds., *Reading for Difference: Feminist Perspectives on Women Novelists of Contemporary Spain, Anales de la Literatura Española Contemporanea*, 12 (1987); and Roberto C. Manteiga, Carolyn Galerstein and Kathleen McNerney, eds., *Feminine Concerns in Contemporary Spanish Fiction by Women* (Potomac, Maryland: Scripta Humanistica, 1988).

16. Linda Chown implicates me and other North American critics of the late seventies as persistently focusing our "attention on external circumstances." Though I would disagree with her claim that our blindness was a result of American biases (since my approach was as indebted to Spanish Marxist and social criticism as much as it was to early North American feminist perspectives), she is perceptive in her uneasiness with the partiality of exclusively sociohistorical readings of the contemporary Spanish novel by women. See "American Critics and Spanish Women Novelists, 1942–1980," *Signs* 9 (Autumn 1983): 96–97.

17. David K. Herzberger, "An Overview of Postwar Novel Criticism of the 1970s," *Anales de la narrativa española contemporanea* 5 (1980): 30.

18. Ibid.

19. Fredric Jameson, *The Political Unconscious: Narrative as a Socially Symbolic Act* (Ithaca: Cornell University Press, 1981), 70.

20. Juliet Flower MacCannell, *Figuring Lacan: Criticism and the Cultural Unconscious* (Lincoln: University of Nebraska Press, 1986), 128.

21. Jacques Lacan, *Ecrits: A Selection*, trans. Alan Sheridan (London: Tavistock, 1977), 287. See Vincent B. Leitch, *Deconstructive Criticism: An Advanced Introduction* (New York: Columbia University Press, 1983), for a brief summary of Derrida's complaints about Lacan's theories (Ibid., 30) and Jane Gallop, *Reading Lacan* (Ithaca: Cornell University Press, 1985), for insights into the polemics surrounding the meaning of Lacan's assertion (chap. 6).

22. Lacan, *Ecrits*, 67.

23. The Symbolic Order is often unkind, as Susan Suleiman has described: "the symbolic functions as the realm of the unattainable Other; it is by definition the realm of frustrated relations, of impossible loves." See "Writing and Motherhood," in *The (M)other Tongue: Essays in Feminist Psychoanalytic Interpretation*, ed. Shirley Nelson Garner, Claire Kahane, and Madelon Sprengnether (Ithaca, N.Y.: Cornell University Press, 1985), 367.

24. Roland Barthes seems undaunted by the grim legality of Lacan's Symbolic Order, wresting from the canonical structures of the language a transmutation through what he calls bliss or the disruption of comfortable cultural, historical, and psychological assumptions. See *The Pleasure of the Text*, trans. Richard Miller (New York: Hill and Wang, 1975).

25. Derrida states categorically: "there is no absolute origin of sense in general." See *Of Grammatology*, trans. Gayatri Chakravorty Spivak (Baltimore: The Johns Hopkins University Press), 65.

26. Terry Eagleton, *Literary Theory: An Introduction* (Minneapolis: University of Minnesota Press, 1983), 189.

27. See Derrida, "Edmond Jabès and the Question of the Book," *Writing and Difference*, trans. Alan Bass (Chicago: The University of Chicago Press), 77.

28. See Leitch, *Deconstructive Criticism,* and Mark Krupnick, ed. *Displacement: Derrida and After* (Bloomington: Indiana University Press, 1983) for accessible applications of Derrida's thought to literature.

29. See Jameson, *The Political Unconscious,* 43, 45.

30. See Michel Foucault, *The Archaeology of Knowledge,* trans. A. M. Sheridan Smith (New York: Pantheon Books, 1972), 50.

31. Ibid., 23, 25.

32. Krupnick, "Displacement," 186.

33. Luce Irigaray, *Speculum of the Other Woman,* trans. Gillian C. Gill (Ithaca, N.Y.: Cornell University Press, 1985), 308.

34. See Jonathan Culler, *On Deconstruction: Theory and Criticism after Structuralism* (Ithaca: Cornell University Press, 1982), 173 and passim for an incisive and illuminating discussion of feminist theorists influenced by deconstruction.

35. Ann Rosalind Jones, "Writing the Body," in *The New Feminist Criticism: Essays on Women, Literature and Theory,* ed. Elaine Showalter (New York: Pantheon Books, 1985), 362.

36. Hélène Cixous, "The Laugh of the Medusa," in *New French Feminisms,* ed. Elaine Marks and Isabelle de Courtivron (University of Massachusetts Press, 1980), 252–53.

37. Luce Irigaray, *This Sex Which Is Not One,* trans. Catherine Porter with Carolyn Burke (Ithaca, N.Y.: Cornell University Press, 1985), 143.

38. See Annie Leclerc, "Woman's Word," in *New French Feminisms,* ed. Marks and de Courtivron, 79–86; Elizabeth A. Meese, *Crossing the Double-Cross: The Practice of Feminist Criticism* (Chapel Hill: The University of North Carolina Press, 1986); Rachel Blau DuPlessis, *Writing Beyond the Ending: Narrative Strategies of Twentieth-Century Women Writers* (Bloomington: Indiana University Press, 1985).

39. See especially Annis Pratt, *Archetypal Patterns in Women's Fiction* (Bloomington: Indiana University Press, 1981) as well as articles listed in "Bibliography."

40. Carme Riera, "Literatura escrita por mujeres," Mesa redonda 4, Feria del libro, Madrid, summer 1983.

41. Montserrat Roig, *¿Tiempo de mujer?* (Barcelona: Plaza & Janes, 1980), 158.

42. Carme Riera, "Literatura fememina: ¿Un lenguaje prestado?," *Quimera* 18 (April 1982): 12.

43. Ibid.

44. See Helen Araújo, "¿Escritura femenina?," *Escandalar* 4 (1981): 32–36; Marta Traba, "Hipótesis sobre una escritura diferente," *Quimera* 13 (November 1981): 9–11; Evelyne García, "Lectura: N. Fem. Sing. ¿Lee y escribe la mujer en forma diferente al hombre?," *Quimera* 23 (September 1982): 54–57.

45. See Irigaray, *Speculum,* 308.

46. Ibid.

47. Mari Sarda, "Literatura feminista de los años 60–70: silencio, gritos, indicios," *Camp de l'arpa* 47 (February 1978): 27.

48. See Spivak, "Displacement and the Discourse of Woman," in *Displacement,* ed. Krupnick, 186.

49. Jane Gallop has recently expressed such reservations: "to move beyond the father, the mother looks like an alternative, but if we are trying to move beyond patriarchy, the mother is not outside . . . the institution of motherhood is a cornerstone of patriarchy." See "Reading the Mother Tongue: Psychoanalytic Feminist Criticism," *Critical Inquiry* 13 (Winter 1987): 322.

50. See Empar Pineda, "El discurso de la diferencia. El discurso de la -igualdad," in *Nuevas perspectivas sobre la mujer,* ed. María Angeles Durán (Madrid: Universidad Autónoma de Madrid, 1982), 257–71.

51. Domna C. Stanton, "Difference on Trial: A Critique of the Maternal Metaphor in Cixous, Irigaray, and Kristeva," in *The Poetics of Gender*, ed. Nancy K. Miller (New York: Columbia University Press, 1986), 175. My recurrent use throughout this study of the neologism "an(other)" will be to signify a supplemental, different, even transgressive discourse—a writing beyond the strictest boundaries of phallo(go)centric tradition and convention, especially regarding gender-inflected desire. By bracketing off the second part of this common adjective to separate off the preceding syllable as indefinite article, the word can stress connotations of both otherness and open indefiniteness.

52. I am indebted to Linda Alcoff and her concept of "positionality" in the formation of female identity for this final observation of the positionality of the text. See "Cultural Feminism versus Post-Structuralism: The Identity Crisis in Feminist Theory," *Signs* 13 (1988): 405–36.

53. Though there is much that links and even telescopes these terms—patriarchal, paternal, and phallocentric—my opting for one or the other throughout the following study will often reflect subtle nuances of difference. "Patriarchal" evokes more strongly social or cultural discourse as ideology and/or institution; "paternal" resonates with Lacanian connotations ("name or Law of the Father") as well as with references to the father or father figure as authority or manager of desire; "phallocentric" without the Derridean ("go") shall refer particularly to Lacanian and French feminist notions of symbolic or signifying systems applied to woman by man, especially regarding the structuring, delimiting, and expression of desire; and finally, the Derridean variant ("phallogocentrism") will stress especially the logocentric or binary oppositions that underwrite the structures of phallocentrism.

Chapter 1. The Double Voices of Youth

1. Katherine Dalsimer, *Female Adolescence: Psychoanalytic Reflections on Literature* (New Haven: Yale University Press, 1986), 7.

2. Bruce Lincoln, *Emerging From the Chrysalis: Studies in Rituals of Women's Initiation* (Cambridge, Mass.: Harvard University Press, 1981), 104.

3. Elaine Showalter has gone so far as to assert that "women's writing is a 'double-voiced discourse' that *always* embodies the social, literary, and cultural heritages of both the muted and the dominant." More modestly, this certainly appears to be the case in *this* text at *this* time. (Emphasis is mine.) See "Feminist Criticism in the Wilderness," *Critical Inquiry* 8 (1981): 201.

4. Carmen Kurtz, letter to the author, 16 June 1984.

5. Marta Portal, letter to the author, 6 June 1984.

6. Rosa Romá, letter to the author, 6 June 1984.

7. Susana March, letter to the author, 15 June 1984.

8. Carme Riera, letter to the author, 7 December 1984.

9. Esther Tusquets, letter to the author, 19 June 1984.

10. Carmen Laforet, *Nada* (Barcelona: Destino, 1969), 294. Subsequent citations from this edition of the novel will be indicated parenthetically within the text.

11. Robert Spires, "El papel del lector implícito en la novela española de posguerra," in *Novelistas españoles de postguerra*, ed. Rodolfo Cardona (Madrid: Taurus, 1976), 241–52.

12. See Verena Andermatt Conley, *Hélène Cixous: Writing the Feminine* (Lincoln: University of Nebraska Press, 1984), 115.

13. Prewar ideologue, Bishop Isidro Gomá's *La familia según el derecho natural y cristiano (The Family According to Natural and Christian Law)* (1931) exemplifies the kind of source book that was invoked during the postwar period for substantiating and corroborating the discursive practices of Falangist patriarchy. In it, the bishop enumerates paternal qualities and responsibilities that he deemed essential for the sustenance of family and indeed of civilization: authority, intelligence, power, and the spirit of enterprise. See Carlos Moya, "Familia e ideología política," in *Las ideologías en la España de hoy (Coloquio)*, ed. José Jiménez Blanco (Madrid: Seminarios y Ediciones, 1972), 97–98.

14. These connections are correctly, if ponderously, theorized by Carlos Moya: "a través de esta dimensión 'paternal-ancestral' del titular del poder legítimo se garantiza perfectamente la conexión y la circulación simbólica entre el 'mundo privado-familiar' y el 'mundo público-político,' asegurando así el perfecto funcionamiento de las estructuras familiares al servicio de la reproducción de las imágenes y actitudes básicas de la personalidad que interiorizan psicológicamente la sumisión a la autoridad característica de las sociedades tradicionales" (through this "paternal-ancestral" dimension of the title holder of legitimate power, the connection and the symbolic circulation between the "private-familiar realm" and the "public-political sphere" is perfectly guaranteed, assuring in this way the perfect functioning of familial structures in the service of the reproduction of basic personality images and attitudes that psychologically interiorize submission to the authority characteristic of traditional societies). Ibid., 89–90.

15. Pierre Ullman, "The Moral Structure of Carmen Laforet's Novels," in *The Vision Obscured*, ed. Melvin J. Friedman (New York: Fordham University Press, 1970), 203.

16. Antoni Jutglar, *Mitología del capitalismo* (Madrid: Seminarios y Ediciones, 1971), 58.

17. Patricia Meyer Spacks, "Taking Care: Some Women Novelists," *Novel* (Fall 1972): 49.

18. See an example of this phenomenon in Eliseo Bayo, *Trabajos duros de la mujer* (Barcelona: Plaza Janés, 1970), 42: "El no se enteró nunca de que el dinero que nos dejaba, no era suficiente para mantener tantas bocas. . . . Yo tenía que trabajar casi a escondidas, y entonces éramos muchas las mujeres que trabajábamos a espaldas del marido (He never realized that the money he provided us wasn't sufficient to feed so many mouths. . . . I had to work on the sly, and at that time there were a lot of us women who worked behind the backs of our husbands).

19. Carlos Castilla del Pino, *Cuatro ensayos sobre la mujer* (Madrid: Alianza Editorial, 1971), 44.

20. Werner Beinhauer, *El carácter español* (Madrid: Ediciones Nueva Epoca, 1944), 49.

21. Ibid., 57, 52.

22. Freud expressed a patriarchal wish for women that may well constitute the intertext of Andrea's desire: "Nature has determined a woman's destiny through beauty, charm and sweetness." See Eva Figes, *Patriarchal Attitudes: Women in Society* (London: Faber and Faber, 1970), 28–29. Or from Freud's letters: "But I believe that all reforming activity, legislation and education, will founder on the fact that long before the age at which a profession can be established in our

society, nature will have appointed woman by her beauty, charm, and goodness, to do something else." See *Letters of Sigmund Freud*, ed. Ernst L. Freud, trans. Tania and James Stern (New York: Basic Books, 1960), 76.

23. Sherman Eoff, "*Nada* by Carmen Laforet: A Venture in Mechanistic Dynamics," *Hispania* 25 (1952): 211.

24. From a publication of INLE cited by Valeriano Bozal, "La edición en España. Notas para su historia," *Cuadernos para el diálogo* 14 (May 1969): 91.

✔ 25. Fredric Jameson calls our attention to "generic discontinuities" or generic layering that similarly deconstructs "working" or traditional categories of genre, thus making way for contradictory and heterogeneous ideological meanings in the narrative text. See *The Political Unconscious: Narrative as a Socially Symbolic Act* (Ithaca, N.Y.: Cornell University Press, 1981), 144–45.

26. See Juan Luis Alborg, *Hora actual de la novela española*, I (Madrid: Taurus, 1963); José Corrales Egea, *La novela española actual: Ensayo de ordenación* (Madrid: Edicusa, 1971); Juan Carlos Curutchet, *Introducción a la novela española de la postguerra* (Montevideo: Alfa, 1966); David William Foster, "*Nada* de Carmen Laforet: Ejemplo de neo-romance en la novela contemporánea," *Revista Hispánica Moderna* 32 (1966): 43–55; Iglesias Laguna, *Treinta años de novela española 1938–68*, I (Madrid: Prensa española, 1970); and Dámaso Santos, *Generaciones juntas* (Madrid: Bullón, 1962).

27. Norman N. Holland and Leona F. Sherman, "Gothic Possibilities," in *Gender and Reading: Essays on Readers, Texts, and Contexts*, ed. Elizabeth A. Flynn and Patrocinio P. Schweickart (Baltimore: The Johns Hopkins University Press, ✔ 1986), 220.

28. See Sandra M. Gilbert and Susan Gubar's brilliant essay on *Wuthering Heights* in *The Madwoman in the Attic: The Woman Writer and the Nineteenth-Century Literary Imagination* (New Haven: Yale University Press, 1979), 248–308, in which they reread Heathcliff as an incarnation of raw and untamed nature with more affinity to disenfranchised femaleness than to the maleness of patriarchal legitimacy.

29. Holland and Sherman, "Gothic Possibilities," 224.

30. We might recall here Freud's own inability, especially in the case of Dora, to conceive of anything but marriage as an appropriate conclusion to the narrative of feminine development. See Shirley Nelson Garner, et al., eds., *The (M)other Tongue: Essays in Feminist Psychoanalytic Interpretation* (Ithaca, N.Y.: Cornell University Press, 1985) for current psychoanalytic explorations of Freud's blindness to alternative plots of female development.

31. See Garner, *The (M)other Tongue*, for analyses of how Freud's narratives concerning gender may be overturned, and Nancy Chodorow, *The Reproduction of Mothering: Psychoanalysis and the Sociology of Gender* (Berkeley: University of California Press, 1978), for a discussion of how the mother-daughter bond is never surrendered.

32. Conley, *Hélène Cixous*, 109.

33. Ibid., 114.

34. In *Writing Beyond the Ending: Narrative Strategies of Twentieth-Century Women Writers* (Bloomington: Indiana University Press, 1985), 5, Rachel Blau DuPlessis reminds us that if the romance plot is a trope for the sex-gender system as a whole, then what she calls "writing beyond the ending," or beyond the inevitable closure of heterosexual pairing, is a narrative strategy that expresses critical dissent from dominant narrative and its function as a script for dominant social ideology. DuPlessis only confirms and elaborates the significance of this strategy

as a widespread phenomenon during the twentieth century, while Virginia Woolf earlier dubbed it breaking "the sequence-the expected order." See *A Room of One's Own* (London: Hogarth Press, 1929), 95.

Chapter 2. Feminine Plots and Their Undertow

1. Kathleen Woodward, "The Mirror Stage of Old Age," in *Memory and Desire: Aging-Literature-Psychoanalysis*, ed. Kathleen Woodward and Murray M. Schwartz (Bloomington: Indiana University Press, 1986), 104.

2. Elena Soriano, *La playa de los locos* (Barcelona: Argos Vergara, 1984), 21. Subsequent references to this edition of the novel will be cited parenthetically within the text.

3. Elena Quiroga, *La enferma* (Barcelona: Editorial Noguer, 1962), 99. Subsequent references to this edition of the novel will be cited parenthetically within the text.

4. Ana María Matute, *La trampa* (Barcelona: Ediciones Destino, 1969), 75. Subsequent references to this edition of the novel will be cited parenthetically within the text.

5. Woodward, "The Mirror Stage," *Memory*, 108.

6. Karen Horney, *New Ways in Psychoanalysis* (New York: Norton, 1939), 115.

7. In Ruth and Edward Brecker, *An Analysis of Human Sexual Response* (Boston: Little, Brown & Co., 1966), 252.

8. Albert Camus, *The Stranger*, trans. Stuart Gilbert (New York: Random House, 1946), 154.

9. Albert Camus, *The Myth of Sisyphus and Other Essays*, trans. Justin O'Brien (New York: Random House, 1955), 17.

10. It might be helpful to recall here how the paternal nature of language is exposed in Jacques Lacan's *Ecrits: A Selection*, trans. Alan Sheridan (London: Tavistock, 1977): the "name of the father" is identified with the law; the law, in turn, is identified with culture and language (or the Symbolic Order). Kristeva explores how the symbolic contract demands a sacrificial relationship to it and how recent literature reveals an "antisacrificial current" a "protest against the constraints of the sociosymbolic contract." See Julia Kristeva, "Women's Time," trans. Alice Jardine and Harry Blake, in *Feminist Theory: A Critique of Ideology*, ed. Nannerl O. Keohane, Michelle Z. Rosaldo, and Barbara C. Gelpi (Chicago: University of Chicago Press, 1982), 51.

11. Elizabeth A. Meese, *Crossing the Double-Cross: The Practice of Feminist Criticism* (Chapel Hill: The University of North Carolina Press, 1986), 118.

12. Lacan, *Ecrits*, 55.

13. Hélène Cixous, "The Laugh of the Medusa," in *New French Feminisms*, ed. Elaine Marks and Isabelle de Courtivron (Amherst: University of Massachusetts Press, 1980), 257.

14. Simone de Beauvoir has observed how in the act of defloration, man makes of the female body "unequivocally a passive object, he affirms his capture of it." See *The Second Sex*, trans. H. M. Parshley (New York: Bantam Books, 1970), 144.

15. Laurel Limpus, "Sexual Repression and the Family," in *Womankind: Beyond the Stereotypes*, ed. Nancy Reeves (New York: Aldine Atherton, 1971), 358.

16. It is noteworthy that the Petrarchan image of womanhood constituted a

bugaboo for women until the present post-Franco generation, during which Carme Riera and Carmen Gómez Ojea still engage in struggle to shake off its delimiting power (see chapter 5).

17. Sigmund Freud, *Civilization and Its Discontents*, trans. James Strachey (New York: W. W. Norton & Company, 1961), 44. Subsequent references to this edition of the work will be cited parenthetically within the text.

18. Helene Deutsch, *The Psychology of Women*, I (New York: Bantam Books, 1973), 298.

19. A recent observation by historian Gerda Lerner is apropos here: "women had no history—so they were told and so they believed. And because they had no history they had no future alternatives." See Gerda Lerner, *The Creation of Patriarchy* (New York: Oxford University Press, 1986), 222.

20. Luce Irigaray, *Speculum of the Other Woman*, trans. Gillian C. Gill (Ithaca, N.Y.: Cornell University Press, 1985), 93.

21. See Ibid., 97.

22. Beauvoir, *Second Sex*, 156.

23. See Sigmund Freud, "Femininity," in *The Complete Psychological Works of Sigmund Freud*, XXII (1932–36), ed. James Strachey (London: Hogarth Press, 1964), 124.

24. In spite of the protagonist's ambivalence and seeming willingness to capitulate to the phallocentric structuring of her desire, the mere fact that such a topic was voiced at all did not sit well with the censors when Elena Soriano originally submitted her manuscript for publication in 1955. The story of its rejection, told in an interview with me and in the introductory pages of the 1984 edition of the novel, is a tragic tale of frustration and silencing, not only of a narrative character but of her creator as well (See Soriano, *La playa*, 1–9).

25. Juan Luis Alborg, *Hora actual de la novela española*, I (Madrid: Taurus, 1963), 208.

26. Lacan, *Ecrits*, 69.

27. Beauvoir, *Second Sex*, 179.

28. Ibid., 152.

29. M. Esther Harding, *Woman's Mysteries* (New York: Bantam Books, 1973), 139.

30. Beauvoir, *Second Sex*, 144.

31. Term borrowed from H. R. Hays, *The Dangerous Sex: The Myth of Feminine Evil* (New York: Pocket Books, 1972), 137.

32. Leslie Fiedler, *Love and Death in the American Novel* (New York: Criterion Books, 1960), 281.

33. Phyllis Chesler cites apropos this situation: "Women in modern Judeo-Christian societies are motherless children. Painting after painting, sculpture after sculpture in the Christian world portray Madonnas comforting and worshipping their infant sons. Catholic mythology symbolizes the enforced splitting of Woman into either Mother or Whore—both of whom nurture and ultimately worship a dead man and/or a 'divine' male child." *Women and Madness* (New York: Avon Books, 1972), 17.

34. Mary Ellmann, *Thinking About Women* (New York: Harcourt Brace Jovanovich, 1968), 136.

35. Julia Kristeva, *Desire in Language: A Semiotic Approach to Literature and Art*, ed. Leon S. Roudiez, trans. Thomas Gora, Alice Jardine, and Leon S. Roudiez (New York: Columbia University Press, 1980), 241–42.

36. Cited by Jane Gallop, in *The Daughter's Seduction: Feminism and Psychoanalysis* (Ithaca, N.Y.: Cornell University Press, 1982), 123, from Julia Kristeva, "L'Autre de sexe," *Sorcières*, 10: 40.

37. Diana Hume George, " 'Who is the Double Ghost Whose Head is Smoke?' Women Poets on Aging," in *Memory and Desire*, ed. Woodward and Schwartz, 148.

38. In a somewhat different context, Derrida calls for a way out of the "double bind" that is suggestive for future texts by women (to begin with, Martín Gaite's interrogation of binary oppositions): "we maintain that it is necessary to seek new concepts and new models, an economy escaping this sytsem of [metaphysical] oppositions. The break with this structure of belonging can be announced only through a certain organization, a certain strategic arrangement which, within the field of [metaphysical] opposition, uses the strengths of the field to turn its own stratagems against it, producing a force of dislocation that spreads itself throughout the entire system, fissuring it in every direction and thoroughly delimiting it." See Jacques Derrida, "Force and Signification," in *Writing and Difference*, trans. Alan Bass (Chicago: The University of Chicago Press, 1978), 19–20. (Bracketing is mine.)

Chapter 3. Talking Herself Out

1. Jacques Derrida interprets Saussure's view of the corruption of speech by writing in *Of Grammatology*, trans. Gayatri Chakravorty Spivak (Baltimore: The Johns Hopkins University Press, 1978), 41.

2. Carmen Martin Gaite, *La búsqueda de interlocutor y otras búsquedas* (Madrid: Nostromo, 1973), 17.

3. Roland Barthes, *Writing Degree Zero*, trans. Annette Lavers and Colin Smith (Boston: Beacon Press, 1970), 87; *The Pleasure of the Text*, trans. Richard Miller (New York: Hill and Wang, 1975), 66–67.

4. Tzvetan Todorov, *Literatura y significación*, trans. Gonzalo Suárez Gómez (Barcelona: Editorial Planeta, 1971), 124.

5. Articles analyzing this aspect of *Retahílas* and *El cuarto de atrás* are almost too numerous to mention, however the following are salient: the studies by Ricardo Gullón, Manuel Durán, Ruth El Saffar, and Gonzalo Sobejano in *From Fiction to Metafiction*, ed. Mirella D'Ambrosio Servodidio and Marcia L. Welles (Lincoln, Neb.: Society of Spanish and Spanish-American Studies, 1983); Luanne Buchanan, "La novela como canto a la palabra," *Insula* 34 (November–December 1979): 13; Manuel Durán, "Carmen Martín Gaite, *Retahílas, El cuarto de atrás*, y el diálogo sin fin," *Revista Iberoamericana* 47 (1981): 233–40; Gonzalo Navajas, "El diálogo y el yo en *Retahílas* de Carmen Martín Gaite," *Hispanic Review* 53 (1985): 25–39; and Kathleen Glenn, "La posibilidad de diálogo: *Retahílas* de Carmen Martín Gaite" (Paper delivered at the Annual Meeting of the American Association of Teachers of Spanish and Portuguese, Madrid, 9–13 August 1986.)

6. Roland Barthes, "From Work to Text," in *Textual Strategies: Perspectives in Post-Structuralist Criticism*, ed. Josué V. Harari (Ithaca, N.Y.: Cornell University Press, 1979), 73–81.

7. Derrida, *Of Grammatology*, 159.

8. See Ibid., 162.

9. The work of Joan Brown has stressed the nonconformity of Martín Gaite's characters, while studies such as those of Robert Spires and Kathleen Glenn in Servodidio and Welles's *From Fiction to Metafiction* address the plurality and playfulness of *El cuarto*'s intertextual inventions. Linda Levine's study in the same volume gestures most toward the interrelationship between gender and textuality in its attentiveness to the ways in which the woman writer of *El cuarto* seeks to "shatter the image of herself created by the male imagination." See "A Portrait of the Artist," in *From Fiction to Metafiction*, 166.

10. As Roman Jakobson has clearly demonstrated, in any speech event, in any act of verbal communication, there is a message sent from addresser to addressee—the ultimate function of any exchange or interplay between interlocutors—and to be operative, the message must be transmitted by means of a code that has as referent a specific context. See "Linguistics and Poetics," in *The Structuralists: From Marx to Levi-Strauss*, trans. Richard T. and Fernande M. De George (New York: Doubleday, 1972), 89.

11. Elaine Showalter, "Feminist Criticism in the Wilderness," in *New Feminist Criticism: Essays on Women, Literature and Theory*, ed. Elaine Showalter (New York: Pantheon Books, 1985), 256.

12. Carmen Martín Gaite, *Retahílas* (Barcelona: Ediciones Destino, 1974), 233. Subsequent references to this edition of the work will be cited parenthetically within the text.

13. Luanne Buchanan, in "La novela como canto a la palabra," and Kathleen Glenn, in "La posibilidad de diálogo," have noted the intertextual resonances of Emilia Pardo Bazán's *Los pazos de Ulloa* and *La madre naturaleza* in the prologue, epilogue, and setting of *Retahílas*.

14. Enrique Sordo, "Carmen Martín Gaite: De la soledad al diálogo," *La Estafeta Literaria* 553 (1974): 1923.

15. My article, which forms the basis for this analysis, is "The Decoding and Encoding of Sex Roles in Carmen Martín Gaite's *Retahílas*," *Kentucky Romance Quarterly* 27 (1980): 237–44.

16. Martín Gaite was herself critical of this kind of feminist expression and may be articulating this problematical aspect of feminism through Eulalia's uneasiness. See Javier Villán, "Carmen Martín Gaite: Habitando el tiempo," *La Estafeta Literaria* 549 (1974): 22.

17. Nancy K. Miller has commented on the nature of Merteuil's sins and consequent punishment: "It seems to me that the sin in question, however, is less intellectual (hubristic) in nature, than sexual. . . . It is a rebellion of the individual spirit against the collective will only insofar as the rebellion challenges the strictures of sexual politics." See "The Exquisite Cadavers: Women in Eighteenth-Century Fiction," *Diacritics* 5 (1975): 41.

18. Esther Harding has shown that the moon goddess belongs to a matriarchal system, that she is not related to any man but is instead her own mistress, virgin, one-in-herself, and that her actions may be unconventional, governed by instinct and creativity. See *Woman's Mysteries* (New York: Bantam Books, 1973), 123, 147 et passim.

19. See Derrida, *Of Grammatology*, 157–64.

20. Jacques Lacan in *Qu'est-ce que le structuralism?*, ed. François Wahl (Paris: Seuil, 1968), 252–53. Quoted by Fredric Jameson, *The Prison-House of Language* (Princeton: Princeton University Press, 1972), 138.

21. Todorov, in his study of *The Thousand and One Nights*, articulates a similar

observation that may well constitute an intertextual source of Eulalia's comment. Demonstrating that a constant in the psychology of the characters of *The Thousand and One Nights* is their obsession with telling and listening to stories, Todorov concludes, "narration equals life: the absence of narration, death." See "Les Hommes-récits," in *Grammaire du Décameron* (The Hague: Mouton, 1969), 92. Quoted by Jameson in *Prison-House,* 199.

22. Germán is doing what Daniel Harris has described in the discourse of male liberation: "It is far easier for a man to confess to a woman that he feels incapable of coping with a given situation than it is for him to make the same confession to another man. It is easier for him to talk with a woman about sexist behavior than it is for him to acknowledge that dodge for what it is. . . ." "Androgyny: The Sexist Myth in Disguise," *Women's Studies* 3 (1974): 182–83.

23. Michel Foucault, *Language, Counter-memory, Practice,* trans. Donald F. Bouchard and Sherry Simon (Ithaca, N.Y.: Cornell University Press, 1977), 90.

24. Ibid.

25. Carmen Martín Gaite, *El cuarto de atrás* (Barcelona: Ediciones Destino, 1978), 25. Subsequent references to this work will be cited parenthetically within the text.

26. Luis Suñen, "Interlocutor intruso y texto total," *Insula* 380–81 (July–August 1978): 11.

27. Barthes, "From Work to Text," in *Textual Strategies,* 75.

28. See Carmen Martín Gaite, "Los malos espejos," in *La búsqueda,* 10.

29. I am indebted to John Sturrock's fine interpretation of Barthes' contrasting responses to a text for my own comparison. See "Roland Barthes" in *Structuralism and Since: From Lévi Strauss to Derrida,* ed. John Sturrock (New York: Oxford University Press, 1979), 72.

30. Linda Levine, "*El cuarto de atrás* de Carmen Martín Gaite: Por fin, el mundo al revés." (Paper delivered at the Annual Convention of the Modern Language Association, San Francisco, December 1979.)

31. Debra A. Castillo has pointed out that *Reivindicación del Conde don Julián* is not only an analogue and possible model for the deconstructive tendencies of *El cuarto,* but that it indeed becomes one of the textual layers of Martín Gaite's novel. Pointing to parallel enumerations of C words in *Reivindicación* and *El cuarto,* Castillo suggests that Martín Gaite "transposed into the context of a feminine experience" Goytisolo's series of words beginning with C. This suggestion that Martín Gaite was playfully dialoguing with Goytisolo's text, and thereby echoing it in her own, might well be born out by my own conversations with her in which she admitted her strong antipathy for writers, like Goytisolo, who insist on writing so that no one can understand them. In light of the author's own preferences, the series contrasted by Castillo is telling: in response to Goytisolo's "culebra, culpa, cupletista" etc., Martín Gaite enunciates less abstract, more domestic words such as "casa, cuarto, cama." See Debra A. Castillo, "Never-Ending Story: Carmen Martín Gaite's *The Back Room,*" *PMLA* 102 (1987): 824.

32. See Carmen Martín Gaite, *Usos amorosos del dieciocho en España* (Barcelona: Editorial Lumen, 1981).

33. Julian Palley, "El interlocutor soñado de *El cuarto de atrás* de Carmen Martín Gaite," *Insula,* 404–5 (July–August 1980): 22.

34. Here, too, the fictional text seems to incorporate its author's personal peeves. In an interview with me in 1980, Martín Gaite expressed in no uncertain terms how man can be tedious or boring ("pesado") and too abstract, too immersed in terminology and theory. Though she is well-informed and read in

structuralist and poststructuralist theory, Martín Gaite declares her preference for writing without the imposition of abstract theory. Things are narrated well or badly and that is all, she maintains.

35. Tzvetan Todorov, *The Fantastic: A Structural Approach to a Literary Genre,* trans. Richard Howard (Cleveland: The Press of Case Western Reserve University, 1973), 139.

36. From *The Diary of Anaïs Nin,* II (August 1937), quoted in *Woman as Writer,* ed. Jeanette L. Webber and Joan Grumman (Boston: Houghton Mifflin, 1972), 34–35.

37. Shortly after the publication of *El cuarto,* Julia Kristeva expressed views not unlike those of Martín Gaite and, before her, Anaïs Nin. In her consideration of how woman's desire for affirmation manifests itself in literary creation, Kristeva, too, observes how literature may reveal the nocturnal, secret, unconscious universe repressed by the social contract. In "exposing the unsaid, the uncanny," and in making "a game, a space of fantasy and pleasure, out of the abstract and frustrating order of social signs," women express their desire "to nourish our societies with a more flexible and free discourse," suggests Kristeva. See Julia Kristeva, "Women's Time," trans. Alice Jardine and Harry Blake, in *Feminist Theory: A Critique of Ideology,* ed. Nannerl O. Keohane, Michelle Z. Rosaldo, and Barbara C. Gelpi (Chicago: University of Chicago Press, 1982), 49–50. From this perspective, the nocturnal space of *Retahílas* emerges even more boldly as a precursor of *El cuarto*'s nocturnal discourse.

38. Suñén, "Interlocutor intruso," 11.

Chapter 4. In Search of Her Mother's House

1. María Elena Bravo has observed: "en 1975 . . . lo que sí se produce es un ambiente mucho más acogedor para lo que hasta ahora podía haber parecido excepcional. La experimentación ocupa la total atención de los novelistas" (in 1975 that which is produced is an environment much more accepting of what before might have seemed exceptional. Experimentation completely occupies the attention of novelists). María Elena Bravo, "Ante la novela de la democracia: Reflexiones sobre sus raíces," *Insula* 38 (November–December 1983): 24.

2. Concha Alós, *Os habla Electra* (Barcelona: Plaza & Janés, 1975), 9. Subsequent references to this work will be from this edition and will be cited parenthetically within the text.

3. Luis Suñén, "El mito en el espejo," *Insula* 382 (September 1978): 5.

4. See Fredric Jameson, *The Political Unconscious: Narrative as a Socially Symbolic Act* (Ithaca, N.Y.: Cornell University Press, 1981), 27, 110.

5. Jacques Derrida, *Writing and Difference,* trans. Alan Bass (Chicago: The University of Chicago Press, 1978), 286.

6. Salient characteristics of the matrilinear or "Green World," as identified by Annis Pratt, are freedom, a oneness with nature, and the presence of a Green World or nonpatriarchal lover. Patriarchal counteraspects of such matrilinear archetypes are enclosure, rape, and imposed "femininity." Opposed to matrilinear figures such as wise old women or figures engaged in herbal lore and healing are "policing" women and the domesticated activities of cooking and nursing as they have been formulated and practiced by patriarchal cultures. (This schema of matrilinear aspects and patriarchal responses or counteraspects

was initially introduced by Pratt in "Feminist Archetypal Theory: Some Definitions," a paper delivered at the Annual Convention of the Midwest Modern Language Association, St. Louis, 4–6 November 1976. When I use the word "matrilinear"—as opposed to matrilineal—I shall be signaling my specific reference to Pratt's supplementary archetypal formulations. Also my recurrent use of the term or concept "Green World" will be borrowed from Pratt's suggestive terminology.)

7. As an aid to the reader, I briefly outline here the Frye quest paradigm, followed by Pratt's revision, in order to underscore differences in the female quest. A. Phases of the Quest-Romance from Northrop Frye, *Anatomy of Criticism* (New York: Atheneum, 1968), 198–203: 1. Myth of the Birth of the Hero; 2. Innocent youth of the hero: pastoral, Arcadian world; 3. Quest theme, struggle against adversaries such as witches, "terrible mother"; 4. Happier society more or less visible through the action; 5. Reflective, idyllic view of experience from above; 6. Penseroso phase, the end of a movement from active to contemplative adventure; cosmic disaster and life beginning anew. B. The Inner Journey of the Female Hero from Pratt, "Feminist Archetypal Theory: Some Definitions": 1. The Green World remembered; 2. The Green World lover recalled or met; 3. Confrontation with parents within the mind; 4. Final agon leading to 5. Elixir of androgyny and 6. Return to patriarchy, backlash.

8. See Frye, *Anatomy,* 186–206.

9. One might conjecture if Kant bears any resemblance to the philosopher of the same name. Certainly a meditation of Luce Irigaray on the philosopher is suggestive in this novel's context: "And, in the suffering made necessary by his pleasure, shall we place Kant next to Sade? Or, if the subtlety of his mind is given one quarter turn of the screw more—in or out—next to Masoch? The lawgiver is the cruel instrument implementing the rule, of course, but he is also forced into a painful respect for Nature. . . ." See Luce Irigaray, *Speculum of the Other Woman,* trans. Gillian C. Gill (Ithaca, N.Y.: Cornell University Press, 1985), 212.

10. The daughter's symbolic recreation of her mother in this way recalls an essential attribute of matriarchal societies as conceived by Robert Briffault: "Those societies where the influence and power wielded by women have been greatest, are uniformly characterised by greater sexual freedom as compared with patriarchal societies." See *The Mothers,* Vol. III (New York: The Macmillan Company, 1927), 256. In fact, as J. J. Bachofen has also summarized, matriarchal people are characterized by "their aversion to restrictions of all sorts." See *Myth, Religion and Mother Right,* trans. Ralph Manheim (Princeton: Princeton University Press, 1967), 88. In the context of these discourses on matriarchal attitudes and values, the condition of being a bastard can be viewed with pride and admiration (Electra's progeny as "tan libres y bellamente bastardos" [so free and beautifully bastardly]) (70), for it implies the mother's power to freely consider man as progenitor, not as protector nor proprietor as the restrictions of patriarchal discourse would define him.

11. See Helen Diner, *Mothers and Amazons: The First Feminine History of Culture,* trans. John Philip Lundin (New York: Anchor Press, 1973), 36.

12. Bachofen, *Mother Right,* 91.

13. Briffault discusses the widespread association with women of rites designed to produce and control rainfall in *The Mothers,* 10.

14. See Joseph Campbell, *The Masks of God: Occidental Mythology* (New York: Penguin Books, 1984), 106.

15. See Evelyn Reed, *Woman's Evolution* (New York: Pathfinder Press, 1975), 339.

16. Phyllis Chesler writes apropos the oppressive conditions of the mental institution: "The patriarchal nature of psychiatric hospitals has been documented. . . . At their worst mental asylums are families bureaucratized: the degradation and disenfranchisement of self, experienced by the biologically owned child (patient, woman), takes place in the anonymous and therefore guiltless embrace of strange fathers and mothers." Phyllis Chesler, *Women and Madness* (New York: Avon Books, 1972), 34–35.

17. Joseph Campbell, *The Hero with a Thousand Faces* (New York: Bollingen Series XVII, 1953), 71.

18. Suñen, "El mito," 5.

19. Esther Tusquets, *El mismo mar de todos los veranos* (Barcelona: Editorial Lumen, 1978), 12. Subsequent references to this novel will be cited parenthetically within the text.

20. Diner, *Mothers and Amazons*, 36.

21. See Bachofen, *Mother Right*, 88–112 for a discussion of this spiritual evolution in Western culture. Also see Gerda Lerner, *The Creation of Patriarchy* (New York: Oxford University Press, 1986), for more recent, though similar, views on cultural transformations leading from the supremacy to the subordination of goddesses powerful in their own right.

22. Bachofen reminds us that Luna (Selene in Greek mythology) is the prototype of the matriarchal woman (*Mother Right*, 115). Though Dionysus is often associated with the matriarchal Demeter, and is a sacrificial victim himself, here the young woman as Ariadne becomes herself a passive, sacrificial victim, caught metaphorically between the Scylla and Charybdis of man's repressed and unclaimed bestiality (the Minotaur) and the redeeming, protective husband, Dionysus. Bachofen identifies Dionysus as "foremost among the great adversaries of matriarchy" and as calling for fulfillment of the marriage law (*Mother Right*, 100).

23. Rachel Blau Du Plessis, "Washing Blood," *Feminist Studies* 4 (June 1978): 10.

24. Campbell, *The Hero*, 37.

25. Ibid.

26. Cristina Peri Rossi's Ariadna is suggestive in this sense: "triunfante navegaba, esta vez, por sus propios periplos elegidos, conduciendo su nave y su timón con independencia" (triumphantly, this time, according to her own itinerary, steering her own vessel and her helm with independence). See *Los museos abandonados* (Barcelona: Editorial Lumen, 1974), 102.

Chapter 5. Writing "Her/story"

1. Ymelda Navajo assesses some influences on Spanish women writers during the early eighties: "In my opinion, the influence exercised by authors like Virginia Woolf, Simone de Beauvoir, Doris Lessing or Mary MacCarthy has contributed toward 'universalizing' to a certain extent the uneasiness or projects of the immense majority of women who are publishing at this time. I would even say that many of the narratives . . . more closely approach the work of young

American or British women writers than the feminine fiction of the Spanish postwar period." See *Doce relatos de mujeres* (Madrid: Alianza Editorial, 1983), 12. Translation is my own.

2. See Hayden White, "The Historical Text as Literary Artifact," *Clio* 3 (1974): 277–303.

3. Yurij Lotman and B. A. Uspensky, "On the Semiotic Mechanism of Culture," in *Critical Theory Since 1965*, ed. Hazard Adams and Leroy Searle (Tallahassee: Florida State University Press, 1986), 413.

4. Carme Riera, *Una primavera para Domenico Guarini*, trans. Luisa Cotoner (Barcelona: Montesinos, 1981), 107. Subsequent citations will be from the same edition and will be indicated parenthetically in the text.

5. Gary Saul Morson, "Who Speaks for Bakhtin?: A Dialogic Introduction," *Critical Inquiry* 10 (December 1983): 236.

6. Gayatri Chakravorty Spivak, "Finding Feminist Readings: Dante-Yeats," in *American Criticism in the Poststructuralist Age*," ed. Ira Konigsberg (Ann Arbor: University of Michigan Press, 1981), 54.

7. See Annis Pratt's pertinent consideration of the myth of Daphne and Apollo in *Archetypal Patterns in Women's Fiction* (Bloomington: Indiana University Press, 1981), 3–12.

8. "Primavera" was originally painted for Lorenzo de Pierfrancesco, when this patron of Botticelli was a boy of some fourteen to fifteen years of age. And though, according to E. H. Gombrich, there are few, if any, fixed meanings in the painting, Gombrich's exegesis, as well as the one we find in the novel, make most sense when we know that the recipient of the painting and of its message was a boy. Venus, "as a guide to the love of men," and the other mythological figures of her entourage were supposed to "speak" to the boy, provide an ambiguous, sometimes even arcane lesson in the practical and spiritual virtues of Renaissance manhood. This suggests a possible problem in interpretation when the viewer or "reader" of the painting happens to be female and contemporary. See E. H. Gombrich, "Botticelli's Mythologies: A Study in the Neoplatonic Symbolism of his Circle," *Journal of the Warburg and Courtauld Institutes* 8 (1945): 17.

9. Spivak, "Finding Feminist Readings," 51.

10. Gombrich leans, for historical reasons, toward Venus Humanitas as the central figure of "Primavera," See "Botticelli's Mythologies," 19.

11. See Jane Gallop, *The Daughter's Seduction: Feminism and Psychoanalysis* (Ithaca, N.Y.: Cornell University Press, 1982), 113–131, for a discussion of the phallic Mother.

12. Ibid., 31.

13. Interestingly apropos this character, Riera cites Annie Leclerc's attempts to invent new words "en mi vientre" (in my womb). See Carme Riera, "Literatura femenina: ¿Un lenguaje prestado?" *Quimera* 18 (April 1982): 10.

14. Julia Kristeva, *Desire in Language: A Semiotic Approach to Literature and Art*, ed. Leon S. Roudiez, trans. Thomas Gora, Alice Jardine, and Leon S. Roudiez (New York: Columbia University Press, 1980), 240.

15. Riera, "Literatura femenina," 12.

16. Carmen Gómez Ojea, *Otras mujeres y Fabia* (Barcelona: Argos Vergara, 1982), 13. Hereafter page references will be indicated parenthetically within the text.

17. Milagros Sánchez Arnosi, "El mundo de los libros: Gómez Ojea, *Otras mujeres y Fabia*," *Insula* 431 (October 1982): 8.

18. Pratt, *Archetypal Patterns*, 127.

19. Elaine Showalter, "Feminist Criticism in the Wilderness," *Critical Inquiry* 8 (1981): 201.

20. Virginia Woolf, *A Room of One's Own* (London: Hogarth Press, 1929), 146.

21. In my "Narrative Texts by Ethnic Women," I observe an aspect of Maxine Hong Kingston's *The Woman Warrior* that provides a suggestive analogy here: "the new Woman Warrior is a writer, a re-teller of ancient tales so that women may emerge hero of her own destiny, her own text." See Elizabeth Ordóñez, "Narrative Texts by Ethnic Women: Rereading the Past, Reshaping the Future," *MELUS* 9 (1982): 26.

22. Sánchez Arnosi, "El mundo de los libros," 8.

23. Richard King reminds us that Mitchell "thought it obvious" that Scarlett's letter "S" was for "survival." See Richard King, "The 'Simple Story's' Ideology: *Gone with the Wind* and the New South Creed," in *Recasting: Gone with the Wind in American Culture*, ed. Darden Asbury Pyron (Miami: University Press of Florida, 1983), 180–81.

24. Helen Deiss Irvin, "Gea in Georgia: A Mythic Dimension in *Gone with the Wind*," in Ibid., 68.

25. May Sarton, *Journal of a Solitude* (New York: W. W. Norton, 1977), 113.

26. Bernard F. Reilly, *The Kingdom of Leon-Castilla Under Queen Urraca: 1109–1126* (Princeton: Princeton University Press, 1982), 353.

27. Juan de Dios de la Rada y Delgado, *Mujeres célebres de España y Portugal* (Buenos Aires, Espasa Calpe, 1954), 55–84.

28. E. L. Miron, *The Queens of Aragon: Their Lives and Times* (New York: Kennikat Press, 1970), 43–61. Reilly's more recent evidence cites the Count of Lara as Urraca's "lover and her companion until her death." See *The Kingdom*, 353.

29. As communicated to me by Lourdes Ortiz in personal correspondence, 13 October 1983.

30. Jane Tibbetts Schulenburg, "Clio's European Daughters: Myopic Modes of Perception," in *The Prism of Sex: Essays in the Sociology of Knowledge*, ed. Julia A. Sherman and Evelyn Torton Beck (Madison: The University of Wisconsin Press, 1977), 42.

31. Lourdes Ortiz, *Urraca* (Madrid: Puntual Ediciones, 1982), 12. Subsequent citations from this novel will be included parenthetically within the text.

32. Roland Barthes, *The Pleasure of the Text*, trans. Richard Miller (New York: Hill and Wang, 1975), 14.

33. Ibid.

34. See Reilly, *The Kingdom*, 346–49.

35. Mary Jacobus, "The Difference of View," in *Women Writing and Writing About Women*, ed. Mary Jacobus (London: Croom Helm, 1979), 12.

36. See Beth Miller, "Introduction: Some Theoretical Considerations," in *Women in Hispanic Literature: Icons and Fallen Idols*, ed. Beth Miller (Berkeley: University of California Press, 1983), 8, for a succinct overview of the polarization of female characters in male-authored Hispanic literature.

37. From Gallop, *The Daughter's Seduction*, 49–50.

38. In medieval writings fear and suspicion of the menstruating woman are common. Shulamith Shahar writes: "One of the pupils of Albertus Magnus writes that woman's menstrual blood is injurious to the penis and to any plant she touches. Thomas Aquinas writes that the gaze of a menstruating woman can dim and crack a mirror." See *The Fourth Estate* trans. Chaya Galai (London: Methuen, 1983), 73. Barbara G. Walker adds to our knowledge of these Chris-

tian beliefs and superstitions about menstruating women: "St. Jerome wrote: 'Nothing is so unclean as a woman in her periods; what she touches she causes to become unclean.' From the 8th to the 11th centuries, many church laws denied menstruating women any access to church buildings. In 1298 the Synod of Wurzburg commanded men not to approach a menstruating woman." See *The Woman's Encyclopedia of Myths and Secrets* (San Francisco: Harper & Row, 1983), 643.

39. Gallop, *The Daughter's Seduction,* 83. Walker confirms this view by citing examples of how "menstrual blood occupied a central position in matriarchal theologies" (*The Woman's Encyclopedia,* 641). She also cites historical evidence that "medieval peasants thought it could heal, nourish, and fertilize" (ibid., 644). Also see Ernest Crawley, *The Mystic Rose* (New York: Meridian Books, 1960), 241.

40. Hélène Cixous, "The Laugh of the Medusa," in *New French Feminisms,* ed. Elaine Marks and Isabelle de Courtivron (University of Massachusetts Press, 1980), 256.

41. Hayden White, "The Value of Narrativity in the Representation of Reality," *Critical Inquiry* 7 (Autumn 1980): 23.

42. Cixous, "The Laugh," in *New French,* 250.

43. Evelyne García, "Lectura: N. Fem. Sing. ¿Lee y escribe la mujer en forma diferente al hombre?" *Quimera* 23 (September 1982): 57.

Chapter 6. Parody and Defiance

1. See M. M. Bakhtin, *The Dialogic Imagination,* ed. Michael Holquist, trans. Caryl Emerson and Michael Holquist (Austin: The University of Texas Press, 1981), 68–83.

2. Julia Kristeva characterizes parody as the introduction of "a signification opposed to that of the other's word." See Julia Kristeva, *Desire in Language: A Semiotic Approach to Literature and Art,* ed. Leon S. Roudiez, trans. Thomas Gora, Alice Jardine, and Leon S. Roudiez (New York: Columbia University Press, 1980), 73. Wayne Booth, through Shakespeare, indicates how parody establishes its superiority to convention. See Wayne C. Booth, *A Rhetoric of Irony* (Chicago: The University of Chicago Press, 1975), 125.

3. Maria Luz Diéguez, "Entrevista con Paloma Díaz-Mas (febrero de 1987)," *Revista de Estudios Hispánicos* 22 (January 1988): 80.

4. See Barbara G. Walker, *The Woman's Encyclopedia of Myths and Secrets* (San Francisco: Harper & Row, 1983), 378–79.

5. Paloma Díaz-Mas, *El rapto del Santo Grial* (Barcelona: Anagrama, 1984), 11. Subsequent citations from this work will be from this edition and will be indicated parenthetically within the text.

6. Maurice Keen demystifies the traditional qualities of knighthood, such as service, courage, and prowess, as having "quintessentially martial associations rather than religious ones." See Maurice Keen, *Chivalry* (New Haven: Yale University Press, 1984), 81. Martín de Riquer has advanced the proposition that Chrétien's Grail narrative was grounded not so much on Celtic mythologies or a realm of idealized fiction as on contemporary struggles of real men for political power. See Martín de Riquer, *La leyenda del graal y temas épicos medievales* (Madrid: Prensa Española, 1968), 122–33. These more militaristic aspects of chivalry were particularly marked in peninsular versions of Grail material, as William Entwistle

rather quaintly describes the heroes of the Portuguese *Demanda do Santo Graal:* "nobody cares for the Holy Vessel; nobody has any purpose save cuffs and blows. Galahad is as absurdly pugilistic as any other knight." See William J. Entwistle, *The Arthurian Legend in the Literatures of the Spanish Peninsula* (Millwood, N.Y.: Krause Reprint Company, 1975), 165. María Rosa Lida de Malkiel reaches a similar conclusion: she marks particularly the "preference for duels and knightly deeds" of the Castilian *Demanda,* chastizing its "mania for piling up mere feats of chivalry." See María Rosa Lida de Malkiel, "Arthurian Literature in Spain and Portugal," in *Arthurian Literature in the Middle Ages,* ed. Roger Sherman Loomis (Oxford: Oxford University Press, 1959), 412. And more recently, J. B. Hall concludes that the glorification of martial exploits in chivalric literature propped up a very real consolidation of economic power among the Castilian nobility. See J. B. Hall, "La Matiere Arthurienne Espagnole," *Revue de Littérature Comparée,* 56 (1982): 435.

7. Annis Pratt, *Archetypal Patterns in Women's Fiction* (Bloomington: Indiana University Press, 1981), 174.

8. See Per Nykrog, "Trajectory of the hero: Gauvain paragon of chivalry 1130–1230," in *Medieval Narrative: A Symposium,* ed. Hans Bekker-Nielsen (Odense: Odense University Press, 1978), 92.

9. See Wayne Booth's observations on these functions of parody in *A Rhetoric of Irony,* 71–72.

10. Annie Leclerc, "Woman's Word," in *New French Feminisms,* ed. Elaine Marks and Isabelle de Courtivron (Amherst: University of Massachusetts Press, 1989), 82 and 85.

11. See Walker, *The Woman's Encyclopedia of Myths,* 829.

12. Ibid., 1043–44.

13. See Jessie L. Weston, *From Ritual to Romance* (Garden City: Doubleday Anchor, 1957) and *The Quest of the Holy Grail* (New York: Haskell House, 1965); and Roger Sherman Loomis, "The Origin of Grail Legends," in *Arthurian Literature in the Middle Ages,* ed. Roger Sherman Loomis (Oxford: Oxford University Press, 1959), 274–94.

14. Hélène Cixous, "The Laugh of the Medusa," in *New French Feminisms,* ed. Marks and de Courtivron, 257.

15. María Luz Diéguez has also identified the tragic incommunicability between the discourses of the "Doncella" and Pelinor ("Entrevista," 86–87).

16. Díaz-Mas has commented upon the complexity of factors enmeshing both woman and man in a system of deadly requirements: "la pareja más idealizada es víctima de un juego de intereses enormemente sucio que se sirve de Pelinor para que la mate a ella y luego sacrifica a Pelinor. Así, la mujer no es la única víctima; también el varón correspondiente es víctima de la situación" (the most idealized pair is victim of enormously dirty vested interests that are using Pelinor to kill her and then sacrifice Pelinor. Thus, woman is not the only victim; the corresponding male is also victim of the situation) (ibid., 85).

17. When Pelinor departs in service to King Arthur he dubs himself Caballero de la Verde Oliva, "símbolo de la paz en la que creo" (symbol of the peace in which I believe) (Díaz-Mas, *Rapto,* 24). This assertion is obviously meant to prove ironic after his violent encounter with the Purple Knight.

18. Madeleine Gagnon observes how man is constantly confronting himself, setting up mirrors, projecting his fantasm in his attempt to master himself and diminish others. Woman, in contrast, just lets herself flow. Madeleine Gagnon, "Body I," in *New French Feminisms,* Marks and de Courtivron, 179–80.

19. Chantal Chawaff, "Linguistic Flesh," in *New French Feminisms*, Marks and de Courtivron, 177.

20. Weston, *From Ritual to Romance*, 47.

21. Joseph Campbell, *The Masks of God: Creative Mythology* (New York: Penguin Books, 1984), 459.

22. Elizabeth Gould Davis, *The First Sex* (Baltimore: Penguin Books, 1971), 97. Davis maintains that "it was not until the patriarchal revolution that phallus worship became the purely masculine preoccupation that it remains to this day." (*First Sex*, 98.)

23. See Walker, *The Woman's Encyclopedia*, 862.

24. Helen Diner, *Mothers and Amazons: The First Feminine History of Culture*, trans. John Philip Lundin (New York: Anchor Press, 1973), 203.

25. Weston, *Quest*, 93.

26. Weston, *From Ritual to Romance*, 75.

27. Viviane Forrester, "What Women's Eyes See," in *New French Feminisms*, ed. Marks and de Courtivron, 181.

28. Carmen Gómez Ojea, *Los perros de Hécate* (Barcelona: Grijalbo, 1985), 8–9. Subsequent references to this novel will be indicated parenthetically within the text.

29. Elizabeth A. Meese, *Crossing the Double-Cross: The Practice of Feminist Criticism* (Chapel Hill: The University of North Carolina Press, 1986), 17.

30. Michel Foucault, *The History of Sexuality, Vol. I: An Introduction*, trans. Robert Hurley (New York: Vintage Books, 1980), 39–40.

31. Jane Gallop, *The Daughter's Seduction: Feminism and Psychoanalysis* (Ithaca, N.Y.: Cornell University Press, 1982), 89.

32. Edward W. Said, "The Text, the World, the Critic," in *Textual Strategies: Perspectives in Post-Structuralist Criticism*, ed. Josué V. Harari (Ithaca, N.Y.: Cornell University Press, 1979), 179.

33. See Cixous, "The Laugh," in *New French Feminisms*, ed. Marks and de Courtivron, and Nancy K. Miller, "Women's Autobiography in France: For a Dialectics of Identification," in *Women and Language in Literature and Society*, ed. Sally McConnell-Ginet, Ruth Borker, and Nelly Furman (New York: Praeger, 1980), 258–73, wherein these ideas are expressed.

34. See Walker, *The Woman's Encyclopedia*, 378–79.

35. See ibid., 168–69 and 628 for these nonpatriarchal revisions of Circe and Medea.

36. I borrow the concept of "refusing the authority of the signified" from Nelly Furman, "Textual Feminism," in *Women and Language*, ed. McConnell-Ginet et al., 49.

Chapter 7. Beyond the Father

1. Tzvetan Todorov, *The Fantastic: A Structural Approach to a Literary Genre*, trans. Richard Howard (Cleveland: The Press of Case Western Reserve University, 1973), 25.

2. Ibid., 138.

3. Fredric Jameson, *The Political Unconscious: Narrative as a Socially Symbolic Act* (Ithaca, N.Y.: Cornell University Press, 1981), 106.

4. See Rosemary Jackson, *Fantasy: The Literature of Subversion* (New York: Methuen, 1981).

5. Ibid., 54.

6. See Ibid. for further analyses of these themes and motifs.

7. Ibid., 104.

8. Andrés Amorós, *Introducción a la novela contemporanea* (Salamanca: Ediciones Anaya, 1966), 159.

9. Adelaida García Morales, *El Sur seguido de Bene* (Barcelona: Ediciones Anagrama, 1985), 6. Subsequent citations from *El Sur* will be from this edition and will be indicated parenthetically within the text.

10. Milagros Sánchez Arnosi, "Adelaida García Morales: La soledad gozosa," *Insula* 472 (March 1986): 4.

11. Jane Gallop, *The Daughter's Seduction: Feminism and Psychoanalysis* (Ithaca, N.Y.: Cornell University Press, 1982), 70.

12. See Norman N. Holland and Leona F. Sherman, "Gothic Possibilities," in *Gender and Reading: Essays on Readers, Texts, and Contexts*, ed. Elizabeth A. Flynn and Patrocinio P. Schweickart (Baltimore: The Johns Hopkins University Press, 1986), 215–33.

13. Rafael Llopis, *Esbozo de una historia natural de los cuentos de miedo* (Madrid: Ediciones Juncar, 1974), 160–61.

14. See Elizabeth Ordóñez, "Paradise Regained, Paradise Lost: Desire and Prohibition in *La madre naturaleza*," *Hispanic Journal* 8 (1986): 7–18 for a more extensive study on the sister-brother bond as a mode of defying the Father's Law.

15. Gallop, *The Daughter's Seduction*, 79.

16. Given certain similarities of theme and tone between *Bene* and Henry James's *The Turn of the Screw*, I have been inspired in many of my observations by Shoshana Felman's brilliant study of this James novel, "Turning the Screw of Interpretation," in *Literature and Psychoanalysis: The Question of Reading—Otherwise*, ed. Shoshana Felman (Baltimore: The Johns Hopkins University Press, 1982), 94–204. Felman's argument rests upon the premise that the James novel never resolves its ambiguity, and from Edmund Wilson's three ways in which the text questions (through its rhetoric, its thematic content, and its narrative structure), she constructs her elaborate examination into this threefold refusal of the Jamesian text to tell all.

17. García Morales, *El Sur seguido de Bene*, 58. Subsequent citations from *Bene* will be from this edition and will be indicated parenthetically within the text.

18. Felman, "Turning the Screw," Felman, 107.

19. Jameson, *The Political Unconscious*, 115.

20. Felman, "Turning the Screw," Felman, 193.

21. Jackson, *Fantasy*, 69.

22. Ibid.

23. Peter Brooks, "The Idea of a Psychoanalytic Literary Criticism," *Critical Inquiry*, 13 (1987): 343.

24. Brooks, "The Idea," 345.

25. Felman, "Turning the Screw," Felman, 133.

26. Adelaida García Morales, *El silencio de las sirenas* (Barcelona: Anagrama, 1986), 51. Subsequent citations from this novel will be from this edition and will be indicated parenthetically within the text.

27. Fredric Jameson has charted this process in Lacanian terms: "In any case, whatever the nature of the Lacanian Symbolic, it is clear that the Imaginary—a kind of pre-verbal register whose logic is essentially visual—precedes it as a stage in the development of the psyche." See "Imaginary and Symbolic in Lacan: Marxism, Psychoanalytic Criticism, and the Problem of the Subject," in *Literature*

and Psychoanalysis, ed. Felman, 353. Though Jameson is thinking here of the "mirror stage" of psychic development when the Imaginary is formed and the subject and its "imago" become forever split, I think it is safe to extrapolate that if the subject sees the image of one it desires, a gap similar to that formed between the subject and its own self, a gap that never can be bridged, may form. This constitutes the desire that becomes the "motor of narrative" and the force impelling Elsa's love story. See Ronald Schleifer, "The Space and Dialogue of Desire: Lacan, Greimas, and Narrative Temporality," in *Lacan and Narration: The Psychoanalytic Difference in Narrative Theory,* ed. Robert Con Davis (Baltimore: The Johns Hopkins University Press, 1983), 884.

28. Juliet Flower MacCannell, *Figuring Lacan: Criticism and the Cultural Unconscious* (Lincoln: University of Nebraska Press, 1986), 135.

29. Barbara Johnson has studied this fearful circumstance of the woman writer whose "autobiographical reflex" often engenders images of monstruousness as a result of the "difficulty in conforming to a female ideal which is largely a fantasy of the masculine, not the feminine, imagination." See "My Monster/My Self," *Diacritics* 12 (1982): 10.

30. Jacques Lacan, *Ecrits: A Selection,* trans. Alan Sheridan (London: Tavistock, 1977), 311.

Chapter 8. Rewriting the Future

1. Ana María Matute, *Primera memoria* (Barcelona: Ediciones Destino, 1971), 243. Subsequent citations from this novel will be indicated parenthetically within the text.

2. Concha Alós, *Los cien pájaros* (Barcelona: Plaza y Janés, 1963), 33. Subsequent citations from this novel will be indicated parenthetically within the text.

3. Alós, as other women writers considered in this study, rejects the stock ending of the "novela rosa": "todo se resuelve en la novela rosa con el cumplimiento del ideal pequeño burgués del matrimonio" (everything is resolved in the sentimental novel with the fulfillment of the petite bourgeois ideal of marriage). Cited by José María Diez Borque in *Literatura y cultura de masas* (Madrid: Al-Borak, 1972), 159–60.

4. Esther Tusquets, *Varada tras el último naufragio* (Barcelona: Editorial Lumen, 1980), 10.

5. Geraldine Cleary Nichols, "The Prison-House (and Beyond): *El mismo mar de todos los veranos*," *Romanic Review* 75 (1984): 369.

6. Montserrat Roig, *La hora violeta,* trans. Enrique Sordo (Barcelona: Argos Vergara, 1980), 17. Subsequent citations from this novel will be indicated parenthetically within the text.

7. Nichols, "The Prison-House (and Beyond)," 374.

8. Catherine G. Bellver, "The Language of Eroticism in the Novels of Esther Tusquets," *Anales de la Literatura Española Contemporanea* 9 (1984): 20, 14.

9. Ibid., 14.

10. Montserrat Roig, *La ópera cotidiana,* trans. Enrique Sordo (Barcelona: Argos Vergara, 1980), 120. Subsequent citations from this novel will be indicated parenthetically within the text.

11. Marta Portal, *Un espacio erótico* (Madrid: Ibérico Europea de Ediciones,

1983), 107. Subsequent citations from this novel will be indicated parenthetically within the text.

12. Julia Kristeva, *Desire in Language: A Semiotic Approach to Literature and Art,* ed. Leon S. Roudiez, trans. Thomas Gora, Alice Jardine, and Leon S. Roudiez (New York: Columbia University Press, 1980), 239.

Bibliography

Primary Sources

Alós, Concha. *Argeo ha muerto, supongo.* Barcelona: Plaza & Janés, 1982.

———. *El asesino de los sueños.* Barcelona: Plaza & Janés, 1986.

———. *Los cien pájaros.* Barcelona: Plaza & Janés, 1963.

———. *Os habla Electra.* Barcelona: Plaza & Janés, 1975.

Díaz-Mas, Paloma. *El rapto del Santo Grial.* Barcelona: Anagrama, 1984.

García Morales, Adelaida. *El silencio de las sirenas.* Barcelona: Anagrama, 1986.

———. *El Sur seguido de Bene.* Barcelona: Anagrama, 1985.

Gómez Ojea, Carmen. *Los perros de Hécate.* Barcelona: Grijalbo, 1985.

———. *Otras mujeres y Fabia.* Barcelona: Argos Vergara, 1982.

Kurtz, Carmen. *Al lado del hombre.* Barcelona: Planeta, 1961.

———. *Cándidas palomas.* Barcelona: Bruguera, 1976.

Laforet, Carmen. *La isla y los demonios.* Barcelona: Destino, 1970.

———. *Nada.* Barcelona: Destino, 1969.

Martín Gaite, Carmen. *El cuarto de atrás.* Barcelona: Destino, 1978.

———. *Entre visillos.* Barcelona: Destino, 1958.

———. *Fragmentos de interior.* Barcelona: Destino, 1976.

———. *Retahílas.* Barcelona: Destino, 1974.

Matute, Ana María. *La trampa.* Barcelona: Destino, 1969.

———. *Primera memoria.* Barcelona: Destino, 1971.

Montero, Rosa. *La función delta.* Madrid: Debate, 1981.

———. *Te trataré como a una reina.* Barcelona: Seix Barral, 1984.

Ortiz, Lourdes. *Urraca.* Madrid: Puntual Ediciones, 1982.

Portal, Marta. *Un espacio erótico.* Madrid: Ibérico Europea de Ediciones, 1983.

Quiroga, Elena. *La enferma.* Barcelona: Noguer, 1962.

———. *Presente profundo.* Barcelona: Destino, 1973.

Riera, Carme. *Palabra de mujer.* Barcelona: Laia, 1980.

———. *Una primavera para Domenico Guarini.* Translated by Luisa Cotoner. Barcelona: Montesinos, 1981.

Roig, Montserrat. *La hora violeta.* Translated by Enrique Sordo. Barcelona: Argos Vergara, 1980.

———. *La ópera cotidiana.* Translated by Enrique Sordo. Barcelona: Planeta, 1983.

———. *Ramona, adiós.* Translated by Joaquín Sempere. Barcelona: Argos Vergara, 1980.

Soriano, Elena. *La playa de los locos.* Barcelona: Argos Vergara, 1984.

Tusquets, Esther. *El amor es un juego solitario.* Barcelona: Lumen, 1979.

―――. *El mismo mar de todos los veranos.* Barcelona: Lumen, 1978.

―――. *Varada tras el último naufragio.* Barcelona: Lumen, 1980.

Secondary Sources

Alborg, Juan Luis. *Hora actual de la novela española,* I. Madrid: Taurus, 1963.

Alcoff, Linda. "Cultural Feminism versus Post-Structuralism: The Identity Crisis in Feminist Theory." *Signs* 13 (1988): 405–36.

Alvarez Palacios, Fernando. *Novela y cultura española de postguerra.* Madrid: Edicusa, 1975.

Amorós, Andrés. *Introducción a la novela contemporanea.* Salamanca: Ediciones Anaya, 1966.

Araújo, Helena. "¿Escritura femenina?" *Escandalar* 4 (1981): 32–36.

Bachofen, J. J. *Myth, Religion and Mother Right.* Translated by Ralph Manheim. Bollingen Series, LXXIV. Princeton: Princeton University Press, 1967.

Bakhtin, M. M. *The Dialogic Imagination.* Edited by Michael Holquist, and translated by Caryl Emerson and Michael Holquist. Austin: The University of Texas Press, 1981.

Barthes, Roland. "From Work to Text." In *Textual Strategies: Perspectives in Post-Structuralist Criticism,* edited by Josué V. Harari, 73–81. Ithaca, N.Y.: Cornell University Press, 1979.

―――. *The Pleasure of the Text.* Translated by Richard Miller. New York: Hill and Wang, 1975.

―――. *Writing Degree Zero.* Translated by Annette Lavers and Colin Smith. Boston: Beacon Press, 1970.

Bayo, Eliseo. *Trabajos duros de la mujer.* Barcelona: Plaza & Janés, 1970.

Beauvoir, Simone de. *The Second Sex.* Translated and edited by H. M. Parshley. New York: Alfred A. Knopf, 1952; Bantam Books, 1970.

Beinhauer, Werner. *El carácter español.* Madrid: Ediciones Nueva Epoca, 1944.

Bellver, Catherine G. "The Language of Eroticism in the Novels of Esther Tusquets." *Anales de la Literatura Española Contemporanea* 9 (1984): 13–27.

Blanchot, Maurice. *Le pas au-delá.* Paris, 1973.

Booth, Wayne C. *A Rhetoric of Irony.* Chicago: The University of Chicago Press, 1975.

Bozal, Valeriano. "La edición en España. Notas para su historia." *Cuadernos para el diálogo* 14 (May 1969): 85–93.

Bravo, María Elena. "Ante la novela de la democracia: Reflexiones sobre sus raíces." *Insula* 38 (November–December 1983): 1, 24.

Brecker, Ruth and Edward Brecker. *An Analysis of Human Sexual Response.* Boston: Little, Brown & Co., 1966.

Briffault, Robert. *The Mothers.* Vol. III. New York: The Macmillan Co., 1927.

Brooks, Peter. "The Idea of a Psychoanalytic Literary Criticism." *Critical Inquiry* 13 (1987): 334–48.

Brown, Joan L. "Nonconformity in the Fiction of Carmen Martín Gaite." Ph.D. diss., University of Pennsylvania, 1976.

———. "The Nonconformist Character as Social Critic in the Novels of Carmen Martín Gaite." *Kentucky Romance Quarterly* 28 (1981): 165–76.

Buchanan, Luanne. "La novela como canto a la palabra." *Insula* 34 (November–December 1979): 13.

Butt, John. *Writers and Politics in Modern Spain.* New York: Holmes & Meier, 1978.

Cadenas, C. B. "Historia de tres mujeres." *Nueva estafeta* 18 (May 1980): 76–77.

Campbell, Joseph. *The Hero with a Thousand Faces.* New York: Bollingen Series XVII, 1953.

———. *The Masks of God: Creative Mythology.* New York: Viking, 1968; Penguin, 1984.

———. *The Masks of God: Occidental Mythology.* New York: Viking, 1964; Penguin, 1976.

Camus, Albert. *The Myth of Sisyphus and Other Essays.* Translated by Justin O'Brien. New York: Random House, 1955.

———. *The Stranger.* Translated by Stuart Gilbert. New York: Random House, 1946.

Castilla del Pino, Carlos. *Cuatro ensayos sobre la mujer.* Madrid: Alianza Editorial, 1971.

Castillo, Debra A. "Never-Ending Story: Carmen Martín Gaite's *The Back Room.*" *PMLA* 102 (1987): 814–28.

Chawaff, Chantal. "Linguistic Flesh." In *New French Feminisms,* edited by Elaine Marks and Isabelle de Courtivron, 177–78. Amherst: University of Massachusetts Press, 1980.

Chesler, Phyllis. *Women and Madness.* New York: Doubleday, 1972.

Chodorow, Nancy. *The Reproduction of Mothering: Psychoanalysis and the Sociology of Gender.* Berkeley: University of California Press, 1978.

Chown, Linda E. "American Critics and Spanish Women Novelists, 1942–1980." *Signs* 9 (Autumn 1983): 91–107.

Cixous, Hélène. *Illa.* Paris: Des Femmes, 1980.

———. "The Laugh of the Medusa." In *New French Feminisms,* edited by Elaine Marks and Isabelle de Courtivron, 245–64. Amherst: University of Massachusetts Press, 1980.

Conley, Verena Andermatt. *Hélène Cixous: Writing the Feminine.* Lincoln: University of Nebraska Press, 1984.

Corrales Egea, José. *La novela española actual: Ensayo de ordenación.* Madrid: Edicusa, 1971.

Crawley, Ernest. *The Mystic Rose.* 2 vols. New York: Meridian Books, 1960.

Culler, Jonathan. *On Deconstruction: Theory and Criticism after Structuralism.* Ithaca, N.Y.: Cornell University Press, 1982.

Curutchet, Juan Carlos. *Introducción a la novela española de la postguerra.* Montevideo: Alfa, 1966.

Dalsimer, Katherine. *Female Adolescence: Psychoanalytic Reflections on Literature.* New Haven: Yale University Press, 1986.

Davis, Elizabeth Gould. *The First Sex.* New York: Putnam, 1971; Baltimore: Penguin, 1973.

Derrida, Jacques. *Of Grammatology.* Translated by Gayatri Chakravorty Spivak. Baltimore: The Johns Hopkins University Press, 1978.

———. *Writing and Difference.* Translated by Alan Bass. Chicago: The University of Chicago Press, 1978.

Deutsch, Helene. *The Psychology of Women,* I. New York: Grune & Stratton, 1944; Bantam Books, 1973.

Diéguez, Maria Luz. "Entrevista con Paloma Díaz-Mas (febrero de 1987)." *Revista de Estudios Hispánicos* 22 (January 1988): 77–91.

Diez Borque, José María. *Literatura y cultura de masas.* Madrid: Al-Borak, 1972.

Diner, Helen. *Mothers and Amazons: The First Feminine History of Culture.* Translated by John Philip Lundin. New York: The Julian Press, 1965; Doubleday, 1973.

Du Plessis, Rachel Blau. "Washing Blood." *Feminist Studies* 4 (June 1978): 1–12.

———. *Writing Beyond the Ending: Narrative Strategies of Twentieth-Century Women Writers.* Bloomington: Indiana University Press, 1985.

Durán, Manuel. "Carmen Martín Gaite, *Retahílas, El cuarto de atrás,* y el diálogo sin fin." *Revista Iberoamericana* 47 (1981): 233–40.

———. "*El cuarto de atrás:* Imaginación, fantasía, misterio; Todorov y algo más." In *From Fiction to Metafiction: Essays in Honor of Carmen Martín Gaite,* edited by Mirella D'Ambrosio Servodidio and Marcia L. Welles, 129–37. Lincoln: Society of Spanish and Spanish-American Studies, 1983.

Eagleton, Terry. *Literary Theory: An Introduction.* Minneapolis: University of Minnesota Press, 1983.

Ellmann, Mary. *Thinking About Women.* New York: Harcourt Brace Jovanovich, 1968.

El Saffar, Ruth. "Liberation and Labyrinth: A Study of the Works of Carmen Martín Gaite." In *From Fiction to Metafiction: Essays in Honor of Carmen Martín Gaite,* edited by Mirella D'Ambrosio Servodidio and Marcia L. Welles, 185–96. Lincoln: Society of Spanish and Spanish-American Studies, 1983.

Engels, Frederick. *The Origin of the Family, Private Property and the State.* Edited by Eleanor Burke Leacock. New York; International Publishers, 1973.

Entwistle, William J. *The Arthurian Legend in the Literatures of the Spanish Peninsula.* Millwood, N.Y.: Krause Reprint Company, 1975.

Eoff, Sherman. "*Nada* by Carmen Laforet: A Venture in Mechanistic Dynamics." *Hispania* 25 (1952): 207–11.

Felman, Shoshana. "Turning the Screw of Interpretation." In *Literature and Psychoanalysis: The Question of Reading—Otherwise,* edited by Shoshana Felman, 94–207. Baltimore: The Johns Hopkins University Press, 1982.

Fiedler, Leslie. *Love and Death in the American Novel.* New York: Criterion Books, 1960.

Figes, Eva. *Patriarchal Attitudes: Women in Society.* London: Faber and Faber, 1970.

Forrester, Viviane. "What Women's Eyes See." In *New French Feminisms,* edited by Elaine Marks and Isabelle de Courtivron, 181–82. Amherst: University of Massachusetts Press, 1980.

Foster, David William. "*Nada* de Carmen Laforet: Ejemplo de neo-romance en la novela contemporánea." *Revista Hispánica Moderna* 32 (1966): 43–55.

Foucault, Michel. *Language: Counter-memory, Practice.* Translated by Donald F. Bouchard and Sherry Simon. Ithaca, N.Y.: Cornell University Press, 1977.

———. *The Archaeology of Knowledge.* Translated by A. M. Sheridan Smith. New York: Pantheon Books, 1972.

———. *The History of Sexuality. Vol. I: An Introduction.* Translated by Robert Hurley. New York: Pantheon, 1978; Random House, Vintage, 1980.

Freud, Sigmund. *Civilization and Its Discontents.* Translated and edited by James Strachey. New York: W. W. Norton & Company, 1961.

———. "Femininity." In *The Complete Psychological Works of Sigmund Freud,* XXII (1932–36), edited by James Strachey, 112–35. London: Hogarth Press, 1964.

———. *Letters of Sigmund Freud.* Edited by Ernst L. Freud, and translated by Tania and James Stern. New York: Basic Books, 1960.

———. "The Uncanny." In *On Creativity and the Unconscious: Papers on the Psychology of Art, Literature, Religion,* translated by Alix Strachey. New York: Harper Torchbooks, 1958.

Frye, Northrop. *Anatomy of Criticism.* New York: Atheneum, 1968.

Furman, Nelly. "Textual Feminism." In *Women and Language in Literature and Society,* edited by Sally McConnell-Ginet, Ruth Borker, and Nelly Furman, 45–54. New York: Praeger, 1980.

Gagnon, Madeleine. "Body I." In *New French Feminisms,* edited by Elaine Marks and Isabelle de Courtivron, 179–80. Amherst: University of Massachusetts Press, 1980.

Gallop, Jane. *Reading Lacan.* Ithaca, N.Y.: Cornell University Press, 1985.

———. "Reading the Mother Tongue: Psychoanalytic Feminist Criticism." *Critical Inquiry* 13 (Winter 1987): 314–29.

———. *The Daughter's Seduction: Feminism and Psychoanalysis.* Ithaca, N.Y.: Cornell University Press, 1982.

García, Evelyne. "Lectura: N. Fem. Sing. ¿Lee y escribe la mujer en forma diferente al hombre?" *Quimera* 23 (September 1982): 54–57.

García Viño, M. *Novela española actual.* Madrid: Prensa Española, 1975.

Garner, Shirley Nelson, Claire Kahane, and Madelon Sprengwether, eds. *The (M)other Tongue: Essays in Feminist Psychoanalytic Interpretation.* Ithaca, N.Y. Cornell University Press, 1985.

George, Diana Hume. "'Who is the Double Ghost Whose Head is Smoke?' Women Poets on Aging." In *Memory and Desire: Aging-Literature-Psychoanalysis,* edited by Kathleen Woodward and Murray M. Schwartz, 134–53. Bloomington: Indiana University Press, 1986.

Gil Casado, Pablo. *La novela social española (1920–1971).* Barcelona: Editorial Seix Barral, 1973.

Gilbert, Sandra M. and Susan Gubar. *The Madwoman in the Attic: The Woman Writer and the Nineteenth-Century Literary Imagination.* New Haven: Yale University Press, 1979.

Glenn, Kathleen. "La posibilidad de diálogo: *Retahílas* de Carmen Martín Gaite." Paper presented at the annual meeting of the American Association of Teachers of Spanish and Portuguese, Madrid, August 1986.

———. "*El cuarto de atrás:* Literature as *Juego* and the Self-reflexive Text." In *From Fiction to Metafiction: Essays in Honor of Carmen Martín Gaite,* edited by

Mirella D'Ambrosio Servodidio and Marcia L. Welles, 149–59. Lincoln: Society of Spanish and Spanish-American Studies, 1983.

Gombrich, E. H. "Botticelli's Mythologies: A Study in the Neoplatonic Symbolism of his Circle." *Journal of the Warburg and Courtauld Institutes* 8 (1945): 7–60.

Goytisolo, Juan. *El furgón de cola.* Paris: Ruedo Ibérico, 1970.

Gullón, Ricardo. "Retahíla sobre *Retahílas.*" In *From Fiction to Metafiction: Essays in Honor of Carmen Martín Gaite,* edited by Mirella D'Ambrosio Servodidio and Marcia L. Welles, 73–91. Lincoln: Society of Spanish and Spanish-American Studies, 1983.

Hall, J. B. "La Matiere Arthurienne Espagnole." *Revue de Littérature Comparée* 56 (1982): 423–36.

Harding, M. Esther. *Woman's Mysteries.* New York: Putnam, 1971; Bantam Books, 1973.

Harris, Daniel. "Androgyny: The Sexist Myth in Disguise." *Women's Studies* 3 (1974): 171–84.

Hayes, H. R. *The Dangerous Sex: The Myth of Feminine Evil.* New York: Putnam, 1964; Pocket Books, 1972.

Herzberger, David K. "An Overview of Postwar Novel Criticism of the 1970s." *Anales de la narrativa española contemporanea* 5 (1980): 27–38.

Holland, Norman N. and Leona F. Sherman. "Gothic Possibilities." In *Gender and Reading: Essays on Readers, Texts, and Contexts,* edited by Elizabeth A. Flynn and Patrocinio P. Schweickart, 215–33. Baltimore: The Johns Hopkins University Press, 1986.

Horney, Karen. *New Ways in Psychoanalysis.* New York: Norton, 1939.

Iglesias Laguna, Antonio. *Treinta años de novela española 1938–68,* Vol. I. Madrid: Prensa española, 1970.

Irigaray, Luce. *Speculum of the Other Woman.* Translated by Gillian C. Gill. Ithaca, N.Y.: Cornell University Press, 1985.

———. *This Sex Which Is Not One.* Translated by Catherine Porter with Carolyn Burke. Ithaca, N.Y.: Cornell University Press, 1985.

Irvin, Helen Deiss. "Gea in Georgia: A Mythic Dimension in *Gone with the Wind.*" In *Recasting: Gone with the Wind in American Culture,* edited by Darden Asbury Pyron, 57–68. Miami: University Press of Florida, 1983.

Jackson, Rosemary. *Fantasy: The Literature of Subversion.* New York: Methuen, 1981.

Jacobus, Mary. "The Difference of View." In *Women Writing and Writing About Women,* edited by Mary Jacobus, 10–21. London: Croom Helm, 1979.

Jakobson, Roman. "Linguistics and Poetics." In *The Structuralists: From Marx to Levi-Strauss,* translated by Richard T. and Fernande M. De George, 85–122. New York: Doubleday, 1972.

Jameson, Fredric. "Imaginary and Symbolic in Lacan: Marxism, Psychoanalytic Criticism, and the Problem of the Subject." In *Literature and Psychoanalysis: The Question of Reading—Otherwise,* edited by Shoshana Felman, 338–95. Baltimore: The Johns Hopkins University Press, 1982.

———. *The Political Unconscious: Narrative as a Socially Symbolic Act.* Ithaca, N.Y.: Cornell University Press, 1981.

————. *The Prison-House of Language.* Princeton: Princeton University Press, 1972.

Johnson, Barbara. "My Monster/My Self." *Diacritics* 12 (1982): 2–10.

Jones, Ann Rosalind. "Writing the Body: Toward an Understanding of 'l'Ecriture féminine." In *The New Feminist Criticism: Essays on Women, Literature and Theory,* edited by Elaine Showalter, 361–77. New York: Pantheon Books, 1985.

Jutglar, Antoni. *Mitología del capitalismo.* Madrid: Seminarios y Ediciones, 1971.

Kafka, Franz. "The Silence of the Sirens." In *Parables and Paradoxes,* edited by Nahum N. Glatzer, 88–93. New York: Schocken Books, 1970.

Keen, Maurice. *Chivalry.* New Haven: Yale University Press, 1984.

King, Richard. "The 'Simple Story's' Ideology: *Gone with the Wind* and the New South Creed." In *Recasting: Gone with the Wind in American Culture,* edited by Darden Asbury Pyron, 167–83. Miami: University Press of Florida, 1983.

Kristeva, Julia. *Desire in Language: A Semiotic Approach to Literature and Art.* Edited by Leon S. Roudiez, and translated by Thomas Gora, Alice Jardine, and Leon S. Roudiez. New York: Columbia University Press, 1980.

————. "Oscillation between Power and Denial." In *New French Feminisms,* edited by Elaine Marks and Isabelle de Courtivron, 165–67. Amherst: University of Massachusetts Press, 1980.

————. "Women's Time." Translated by Alice Jardine and Harry Blake. In *Feminist Theory: A Critique of Ideology,* edited by Nannerl O. Keohane, Michelle Z. Rosaldo, and Barbara C. Gelpi, 31–53. Chicago: University of Chicago Press, 1982.

Krupnick, Mark, ed. *Displacement: Derrida and After.* Bloomington: Indiana University Press, 1983.

Lacan, Jacques. *Ecrits: A Selection.* Translated by Alan Sheridan. London: Tavistock, 1977.

Leclerc, Annie. "Woman's Word." In *New French Feminisms,* edited by Elaine Marks and Isabelle de Courtivron, 79–86. Amherst: University of Massachusetts Press, 1980.

Leitch, Vincent B. *Deconstructive Criticism: An Advanced Introduction.* New York: Columbia University Press, 1983.

Lerner, Gerda. *The Creation of Patriarchy.* New York: Oxford University Press, 1986.

Levine, Linda Gould. "Carmen Martín Gaite's *El cuarto de atrás:* A Portrait of the Artist as Woman." In *From Fiction to Metafiction: Essays in Honor of Carmen Martín Gaite,* edited by Mirella D'Ambrosio Servodidio and Marcia L. Welles, 161–72. Lincoln: Society of Spanish and Spanish-American Studies, 1983.

————. "*El cuarto de atrás* de Carmen Martín Gaite: Por fin, el mundo al revés." Paper presented at the annual convention of the Modern Language Association, San Francisco, December 1979.

Limpus, Laurel. "Sexual Repression and the Family." In *Womankind: Beyond the Stereotypes,* edited by Nancy Reeves. New York: Aldine Atherton, 1971.

Lincoln, Bruce. *Emerging From the Chrysalis: Studies in Rituals of Women's Initiation.* Cambridge, Mass.: Harvard University Press, 1981.

Lipking, Lawrence. "Aristotle's Sister: A Poetics of Abandonment." *Critical Inquiry* 10 (1983): 61–81.

Bibliography 237

Llopis, Rafael. *Esbozo de una historia natural de los cuentos de miedo*. Madrid: Ediciones Juncar, 1974.

Loomis, Roger Sherman. "The Origin of Grail Legends." In *Arthurian Literature in the Middle Ages*, edited by Roger Sherman Loomis, 274–94. Oxford: Oxford University Press, 1959.

Lotman, Yurij and B. A. Uspensky. "On the Semiotic Mechanism of Culture." Translated by George Mihaychuk. *New Literary History* 9 (1978): 211–32. Reprinted in *Critical Theory Since 1965*, edited by Hazard Adams and Leroy Searle. Tallahassee: Florida State University Press, 1986.

MacCannell, Juliet Flower. *Figuring Lacan: Criticism and the Cultural Unconscious*. Lincoln: University of Nebraska Press, 1986.

Malkiel, María Rosa Lida de. "Arthurian Literature in Spain and Portugal." In *Arthurian Literature in the Middle Ages*, edited by Roger Sherman Loomis, 406–18. Oxford: Oxford University Press, 1959.

Manteiga, Roberto C., Carolyn Galerstein, and Kathleen McNerney, eds. *Feminine Concerns in Contemporary Spanish Fiction by Women*. Potomac, Md.: Scripta Humanistica, 1988.

Marks, Elaine and Isabelle de Courtivron, eds. *New French Feminisms*. Amherst: University of Massachusetts Press, 1980.

Martín Gaite, Carmen. *La búsqueda de interlocutor y otras búsquedas*. Madrid: Nostromo, 1973.

———. *Usos amorosos del dieciocho en España*. Barcelona: Lumen, 1981.

Martínez Cachero, José María. *La novela española entre 1936–1975*. Madrid: Castalia, 1979.

Meese, Elizabeth A. *Crossing the Double-Cross: The Practice of Feminist Criticism*. Chapel Hill: The University of North Carolina Press, 1986.

Miller, Beth. "Introduction: Some Theoretical Considerations." In *Women in Hispanic Literature: Icons and Fallen Idols*, edited Beth Miller, 1–25. Berkeley: University of California Press, 1983.

Miller, Nancy K. "The Exquisite Cadavers: Women in Eighteenth-Century Fiction." *Diacritics* 5 (1975): 37–43.

———. "Women's Autobiography in France: For a Dialectics of Identification." In *Women and Language in Literature and Society*, edited by Sally McConnell-Ginet, Ruth Borker, and Nelly Furman, 258–73. New York: Praeger, 1980.

Miron, E. L. *The Queens of Aragon: Their Lives and Times*. New York: Kenikat Press, 1970.

Morson, Gary Saul. "Who Speaks for Bakhtin?: A Dialogic Introduction." *Critical Inquiry* 10 (December 1983): 225–43.

Moya, Carlos. "Familia e ideología política." In *Las ideologías en la España de hoy (Coloquio)*, edited by José Jiménez Blanco, 85–108. Madrid: Seminarios y Ediciones, 1972.

Navajas, Gonzalo. "El diálogo y el yo en *Retahílas*." *Hispanic Review* 53 (1985): 25–39.

Navajo, Ymelda, ed. *Doce relatos de mujeres*. Madrid: Alianza, 1983.

Nichols, Geraldine Cleary. "The Prison-House (and Beyond): *El mismo mar de todos los veranos*." *Romanic Review* 75 (1984): 366–85.

Nykrog, Per. "Trajectory of the Hero: Gauvain Paragon of Chivalry 1130–1230."

238   Bibliography

In *Medieval Narrative: A Symposium,* edited by Hans Bekker-Nielsen, 82–93. Odense: Odense University Press, 1978.

Olsen, Tillie. *Silences.* New York: Delacorte, 1965; Dell, 1978.

Ordóñez, Elizabeth. "Narrative Texts by Ethnic Women: Rereading the Past, Reshaping the Future." *MELUS* 9 (1982): 19–28.

———. "Paradise Regained, Paradise Lost: Desire and Prohibition in *La madre naturaleza.*" *Hispanic Journal* 8 (1986): 7–18.

———. "The Decoding and Encoding of Sex Roles in Carmen Martín Gaite's *Retahílas.*" *Kentucky Romance Quarterly* 27 (1980): 237–44.

Palley, Julian. "El interlocutor soñado de *El cuarto de atrás* de Carmen Martín Gaite." *Insula,* 404–5 (July–August 1980): 22.

Pérez, Janet. "Some Desiderata in Studies of Twentieth Century Spanish Fiction." *Siglo XX/20th Century* 1 (1984): 4–6.

Peri Rossi, Cristina. *Los museos abandonados.* Barcelona: Lumen, 1974.

Pineda, Empar. "El discurso de la diferencia. El discurso de la igualdad." In *Nuevas perspectivas sobre la mujer,* edited by María Angeles Durán, 257–71. Madrid: Universidad Autónoma de Madrid, 1982.

Pratt, Annis. "Archetypal Approaches to the New Feminist Criticism." *Bucknell Review* 21 (Spring 1973): 3–14.

———. *Archetypal Patterns in Women's Fiction.* Bloomington: Indiana University Press, 1981.

———. "Aunt Jennifer's Tigers: Notes Toward a Preliterary History of Women's Archetypes." *Feminist Studies* 4 (February 1978): 163–94.

———. "Feminist Archetypal Theory: Some Definitions." Paper presented at the annual convention of the Midwest Modern Language Association, St. Louis, November 1976.

———. "The New Feminist Criticism: Exploring the History of the New Space." In *Beyond Intellectual Sexism: A New Woman, A New Reality,* edited by Joan I. Roberts, 175–95. New York: David McKay, 1976.

Prjevalinsky Ferrer, Olga. "Las novelistas españolas de hoy." *Cuadernos Americanos,* Año 20, Tomo 118 (1961): 211–23.

Rada y Delgado, Juan de Dios de la. *Mujeres célebres de España y Portugal.* Buenos Aires: Espasa Calpe, 1954.

Reed, Evelyn. *Woman's Evolution.* New York: Pathfinder Press, 1975.

Reilly, Bernard F. *The Kingdom of Leon-Castilla Under Queen Urraca: 1109–1126.* Princeton: Princeton University Press, 1982.

Rich, Adrienne. *Of Woman Born.* New York: Norton, 1976; Bantam, 1977.

Riera, Carme. "Literatura escrita por mujeres." Mesa redonda no. 4. Madrid: Feria del Libro, Summer 1983.

———. "Literatura femenina: ¿Un lenguaje prestado?" *Quimera* 18 (April 1982): 9–12.

Riquer, Martín de. *La leyenda del graal y temas épicos medievales.* Madrid: Prensa Española, 1968.

Rodriguez Alcalde, Leopoldo. "Las novelistas españolas en los últimos veinte años." *La estafeta literaria* 25 (1962): 6.

Roig, Montserrat. *¿Tiempo de mujer?* Barcelona: Plaza & Janes, 1980.

Said, Edward W. "The Text, the World, the Critic." In *Textual Strategies: Perspectives in Post-Structuralist Criticism,* edited by Josué V. Harari, 161–88. Ithaca, N.Y.: Cornell University Press, 1979.

Sánchez Arnosi, Milagros. "Adelaida García Morales: La soledad gozosa." *Insula* 472 (March 1986): 4.

———. "El mundo de los libros: Gómez Ojea, *Otras mujeres y Fabia.*" *Insula* 431 (October 1982): 8.

Santos, Dámaso. *Generaciones juntas.* Madrid: Bullón, 1962.

Sanz Villanueva, Santos. *Historia de la novela social española (1942–1975).* Madrid: Alhambra, 1980.

———. *Tendencias de la novela española actual.* Madrid: Editorial Cuadernos para el diálogo, 1972.

Sarda, Mari. "Literatura feminista de los años 60–70: silencio, gritos, indicios." *Camp de l'arpa* 47 (February 1978): 22–28.

Sarton, May. *Journal of a Solitude.* New York: Norton, 1977.

Schleifer, Ronald. "The Space and Dialogue of Desire: Lacan, Greimas, and Narrative Temporality." In *Lacan and Narration: The Psychoanalytic Difference in Narrative Theory,* edited by Robert Con Davis, 871–90. Baltimore: The Johns Hopkins University Press, 1983.

Schulenburg, Jane Tibbetts. "Clio's European Daughters: Myopic Modes of Perception." In *The Prism of Sex: Essays in the Sociology of Knowledge,* edited by Julia A. Sherman and Evelyn Torton Beck, 33–53. Madison: The University of Wisconsin Press, 1977.

Servodidio, Mirella D'Ambrosio and Marcia L. Welles, eds. *From Fiction to Metafiction: Essays in Honor of Carmen Martín Gaite.* Lincoln: Society of Spanish and Spanish-American Studies, 1983.

Servodidio, Mirella D'Ambrosio. ed. *Reading for Difference: Feminist Perspectives on Women Novelists of Contemporary Spain. Anales de la Literatura Española Contemporanea* 12 (1987).

Shahar, Shulamith. *The Fourth Estate.* Translated by Chaya Galai. London: Methuen, 1983.

Showalter, Elaine. "Feminist Criticism in the Wilderness." In *Critical Inquiry* 8 (1981): 179–205. Reprinted in Showalter, Elaine, ed. *The New Feminist Criticism.* 243–70. New York: Pantheon Books, 1985.

———, ed. *The New Feminist Criticism: Essays on Women, Literature and Theory.* New York: Pantheon Books, 1985.

Sobejano, Gonzalo. "Enlaces y desenlaces en las novelas de Carmen Martín Gaite." In *From Fiction to Metafiction: Essays in Honor of Carmen Martín Gaite,* edited by Mirella D'Ambrosio Servodidio and Marcia L. Welles, 209–23. Lincoln: Society of Spanish and Spanish-American Studies, 1983.

———. *Novela española de nuestro tiempo (en busca del pueblo perdido).* Madrid: Prensa Española, 1975.

Soldevilla, Ignacio. *La novela desde 1936.* Madrid: Alhambra, 1980.

Sordo, Enrique. "Carmen Martín Gaite: De la soledad al diálogo." *La Estafeta Literaria* 553 (1974): 1923.

Spacks, Patricia Meyer. "Taking Care: Some Women Novelists." *Novel* (Fall 1972): 36–51.

Spires, Robert C. "El papel del lector implícito en la novela española de posguerra." In *Novelistas españoles de postguerra*, edited by Rodolfo Cardona, 241–52. Madrid: Taurus, 1976.

———. "Intertextuality in *El cuarto de atrás.* In *From Fiction to Metafiction: Essays in Honor of Carmen Martín Gaite*, edited by Mirella D'Ambrosio Servodidio and Marcia L. Welles, 139–48. Lincoln: Society of Spanish and Spanish-American Studies, 1983.

———. *La novela española de posguerra*. Madrid: Cupsa Editorial, 1978.

Spivak, Gayatri Chakravorty. "Displacement and the Discourse of Woman." In *Displacement: Derrida and After*, edited by Mark Krupnick, 169–95. Bloomington: Indiana University Press, 1983.

———. "Finding Feminist Readings: Dante-Yeats." In *American Criticism in the Poststructuralist Age*, edited by Ira Konigsberg, 42–65. Ann Arbor: University of Michigan Press, 1981.

Stanton, Domna C. "Difference on Trial: A Critique of the Maternal Metaphor in Cixous, Irigaray, and Kristeva." In *The Poetics of Gender*, edited by Nancy K. Miller, 157–82. New York: Columbia University Press, 1986.

Sturrock, John. "Roland Barthes." In *Structuralism and Since: From Lévi Strauss to Derrida*, edited by John Sturrock, 52–80. New York: Oxford University Press, 1979.

Suleiman, Susan Rubin. "Writing and Motherhood." In *The (M)other Tongue: Essays in Feminist Psychoanalytic Interpretation*, edited by Shirley Nelson Garner, Claire Kahane, and Madelon Sprengnether, 352–77. Ithaca, N.Y.: Cornell University Press, 1985.

Sullivan, Constance A. "Re-reading the Hispanic Literary Canon." *Ideologies and Literature: A Journal of Hispanic and Luso-Brazilian Studies* 4 (1983): 93–101.

Suñen, Luis. "El mito en el espejo." *Insula* 382 (September 1978): 5.

———. "Interlocutor intruso y texto total." *Insula* 380–81 (July–August 1978): 11.

Todorov, Tzvetan. *Literatura y significación*. Translated by Gonzalo Suárez Gómez. Barcelona: Planeta, 1971.

———. *The Fantastic: A Structural Approach to a Literary Genre*. Translated by Richard Howard. Cleveland: The Press of Case Western Reserve University, 1973.

Traba, Marta. "Hipótesis sobre una escritura diferente." *Quimera* 13 (November 1981): 9–11.

Ullman, Pierre. "The Moral Structure of Carmen Laforet's Novels." In *The Vision Obscured*, edited by Melvin J. Friedman, 201–19. New York: Fordham University Press, 1970.

Villán, Javier. "Carmen Martín Gaite: Habitando el tiempo." *La Estafeta Literaria* 549 (1974): 22.

Walker, Barbara G. *The Woman's Encyclopedia of Myths and Secrets*. San Francisco: Harper & Row, 1983.

Webber, Jeanette L. and Joan Grumman. *Woman as Writer*. Boston: Houghton Mifflin, 1972.

Weston, Jessie L. *From Ritual to Romance*. Garden City: Doubleday, 1957.

———. *The Quest of the Holy Grail*. New York: Haskell House, 1965.

White, Hayden. "The Historical Text as Literary Artifact." *Clio* 3 (1974): 277–303. Reprinted in Hayden White, *The Tropics of Discourse: Essays in Cultural Criticism*, 81–100. Baltimore: The Johns Hopkins University Press, 1978. Reprinted also in *Critical Theory Since 1965*, edited by Hazard Adams & Leroy Searle, 395–407. Tallahassee: Florida State University Press, 1986.

———. "The Value of Narrativity in the Representation of Reality." *Critical Inquiry* 7 (Autumn 1980): 5–27.

Woodward, Kathleen. "The Mirror Stage of Old Age." In *Memory and Desire: Aging-Literature-Psychoanalysis*, edited by Kathleen Woodward and Murray M. Schwartz, 97–113. Bloomington: Indiana University Press, 1986.

Woolf, Virginia. *A Room of One's Own*. London: Hogarth Press, 1929.

Works Available in Translation

García Morales, Adelaida. *Silence of the Sirens (El silencio de las sirenas)*. Translated by Concilia Hayter. London: Collins, 1988.

———. *Silence of the Sirens*. Translated by Concilia Hayter. London: Flamingo, 1989.

Laforet, Carmen. *Nada*. Translated by Inez Muñoz. London: Weidenfeld and Nicholson, 1958.

———. *Andrea (Nada)*. Translated by Charles F. Payne. New York: Vantage Press, 1964.

Martín Gaite, Carmen. *The Back Room (El cuarto de atrás)*. Translated by Helen R. Lane. New York: Columbia University Press, 1983.

Matute, Ana María. *School of the Sun (Primera memoria)*. Translated by Elaine Kerrigan. New York: Pantheon Books, 1963.

———. *School of the Sun*. Translated by Elaine Kerrigan. New York: Columbia University Press, 1989.

Tusquets, Esther. *Love Is a Solitary Game (El amor es un juego solitario)*. Translated by Bruce Penman. London: J. Calder, 1985.

———. *Love is a Solitary Game*. Translated by Bruce Penman. New York: Riverrun Press, 1986.

———. *The Same Sea as Every Summer (El mismo mar de todos los veranos)*. Translated by Margaret E. W. Jones. Lincoln: University of Nebraska Press, 1990.

Index

242